Hamlyn Illustrated History

LIVERPOOL
1892–1998

Stephen F. Kelly

HAMLYN

Art Director: Keith Martin
Design Manager: Bryan Dunn
Original Design: Brian Thomas
Jacket design: Milton Bayer
Design: Stephen Cary
Picture Research: Zoe Holterman
Publishing Director: Laura Bamford
Senior Editors: Adam Ward and Trevor Davies
Editor: Tarda Davison-Aitkins
Production: Bonnie Ashby

First published in Great Britain in 1987 under the title
You'll Never Walk Alone by Queen Anne Press.

This revised and updated edition published in 1998 by
Hamlyn, an imprint of Reed International Books Ltd,
Michelin House, 81 Fulham Road, London SW3 6RB
and Auckland, Melbourne, Singapore and Toronto

ISBN 0 600 59513 7

A catalogue record for this book is available from the
British Library

Produced by Mladinska knjiga
Printed in Slovenia

Photographic acknowledgements

The Publishers would like to thank the following individuals
and organisations for their kind permission to reproduce the
photographs in this book:

Action Images 178, 180, 190, 196, 198, 200
Allsport 69, 116, 118, 119B, 121, 122B, 142, 147, 148, 149,
150, 152, 155, 156, 159, 217, 226 /Shaun Botterill 177, 201,
210 below left, 221 /Clive Brunskill 204, 205, 207, 211 below
right, 213, 218 /Simon Bruty 188 /David Cannon 179 /Steve
Munday 183 /Gary M. Prior 203 /Ben Radford 202, 215, 223
/Mike Hewitt 222, /Mark Thompson 210–211 above /Alex
Livsey 220,
Hulton /Getty 15, 16, 25, 27T, 27B, 35, 66, 68B, 76B, 82T,
94T, 95.
Colorsport 17, 29, 34, 38T, 39T, 41, 45T, 48, 61, 62, 67B,
68T, 78, 80T, 84, 88, 89B, 93, 94B, 96, 98, 102, 103, 138,
139, 145, 151, 162–3, 166, 169, 170, 172, 173, 175, 176,
181, 182, 184, 185, 186, 189, 191, 192, 193, 194, 195, 196,
197, 199, 206, 208, 209, 212, 214, 216 right, 216 left, 217,
218, 219, 225.
Empics /Neal Simpson 187
Steve Hale 63, 108T, 174
George Higham 6, 10, 12
The Illustrated London News Picture Library 8, 11, 18T,
18B, 19
Liverpool City Libraries 5
Liverpool Daily Post & Echo 14, 23, 24, 28B, 32, 42, 47B,
52, 130, 153, 157
London Cigarette Card Co. 22, 27 inset, 28T
Popperfoto 38-39, 75, 76T, 89T, 89C, 101, 104, 105
The Photo Source 33T, 33BL, 33BR, 36, 46, 49, 51, 53, 54,
56B, 59T, 60, 82B, 87, 107, 108B, 109, 112
Sporting Pictures (UK) Ltd 70L, 70R, 71, 72B, 73, 117T,
119T, 120
Bob Thomas Sports Photography 47T, 50, 57B, 58, 67T,
72T, 74, 77, 79, 85, 99, 100, 110, 115, 117B, 122T, 123, 126,
127, 129, 131, 133, 135T, 135B, 136-7, 143, 144, 154, 154,
160, 161, 165, 167
Topham 35 inset, 44, 56T, 57T, 90-91, 141, 146
Steve Hale 224 Bottom, 224 Top, 226 Bottom

Contents

INTRODUCTION

The statistics are simply staggering. Even before Bill Shankly arrived at Liverpool Football Club in 1959 they boasted a long and proud tradition with five League titles and more than three-dozen international players packing their seventy-year history. But since Shankly's Messianic arrival the club has gone on to capture more silverware and honours than anyone could have dreamed of.

As you wind your way up Everton Valley or across Stanley Park on a match day, people pour out of the back-to-back houses in the narrow terraced streets or from the corner pubs to join the long procession. The talk is always the same: who will be substitute, why don't they play so-and-so and wasn't the left back rubbish last week. And then quite unexpectedly you have arrived, the Kop jutting out, a new modernistic steel structure towering over the nearby streets. The famous old Kop, for so long the symbol of Liverpool Football Club, has now gone and in its place is a glass fronted edifice with seating for more than 10,000 supporters, still capable ol generating a sound as vocal and passionate as any in Britian or Europe. It is here that the football worshippers of Liverpool have gathered since the club was formed. At one time as many as 30,000 could pack in under its roof. And anyone wanting to discover the Liverpool secret could do no better than to begin their search here. It has been said that the Kop is worth a goal start and no-one would argue with that. Its fanatical, roaring support, particularly when Liverpool fall a goal behind, has pulled them back on many occasions.

But what else has contributed to the success story? Undoubtedly the management of the team has inspired and pervaded all corners of the club. The Shankly broom swept through the corridors and set a trend that has continued over the years. Training facilities were improved with a new emphasis on fitness and stamina to cope with the rigours of European soccer as well as sixty games a season. Professionalism in the club's administration accelerated the smooth running of the operation, helping to overcome the problems faced by European travel and the disappointments of losing managers and players. And yet no player is bigger than the club. The continuity which the club established with the appointment of Bob Paisley was surely one of the most crucial decisions it has ever made. That was repeated with the promotion of both Joe Fagan and Kenny Dalglish but was then disrupted by the appointment of another old boy as manager, Graeme Souness, who tried to change the old ways, but only brought discord and confusion. Liverpool slumped and in the end Souness and the club were forced to part company. But now the harmony has returned with the appointment of Roy Evans, another bootroom boy, as the new man in charge.

Tradition in the famous bootroom has meant a stability uncommon to any other football club, though it should be emphasised that it is nothing new at Anfield where only fourteen men have occupied the managerial chair in more than a century and only two of those have been sacked. Most have retired through ill health or age.

If those behind the scenes and those on the Kop are vital ingredients, then what of the players? Shankly initiated a policy of searching for talent among the lower divisions and buying cheaply which has been continued through the years reaping success upon success. Home grown players have continued to emerge like Hunt, Lee, Thompson, Smith, Lawler, McManaman and Fowler.

But it has also been to Scotland that the club has searched for some of its finest talent. The first-ever Liverpool side, cobbled together by John McKenna, was entirely Scottish and the trend has continued. No other country has contributed so much talent to Liverpool than Scotland. The net has also been cast abroad making Liverpool a truly cosmopolitan club.

And when Liverpool have plunged into the transfer market it is usually unexpectedly, with few press predictions and rarely revealed until the contract is signed and sealed. Players are chosen carefully and not simply for their footballing skills.

But the club has also suffered tragedy, none more so than in recent years with the Heysel disaster and the tragedy at Hillsborough. Under the glaring lights of international criticism following Heysel, many clubs would have sunk beneath the welter of outrage and humiliation. Yet Liverpool picked themselves up and went on to achieve their greatest domestic success, the double. And then of course, the Hillsborough disaster, when the tragic loss of so many lives, devastated not only the club but the people of Liverpool. No football club has ever experienced such tragedies, but the response was exemplary.

It is perhaps that quality of never surrendering that has been instilled in the club, its players and supporters over the years which has led to so many triumphs. In the end, it is probably no single ingredient that has made Liverpool so successful but rather a combination of many factors. How the club developed its style, skills and character is a fascinating story which did not begin simply with Shankly. It goes back many years to the roots of the club in a history which is rich in incident, where trophies have been won and lost by a single goal, where tears have been shed in disappointment and where scandals have ruined careers. This then is the story of Liverpool Football Club.

1

IT BEGAN WITH EVERTON...

Ironically, the history of Liverpool Football club begins with their greatest rivals and neighbours, Everton, for it was from a dispute with Everton that Liverpool Football Club was born. But the story goes back even further than this. It begins with the building of a new church and Sunday School to replace three old Methodist churches in the city which were in a bad state of repair. The site chosen for the building was Breckfield Road North in Everton and in May 1870 the new chapel of St Domingo was formally consecrated.

At a time when the church was central to working class communities with many of the younger and more enlightened curates preaching the virtues of athletisism as a means to combat urban degeneration, sport was a vital ingredient in the church's activities. Sunday Schools thrived and young people were keen to represent their church in various sporting leagues organised on a diocesal basis. St Domingo's was no exception and very soon a cricket club was regularly playing games against other Sunday schools in the city. But cricket was a summer sport, as was another favourite, baseball, and so it was hardly surprising when a group of enterprising young lads asked the Reverend Chambers if they could set up a football club. Rugby remained the most popular winter sport in the city but football was being played increasingly and the Reverend Chambers was only too delighted to give them the go-ahead. So, St Domingo's Football Club was founded in 1878. Despite the popularity of rugby, football prospered growing from a handful of clubs in 1878 to more than 150 by 1886. Flushed with success after only one year, St Domingo's decided to spread its catchment area and assumed the more ambitious name of Everton Football Club. And under its new title Everton played its first game against St Peter's on 23 December, 1879 and recorded its first ever victory.

By 1880 a flourishing Everton had joined the Lancashire Association and was playing teams as far away as Bolton and Birkenhead with home games still played on the public pitch in Stanley Park. However, a new ruling in 1882 forced the club to find an enclosed ground for their matches. A meeting was held in John Houlding's Sandon Hotel in Everton where it was agreed to rent a field off Priory Road. Houlding, a keen football follower and a future Mayor of Liverpool, was to have a dramatic influence on the fortunes of Everton over the next few years and later on Liverpool Football Club. He was a self-made man who had begun his working life in a brewery soon venturing out on his own to purchase a small public house. His business became so successful that he then bought out a small brewery from which he made a comfortable living for the remainder of his life. He became prominent in the Working Men's Conservative Association and was elected to the City Council as a Conservative representing the Everton ward, finally being appointed Mayor in 1897.

Houlding was now playing a considerable role in the affairs of the club and was even able to secure a new pitch when the owner of the ground off the Priory Road asked them to leave. The new field was to be rented from a fellow brewer of Houlding called John Orrell who agreed to let them have a pitch at Anfield Road for a small rent. On 28 September, 1884 Anfield witnessed its first game when Everton took on Earlstown and duly beat them 5 – 0.

John Houlding, self-made businessman, Conservative councillor, city mayor and the man who founded Liverpool Football Club.

For the next eight years Everton thrived as Houlding poured money into the club. Stands were erected, gates topped 8,000, results improved and in 1888 Everton became founding members of the new Football League. Now they were playing matches all over the country, visiting Wolverhampton, Sunderland and Notts County. Professionalism had been introduced in 1885 and by 1891 the leading players were earning £3 a week. Football in the city was given a further boost in April 1890 when dock workers successfully won the struggle for a five and a half day week. With Saturday afternoon free, thousands more could attend the weekly game.

But behind the scenes there were murmurings that all was not well. 'King John', as Houlding was affectionately known, was becoming increasingly proprietorial. He frequently insisted on his own way and even increased the rate of interest on his loan to the club. To add to the complaints the players were forced to use his public house, The Sandon for changing before and after games. The first hint of a rift cropped up in 1891 when John Orrell threatened to withdraw the tenancy of Anfield Road unless certain alterations were undertaken. Houlding came up with a plan to answer Orrell. He would form a limited liability company and purchase the ground. But there was a snag. Orrell was willing to sell – at a price – but it also transpired that Houlding had bought land adjoining Orrell's plot and intended that the new limited company should also purchase this land at the same price. Houlding stood to make a considerable gain and there was a bitter argument when the club's 279 members met in January 1892. In the event, Houlding's proposal was rejected and the club were given notice to quit Anfield. Houlding also registered the name of Everton Football Club with himself so that for a short period there were two Everton Football Clubs.

A further meeting was held on 15 March, 1892 and with Houlding outvoted his opponents decided to leave Anfield Road and form a new club. A building fund was immediately set up and £1,517 quickly raised to purchase a new ground. The site chosen was at Goodison Park on the north side of Stanley Park and it was duly purchased for £8,000. While Everton were busily constructing their new stadium, Anfield remained shamefully empty and still in the possession of John Orrell and a very angry Houlding. The ground from which they had anticipated a rich profit had turned into a white elephant. But Houlding was not to be outsmarted. If you own an empty football ground, there is only one answer, he decided, to form a football club. And that is precisely what he did. Along with a handful of Anfield loyalists who had not departed to Goodison, he formed the Liverpool Association Football Club in May 1892

and cheekily applied for membership to the Football League. It was a move greeted with astonishment. How could a city support two football teams, asked the local papers while others wondered where all the football talent would come from. The answer to that question was supplied by John McKenna.

McKenna, an Irishman, was a friend of Houlding who had remained with him during the split. A self-made businessman and former rugby player, the handsome, moustached McKenna had become a regular visitor and supporter at Anfield, always recognisable in his bowler hat and velvet-collared overcoat. He had a keen knowledge of football and knew precisely where to find players. Unfortunately for Houlding, the Football League were not too impressed by his application and refused to admit the newly formed club. So, Liverpool were forced to join the Lancashire Association. McKenna's contacts lay in Scotland, particularly Glasgow with its divided Irish population, and it was here that McKenna journeyed to tap the stream of footballing talent.

On the Thursday evening of 1 September, 1892 while Everton were playing their first game at Goodison Park – a friendly against Bolton Wanderers – Liverpool Football Club also played its first ever game – another friendly against Rotherham Town at Anfield. The directors of the club had confidently predicted a fine

John McKenna, perhaps the greatest driving force during Liverpool's early history. The club's first manager he also enjoyed two spells as chairman.

start with the *Liverpool Echo* reporting that 'the old Anfield ground will be occupied by the newly organised club known as the Liverpool Association and the officials claim for it that no better game will be witnessed on any of the plots in the neighbourhood.' In the event, they were probably correct for although Everton won comfortably by four goals to two, Liverpool trounced their opponents from the Midland League by seven goals to one.

'Amidst applause Councillor J. Houlding started the ball,' read the *Liverpool Daily Post*'s first-ever report of a Liverpool match. Hannah won the toss and Liverpool's team of Ross, Hannah, McLean, Kelso, McQueen, McBride, Wyllie, Smith, Miller, McVean and Kelvin set into action the long and outstanding history of Liverpool Football Club. Early into the first half McVean clinched the honour of scoring Liverpool's first goal with Kelvin and Wyllie soon adding to the scoreline and by half-time they were five goals up. 'It is much to be feared that they will win most of their engagements in the same easy fashion,' reported the *Liverpool Football Echo* a few days later. The game was marred only by the poor attendance with no more than a handful of interested spectators while Goodison was crammed with over 10,000 supporters.

Two days later in their second home game and their first in the Lancashire League against Higher Walton, Liverpool repeated their goalscoring feats with an 8–0 victory. McVean was captain that day and with the opposition arriving forty-five minutes after the scheduled kick-off it was hardly surprising that once more there was a poor attendance with 'a miserable array of empty benches.' In fact, only 200 people turned up. Within a week, however, news of Liverpool's winning habits had spread throughout the city and when Liverpool defeated Stockton on 10 September to go top of the league more than 3,000 were at Anfield.

It was ironic that in the first team Liverpool ever fielded there was not a single Englishman. All eleven had arrived via McKenna's trip north and Liverpool soon became known as the 'team of the macs'. Duncan McClean and John McBride had come from Renton while Malcolm McVean joined from the crack Scottish club, Third Lanark. They teamed up with Hugh McQueen, Matt McQueen, John McCartney, Bill McOwen and Joe McQue, making eight Macs in all from the thirteen signatures which had resulted from McKenna's Scottish journey. Almost a century later when Liverpool were to clinch the magic double, they would again field a team without any Englishmen.

Liverpool's first season in the Lancashire League could hardly have been more auspicious. Playing against teams such as Blackpool, Southport and Bury, they headed the table at the end of the season on goal average and also won the Liverpool Cup defeating a 'mixed' Everton side. They then managed to have both trophies stolen and had to purchase two new ones at a cost of £150. They had played twenty-two games, winning seventeen, losing three and drawing two. Sixty-six goals were scored with only nineteen conceded. But unfortunately, their team of Scotsmen was attracting few supporters to Anfield although away games were drawing crowds of up to 8,000. Spurred on by the early flush of success, McKenna now acting as secretary of the club, telegraphed the Football League: 'Liverpool make application to the Second Division of the League,' he wrote, determined that the Anfield club should take the place of Accrington Stanley who had just resigned from the Second Division. Bootle also resigned from the division a short time later, the day the season kicked off. They were a local side who had enjoyed a flourishing early history. Known as 'Brutal Bootle' because of their style of play, they had spent just one season in the League, finishing eighth before encountering financial difficulties. Somewhat to Liverpool's surprise, especially as McKenna had told nobody of his plan, the reply came back from the Football League, 'Liverpool elected. Come to London at 3pm tomorrow to arrange fixtures.' And so, on 2 September, 1893 Liverpool Football Club played its first game in the Football League away to Middlesbrough Ironopolis. Fittingly, before a 'large and enthusiastic crowd' they won by two goals to nil in brilliant sunshine. After a tough, goalless first half Liverpool began to dominate the match and after an hour's play McVean scored Liverpool's first ever League goal.

In their opening home fixture at Anfield on 9 September, 1893 in front of 5,000 spectators they beat Lincoln City by four goals to nil. It was a remarkable start which was all the more impressive at the end of the season with Liverpool unbeaten in twenty-eight matches. They had won twenty-two of these, drawing the other six and had scored seventy-seven goals with only eighteen against. They topped the League but with no automatic promotion in those days they entered a knockout tournament with the bottom three clubs of the First Division known as the 'Test Match System'. In their final match Liverpool beat Newton Heath, later to become Manchester United, by two goals to nil, and duly took their place in the First Division.

However, life in the First Division turned out to be harder than they had anticipated. They made a poor

First goal for Liverpool

The first of Davy Hannah's goals in a hat-trick that gave Liverpool a 3-0 win over Sunderland at Anfield in November 1896.

start, losing four and drawing the other four of their first eight games although with gates up to around 20,000 there was at least clear evidence that the city could support two teams. In their ninth match on 13 October, Liverpool faced Everton at Goodison Park in their first League derby. Liverpool took the game so seriously that they went off to Hightown for a week's training whereas Everton casually remained at home. The *Liverpool Echo*

referred to it as the 'great football match' and immediately prior to kick off the crowd were entertained with a schoolboy game between Liverpool and Nottingham. The derby itself was watched by 44,000 spectators, including the Lord Mayor and other City dignatories, who saw a bruising battle, Liverpool tackling hard and showing little respect for their more elegant neighbours. When the final whistle blew with the two teams playing in semi-darkness, Everton had won 3 – 0. The third Everton goal had been an own goal put in by one of the Liverpool full backs while Bradshaw had missed a sitter. The return game on 17 November at Anfield was a better result for Liverpool who managed a 2 – 2 draw in front of 30,000. The first derby blood then had gone to Everton.

Liverpool went from bad to worse. They were hit by injuries and a hard winter made playing conditions treacherous. At the end of the season they were propping up the rest of the table having won only seven of their thirty matches and went into the deciding promotion-relegation Test Match. In the crucial game against Bury played at Blackburn's smart new ground they fared no better losing 1 – 0, even though the Bury goalkeeper had been sent off, and were consequently relegated. But as they went down, John McKenna, now ruling Liverpool's affairs with W.E. Barclay alongside him as the club's first secretary/manager, swore that their stay in the lower division would be a short one and that they would return within twelve months. It was perhaps the

first example of the fighting spirit of the club that would become renowned in the years ahead. McKenna's prediction was fulfilled but not before he had taken a number of actions to support it. More Scotsmen were recruited including George Allan, a young centre forward from Leith Athletic, who was to become the club's first Scottish international in 1897 when he was capped for his country against England. Sadly he died when he was only twenty-four.

McKenna also built a new stand for the crowds that were flocking into Anfield and by the end of the season, 1895 – 96 they had been rewarded when Liverpool topped the League having lost just six games. And in the subsequent test matches Liverpool easily gained promotion to the highest reaches. They scored 106 goals, the first and only time they have topped a century of goals in a season. Their most notable win was a 10 – 1 victory over Rotherham Town with George Allan scoring four. During the season Frank Becton was honoured with an appearance at inside left for the Football League against the Scottish League in a game at Goodison Park before 16,000 spectators. The club was now becoming a force within the Football League and for the next eight years would remain in the top division and claim their first championship.

CHAMPIONSHIP WIN—THE FIRST OF MANY

In their first season back in Division One Liverpool finished a creditable fifth, above Everton for the first time and made their first appearance in the semi-finals of the FA Cup. They were drawn against Aston Villa, the League Champions at Bramall Lane while in the other semi-final Everton faced Derby County. For the first time there was the serious prospect of an all Merseyside final. But it was not to be. While Everton won their tie, Liverpool were overwhelmed by three goals to nil. 'Agony for Liverpool' read the headline in the *Liverpool Football Echo*, 'Watched With Almost Painful Anxiety And Interest'. The week's training at St Anne's had done them little good and battling in the blustery conditions at Sheffield 'the Anfielders had lost all heart and were overplayed'. More importantly that season, John McKenna persuaded the secretary of Sunderland, Tom Watson to join him at Anfield as the club's assistant secretary. It was a shrewd move which would pay rich dividends over the next twenty-four years and bring a new professionalism to Anfield.

International honours were also bestowed on the club for the first time with Harry Bradshaw becoming the first Liverpool player to win a cap when he played for England against Ireland in February 1897. Two months later the former Preston North End recruit, Frank Becton also played for England while George Allan won a Scottish cap helping his country to a 2−1 victory over England.

The season 1898−99 saw Liverpool change from their blue and white quartered shirts to new colours of red and also the signing a couple of new players. One was Rab Howell, a genuine Romany gipsy who came from Sheffield and over the next few years brought the club considerable luck as well as playing for England. Their other signing was their first star player and not surprisingly he was Scottish. Alex Raisbeck was one of seven brothers from a mining family in Stirlingshire and had been on the books of Edinburgh Hibernian for a number of years. In 1897 he had played for Scotland against the English League and enjoyed a brief spell with Stoke in the First Division but only appeared in a handful of games before returning north of the border. During his time at Stoke, however, he was spotted by the ever-alert John McKenna. When McKenna heard that Raisbeck had returned to Scotland he immediately packed Tom Watson off to Edinburgh telling him not to come back without the lad. Fortunately, his mission was

Alex Raisbeck, the Scottish international was Liverpool's first star player, making 340 appearances for the club.

a success and over the next ten years Raisbeck was to play a major role in the fortunes of Liverpool Football Club. He was capped eight times by his country and hailed as one of the finest centre halves of the era. He was aggressive, a tough tackler and although only 5 feet 9 inches could out-jump any opponent. Among the Anfield faithful he was a favourite and his name still ranks alongside those of the later Liverpool Scots: Liddell and Dalglish.

With the fair-haired Raisbeck inspiring them Liverpool began to impress and in 1899 looked set to clinch the double as the season wound up to an exciting climax. With just three games to go Liverpool were top of the table, well ahead of Aston Villa on goal average but while Liverpool won two of those games only marginally, Villa hit thirteen goals and edged in front of the Reds by the merest of fractions. All rested on the final match of the season which by coincidence pitted Liverpool against Villa at Villa Park. A crowd of more than 40,000 turned up for the battle, Liverpool confident that they could repeat their previous encounter at Anfield which they had won by three goals to nil. In the event, Villa thrashed Liverpool 5−0 scoring all five in the first half and Liverpool had to be content with the runners-up spot. It had been Liverpool's sixteenth game in forty-three days and the players looked visibly tired, so it was hardly surprising that they lost.

A game Liverpool would want to forget. On the verge of winning their first championship in 1899 they faced their leading challengers, Aston Villa in the final match of the season at Villa Park but went down by five goals to nil.

In the Cup Liverpool's fortunes also faded at the penultimate hurdle when Sheffield United beat them in the semi-final at the fourth attempt. The teams shared four goals at Nottingham and eight at Bolton where Liverpool had twice led by two goals. The third game was played at Fallowfield in Manchester on a Monday afternoon. The ground was far too small for the 30,000 who turned up and the crowd kept spilling on to the pitch. At half-time the referee decided to call a halt and abandoned the game. The half had lasted 105 minutes and Liverpool were leading 1−0 with a goal from George Allan. In the fourth game at Derby, Sheffield scored five minutes from the end to win by the only goal. There were no prizes for second best but it would not be very long before Liverpool could consider themselves the best.

In fact, it would only be two seasons. In 1899−1900 they finished a miserable tenth although they were above Everton, and again failed to make much progress in the FA Cup. The following season they clinched their first League Championship with a stirring late run. In mid-February they hardly had the look of champions, having lost eight games and conceded thirty-one goals. But in the next twelve matches they put together a thrilling

finish, conceding only four goals in nine wins and three draws. The most vital win had come in mid-April against Manchester City at Anfield when despite a Billy Meredith goal, Liverpool beat their Lancashire rivals by three goals to one. In the final game of the season on the Monday evening of 29 April the destination of the championship rested on Liverpool beating bottom-placed West Bromwich Albion at the Hawthorns. Albion fought like tigers and, although Walker scored for Liverpool in the first half after a Raybould shot had been only half saved, Albion battled every inch of the way. In the second half they bombarded the Liverpool goal but somehow Liverpool's luck held out and the title went to Anfield.

Liverpool's team that day was: Perkins, Dunlop, Robertson T., Goldie, Raisbeck, Wilson, Fox, Satterthwaite, Raybould, Walker, Robertson J. Of the thirty-four games they had played in the championship winning season of 1900−01, nineteen were won, seven drawn, and eight lost with fifty-nine goals scored and thirty-five conceded. They had won more games and scored more goals than any of their rivals and while tributes were spread among the players, it was Raisbeck who had been the driving force and the hero of the season and it was Raisbeck who was lofted shoulder high by his teammates clasping the shining championship trophy for the first time. As the *Liverpool Football Echo* reported, 'it did not look as if they had any prospects but when the old century closed the men bucked up.' When the team arrived back at Central station shortly before midnight that Monday evening, thousands were waiting to greet them. A drum and fife band met them on the platform, playing 'The Conquering Hero' and the team paraded through the crowded streets with the trophy. Raisbeck was again carried shoulder-high along with most of his teammates – only Tom Watson's vast girth proved too much for the excited fans. The team eventually arrived back at Anfield in the small hours of the morning and the trophy was placed proudly in the old boardroom where it was admired well into the night by Houlding and McKenna. But they need have no fears that it might never appear again.

Sadly, Big John Houlding would never see the League Championship trophy again. He died in 1902 at the age of seventy in the south of France having served the club energetically for almost twenty years although in his latter years he had not been quite so active. When his funeral cortege passed through the streets of Anfield and Everton, residents stood bareheaded, at the two grounds flags fluttered at half-mast and as a mark of his involvement with the clubs his pall-bearers were players from Everton and Liverpool. In later life he admitted that the split with Everton which had initiated the formation of Liverpool had more to do with his opposition to the teetotal fanaticism that had gripped the club's members.

After their League Championship win Liverpool slumped. The main problem was the introduction of the £4 maximum weekly wage on, of all days, April Fools Day, 1901. Liverpool had attendances topping 18,000 and could therefore afford to pay their players a lucrative bonus scheme which in good weeks meant they could earn as much as £10. McKenna was a fierce critic of the maximum wage policy which remained in force until 1960 and resulted in some of the current players seeking transfers while others decided to quit the game altogether. But the club did manage to hang on to Alex Raisbeck by paying him extra money for acting as the bill inspector and checking all the advertisements around the pitch.

The following season they finished in the middle of the table despite beating Stoke City 7 – 0 in early January 1902. The Stoke team had stayed at the Adelphi Hotel and following an expensive meal most of the players suffered food poisoning. At one stage during the game Stoke were down to seven men and ended the game with only nine players still on the field. In 1902 – 03 Liverpool climbed up to the fifth spot only to finish one place from bottom in the next season. With the 'Test Match' system abolished in 1898, they were duly relegated along with West Bromwich Albion.

In the expectation of goals a new stand had been constructed at the Anfield Road end but behind the scenes there were arguments among the players, usually over money. Some of the more disenchanted left while new talent was recruited. Yet another Scot, George Fleming was transferred from Wolves along with Bowen while Ned Doig, the veteran Scottish international goalkeeper arrived from Blackburn. Doig was to be the first in a long history of outstanding and popular goalkeepers that would wear the colours of Liverpool. It was no accident that Liverpool's telegraphic address should become 'goalkeeper'! A few years later Doig was replaced by a young 'keeper from Chesterfield by the name of Sam Hardy. In a career that spanned the next decade and more, Hardy won fourteen England caps while at Liverpool, making 218 appearances for the club before being transferred to Aston Villa. In the years to come he would be replaced by many a fine goalkeeper.

Liverpool's second title winning team in 1905-06 rattled in seventy-nine goals to clinch the First Division championship by four points from Preston North End. Joe Hewitt was the leading marksman with twenty-three goals. Back row (left to right): Connell (trainer), Hewitt, Wilson, Hardy S., Parry, Doig, Dunlop, Hardy J. Middle row: Robinson, Gorman, Murray, Hughes, Raisbeck, Cox, Fleming, Raybould, West. Front row: Goddard, Latham, Carlin.

Edgar Chadwick, the former Everton and England international forward also returned to Merseyside and enjoyed a short spell at Anfield and a local boy, Jack Parkinson who later won two England caps signed up. They joined George Livingstone and a useful centre forward called Sam Raybould who had scored sixteen goals in the championship winning team of 1900–01. In 1902–03 Raybould was the League's leading scorer with thirty-one goals. To cement the Scottish connection Liverpool invited Glasgow Celtic and Hibernian to play a couple of games at Anfield while neighbours Everton invited Glasgow Rangers.

Over the years a myth has grown up concerning the sectarian nature of Merseyside football with Everton alleged to be the Catholic club and Liverpool the Protestant one. But there is virtually no evidence to support this theory. Everton would hardly have been organising friendly fixtures against the overtly Protestant Glasgow Rangers had this been the case. The myth probably stems from the politics of Houlding and McKenna who were prominent Freemasons and Conservatives. Houlding was also a well-known Orangeman. If anything, at the turn of the century, Everton was largely a Protestant club although it did employ a Catholic doctor and was said to be Tory to the backbone. Liverpool's Protestant association probably developed through Houlding's links with the Protestant-inclined Conservative Working Men's Associations and the large number of Scottish players recruited by McKenna but even here there is clear evidence that some of these players were Catholic. During the 1950s Everton forged strong links with the Republic of Ireland, engaging a number of Catholic Irish players. But weighing up all the facts, it is quite clear that it is no more than a myth, encouraged by one or two snippets of evidence and fanned by those who wished to intensify the rivalry between the two clubs. Indeed the managements of the two clubs have traditionally been close even sharing the same match programme for almost fifty years and at Houlding's funeral his coffin was carried by players from both clubs.

The reconstruction of the side reaped dividends and after just one year in Division Two Liverpool were promptly promoted, losing only three games. They notched up ninety-three goals with only twenty-five conceded and failed to score in only one game with their highest win an 8–1 victory over Port Vale. The next season they achieved a first in football history by winning the Second Division and First Division championship in successive years. For Merseyside the 1905–06 season was to be the most memorable and exciting to date.

The season began moderately well as the Reds confidantly continued with their free-scoring habits of Division Two. A couple of injuries then led to a sudden loss of form throwing doubt on their ability to sustain a challenge. But, as with their previous title win, Liverpool came through with a challenging late run that saw them lose only two of their last ten games to clinch their second championship from Preston by four points. Away from home Liverpool had lost eight games, conceding thirty goals, and even losing 5–0 to Aston Villa. Thankfully their home record was considerably better, winning fourteen, drawing three and losing only two.

As if all this was not exciting enough Liverpool's rush of form in the spring led to a fine run in the FA Cup as well. In the first round they nervously overcame Leicester Fosse 2–1 at Anfield, then beat Barnsley 1–0 away. In the third round they came up against non-league Brentford who were comfortably disposed of and then drew another non-league side Southampton in the quarter-final. Southampton were beaten 3–0 at Anfield and Liverpool looked to be striding towards the double. So far they had not faced a First Division side but in the semi-final fate played its cruel hand when Liverpool drew none other than their greatest rivals, Everton. In the League Liverpool had visited Goodison in the autumn and lost a stirring game by four goals to two. All seemed to augur well for the crucial clash. The *Liverpool Echo* ran a competition for the best poems and tales and there were daily reports on the two teams. Merseyside for the first time was gripped by football fever. Liverpool went to Tamworth for a week's training while Everton's directors took their team to Stafford and Northwich for 'hard brine baths'. The game was played at Villa Park before 50,000 fans most of whom had travelled down from Liverpool. The first excursions began arriving at Birmingham shortly after 10.00am with the *Liverpool Echo* reporting that 'the hardware capital was astonished' by so many supporters. 'The roads were congested and the ground full by 2.00pm'.

Liverpool's left winger, Jack Cox was suffering from an injury so the directors met to choose a replacement and also decided to omit Raybould from the team. By all accounts it was a thrilling game, both sides matching each other for skill and determination. In the end, it was luck which broke the deadlock. A weak shot part-way through the second half from Everton's Abbott took a deflection off Dunlop, the Liverpool defender and Sam Hardy was left helpless. With Liverpool angry and cursing their misfortune, Everton struck again within a minute. Hardman, Everton's English international winger volleyed a fierce shot which Hardy could only

13

The 1905-06 season saw a Merseyside double with Liverpool winning the League and Everton the FA Cup.

parry away to the oncoming Sharp who in turn crossed the ball back to Hardman who made no mistake this time. Liverpool had lost 2 – 0 and Everton went on to beat Newcastle in the final, bringing the FA Cup home to Merseyside for the first time. With the League title and the FA Cup safely secured in the city of Liverpool, it could be reasonably suggested that Merseyside was now the home of English football.

After their magnificent championship win a golden age of Liverpool football drew to a close. There were to be no more trophies for sixteen years, only a Cup final appearance. It was a period of consolidation with the Reds usually to be found somewhere in mid-table. The directors celebrated the championship triumph by taking the players on a short trip to Paris and rewarded the spectators in 1906 by building the Spion Kop. In 1907 – 08 Liverpool finished eighth, the highlight of the season being a thrilling 7 – 4 win over prospective champions Manchester United who included Billy Meredith at outside right. It was also the season when singing was first officially reported at Anfield though surprisingly it did not come from the Liverpool supporters but from Backburn Rovers followers standing on the Kop. There is a legend that singing really began the season Liverpool won their second title, 1905 – 06 but this has never been confirmed. Before 1905 it had been rare to spot anyone wearing the colours of their team but after 1907 it became increasingly fashionable to sport coloured rossettes and scarves.

In 1909 – 10 Liverpool finished as runners-up but were never really challenging the eventual title winners, Newcastle United by six goals to five at Anfield after being 5 – 2 down at half-time. They also beat Manchester United 4 – 3 at the opening of the Old Trafford ground and later put seven goals past Nottingham Forest. Jack Parkinson, the club's free-scoring centre forward, hit thirty goals in only thirty-one games during the season and in a career which spanned 181 games between 1904 and 1914 he scored 116 goals. No other player in Liverpool's history has ever scored at such a phenomenal rate.

Some of the great old names disappeared. Alex Raisbeck who had inspired Liverpool to two championships eventually stepped down in 1910 to be replaced by James Harrop, a young centre half signed from Rotherham for £250. He was a complete contrast to Raisbeck, slim with jet black hair and skilful rather than tough. Raisbeck went off to Hamilton Academicals as manager, moving later to Bristol City, Halifax Town and Chester. Eventually he wound up back at Anfield as chief scout and died a poor man in Liverpool in 1949. In 1912 Sam Hardy also moved on to Aston Villa but still continued to keep goal for England. For thirteen years he was England's regular 'keeper winning a grand total of twenty-one caps. For the next few years Ken Campbell kept goal for Liverpool. He had joined the club in 1911 from Cambuslang as understudy to Hardy and although he won eight Scottish caps, he was soon overshadowed by one of the finest goalkeepers of all time. He was still an international goalkeeper when he left Liverpool and it was a tragedy that his career should have been sandwiched between that of two outstanding 'keepers.

In 1912 Liverpool signed an Irishman from Belfast Celtic who was to become a legend among goalkeepers. He was Elisha Scott who for the next twenty years was to stand solidly behind Liverpool's defence. During the 1920s the Liverpool – Everton derbies were always billed as a clash between Scott and Dixie Dean. It was once reported that when they met casually one day in the street, Dean nodded politely to Scott and the great Irish goalkeeper leaped into the air to save some imaginary ball. Scott was also said to arrive in the dressing-room some two hours or more before kick-off and be dressed and ready before his teammates had appeared. He would then spend an hour or so hurling the ball against the wall and catching it but nobody every recorded how his teammates reacted to this. He always wore two pairs of socks and three sweaters, even in the autumn and spring, while in winter a pair of darkened long-johns and knee pads were added.

ABOVE Full back Don McKinlay leading Liverpool out in 1926. McKinlay, a Scottish international, made over 400 appearances for Liverpool.

PREVIOUS PAGE TOP Inside forward Dick Forshaw (left) was ever present in the two championship winning teams of 1921-22 and 1922-23, scoring forty goals over the two seasons. Kenny Campbell (right) succeeded the great Sam Hardy in goal, making 142 appearances between 1911 and 1920 but in turn was ousted by his understudy, Elisha Scott.

BOTTOM Elisha Scott saves bravely from the Chelsea attack.

Another significant signing during this period was Ephraim Longworth who came from Leyton after a spell at Bolton Wanderers. A full back, he later captained England winning five caps and was rated as one of the finest defenders of the time. Bill Lacey, signed in 1912, had the dubious distinction of being one of the first players to move directly from Goodison to Anfield. He was an Irish international who was swapped for two Liverpool players, Tommy Gracie and Harol Uren, and continued to win international honours while at Liverpool before moving on to Third Division New Brighton in 1924 where he even won a couple more caps. Henry Lowe, a centre half from Derbyshire joined the Reds in 1911 and went on to captain them.

Despite these new signings the results still continued to dismay the crowds. In February 1912 the one penny match programme for the Sheffield Wednesday game slammed the side commenting that 'once more the Liverpool team is drifting towards the clutches of the Second Division with feeble displays'. Since their semi-final appearance against Everton, Liverpool had shown little inclination in the Cup but in 1914 as the War clouds gathered darkly over Britain, Liverpool reached their first final. In the opening round they were drawn at home to Second Division Barnsley who had won the cup two years previously and on a wet afternoon managed to scrape a draw with their gritty Yorkshire visitors. At this point it might well have looked as if Liverpool's cup prospects were over barely before they had begun. But they travelled to Oakwell and with apparently even greater luck won 1 – 0. In the next round Liverpool again had a home draw, this time against Gillingham of the Southern League who that season had changed their name from New Brompton. Eventually they were overcome by two goals to nil. The third round pitted Liverpool against another Southern League side, West Ham who held Liverpool to a gallant 1 – 1 draw. But the replay was a very different affair as the Reds rattled in five goals. As if Liverpool had not seen enough of the Southern League, they went and drew Queens Park Rangers for their next tie but the Southern League side

The Liverpool side which reached the 1914 FA Cup final against Burnley. Kenny Campbell (back row, centre) could do little to stop Freeman's outstanding goal which won Burnley the Cup, 1-0.

were easily defeated at Anfield. This put Liverpool into the semi-final for the third time in their history but the prospects did not look too bright. Their opponents were favourites Aston Villa, Cup winners the previous year, champions in 1910 and runners up in 1911 and 1913. And to crown it all Sam Hardy was now keeping goal for them and by all accounts playing just as bravely and safely as he had at Anfield.

Liverpool travelled to White Hart Lane somewhat in awe of their Midland challengers and although the Villa were quick to demonstrate the skilful touches which had made them so popular and successful, Liverpool kept their head and plugged away in the warm sunshine. Their pragmatic approach paid off when James Nicholl, a newly-signed Scot headed in a perfectly-centred Sheldon corner after just half an hour and then rounded off a brilliant personal display with another goal in the second half. Kenny Campbell gave what was said to be the goalkeeping performance of his lifetime and Liverpool were in the final. The crowd went wild and for the first time chanting was reported at a football match. There was even cheering back at Goodison when

the score was put up on the result board and the *Liverpool Football Echo* ran the headline, 'Villa's Cup Pride Goes Before A Fall. Bravo, Liverpool!'

FA Cup Final 1914 Liverpool v Burnley

Liverpool's opponents in the final were North Lancashire neighbours, Burnley who were also making their first appearance in a final. Founding members of the Football League, Burnley had finished the season four places up the table from Liverpool so a close contest was always in prospect. To add glitter to the occasion, His Majesty King George V was to present the prize, the first time a reigning monarch had attended a Cup final.

'London Invaded' ran the headline in the *Sunday Times* and although fewer spectators attended than the previous year when a record crowd of 122,000 had packed the terraces, there were still officially more than 72,000 crammed into the Crystal Palace ground. Some newspapers even estimated the crowd at over 100,000 and judging from the number of trains and coaches arriving in London they could have been close. Fans could be spotted perched dangerously on telegraph poles outside the ground while others clung precariously to the branches of the tallest trees surrounding the stadium. Throughout their Cup run, almost a quarter of a million spectators had watched Liverpool with the club earning more than £9,000. It was to be the last time that the

TOP Liverpool supporters secure every vantage point for their first Cup final, even blocking the way to Crystal Palace.

BOTTOM King George V, sporting his red button-hole becomes the first reigning monarch to attend an FA Cup final.

OPPOSITE PAGE A section of the 74,093 crowd which saw Liverpool lose by a single goal to Burnley.

Crystal Palace would host a final after nineteen consecutive years of staging England's premier football occasion.

Cheap football excursions were already a part of the life of the supporter and around 170 special trains steamed out of Burnley and Lime Street stations as dawn broke over Lancashire on Cup final morning of 25 April, 1914. More than 20,000 Liverpool fans were said to have made the long journey south. The *Liverpool Football Echo* which had first appeared in 1889, now published for the first time a special Cup final edition with photographs of all the players as well as team news, features on the players and predictions on the result. The Liverpool team had left the city on the Monday for a few quiet days at Chingford and travelled up to the Crystal Palace on the actual day.

For the great event, Liverpool were without their captain Lowe and called on the one-time Third Lanark player, Bob Ferguson to assume his role. Two other former Third Lanark players, Tom Fairfoul and Tom Miller, played alongside him with another four Scots supporting them. One of those Scots was Don McKinlay, a half back who had joined Liverpool in 1909. He later captained the team and won two Scottish caps. Yet again the Liverpool line-up typically illustrated their scouting raids north of the border. Of the rest, John Sheldon and Henry Lowe hailed from Derbyshire with Lowe a former Manchester United player who had spent years as understudy to the legendary Billy Meredith. Arthur Metcalfe had come from Newcastle United in 1912, scoring fourteen goals in his first twenty-eight games for Liverpool.

Excited crowds blocked the route to the Crystal Palace, delaying the King who sported a red Lancashire rose in his buttonhole especially for the occasion, but there was never any fear that the game would begin without him. Liverpool playing against a strong breeze started well and Nicholl might have scored in the first few minutes when he missed an open goal. Moments later a fierce shot from the Scotsman almost knocked the Burnley full back, Taylor into the back of the net. As it was Taylor lay stunned for some minutes before recovering. In the meantime, Miller screwed a good opportunity wide. Although Liverpool looked the sturdier team, Burnley were dangerous on the breakaway and might well have stolen a goal before half-time when Lindley hit the crossbar. After a goalless first half Liverpool came out determined to finish the job. The wind was now with them and the sun shone brightly on the packed stadium but the goal simply would not come. Then thirteen minutes into the second half Burnley scored what proved to be the decisive goal when Freeman, from a throw-in, drove a thunderous volley wide of the outstretched Campbell. It was a goal fitting to win a Cup final. Liverpool continued to plug away but the Burnley defence remained solid and chances were few.

At the final whistle the score remained 1 – 0 and as the Liverpool players were handed their runners-up medals by His Majesty they could perhaps reckon themselves a trifle unlucky to have lost a rather dour match. But at least they had reached the final and when they returned home, it was as if they had won the Cup with thousands turning out to give them a tumultuous welcome. Bad luck was to dog Liverpool in the Cup for a long time and

it would be thirty-six years before another Liverpool team would grace a final and fifty-one before the Cup would come home to Anfield.

Liverpool Campbell, Longworth, Purcell, Fairfoul, Ferguson, McKinlay, Sheldon, Metcalfe, Miller, Lacey, Nicholl.

Burnley Sewell, Bamford, Taylor, Halley, Boyle, Watson, Nesbitt, Lindley, Freeman, Hodgson, Mosscrop.

SCANDAL!

Within four months of the Cup final and with a new season imminent, Britain was plunged into World War. There was excitement initially and long queues of volunteers stretched outside recruitment offices up and down the land. There was even an advert in the Liverpool match programme for volunteers to enlist with Lord Kitchener's army. For the city of Liverpool the outbreak of War brought brighter prospects with new jobs in the munitions factories and shipyards which were now working at full capacity to meet the crisis demand for new orders. The footballing authorities met in emergency session to review the darkening situation but with the permission of the Government decided to continue with the approaching season.

It was not a season to be remembered. Liverpool's Cup run ended early and they finished the season in mid-table. Everton had better luck winning their second League title. As hostilities worsened and news of death and horror on the War front and in the trenches filtered home, gates fell and more keen men were enlisted. It was hardly a time to be playing football and at the end of the season the Football League took the inevitable decision to postpone professional football until the War was over. The players could see it coming and with their livelihood threatened, some of them foolishly tried to make a quick financial killing by fixing a game.

Unfortunately, one of the clubs involved in the scandal was Liverpool. The game was the Good Friday match at Old Trafford in 1915 against Manchester United. While Liverpool were in a comfortable position half way up the table, United were struggling near the bottom and staring relegation in the face. A win for United would obviously bring two very useful points. More importantly, as far as some players were concerned, if bets could be laid on a correct result it could prove extremely lucrative. Liverpool had already been involved in two fixing inquiries but exonerated on each occasion. In 1911 there had been doubts about a Liverpool game against Newcastle but the inquiry could find no evidence to substantiate the allegations. More seriously, in 1913 the Arsenal chairman publicly accused Liverpool of fixing a match with Chelsea. John McKenna immediately ordered an official inquiry but again there was no evidence and the players were fully exonerated with deep apologies from the Arsenal chairman.

The game against United was played in pouring rain in front of 15,000 spectators with George Anderson putting United into an early lead. In the second half United were awarded a penalty but instead of Anderson stepping up to take it, Patrick O'Connell grabbed the ball and hit his shot wide, well wide. Liverpool looked lethargic all afternoon, barely making an effort to win the ball and when Fred Pagnam, the Liverpool centre forward hit the bar, his teammates visibly showed their anger at him. Pagnam, it was later alleged was not a party to the deal and had warned his teammates against the arrangement. Late in the match Anderson scored a second to give Manchester United a 2 – 0 victory. There was no immediate speculation in the press although all reports of the game mentioned Liverpool's miserable showing with the *Sporting Chronicle* reckoning Liverpool as 'too poor to describe'. It was not until a few weeks later when the *Sporting Chronicle* published the following note from a bookmaker that the football world was alerted to a possible scandal.

£50 REWARD

'We have solid grounds for believing that a certain First League match played in Manchester during Easter weekend was "squared", the home club being permitted to win by a certain score. Further, we have information that several of the players of both teams invested substantial sums on having the correct score of this match with our firm and others. Such being the case we wish to inform all our clients and the football public generally that we are witholding payment on these correct score transactions, also that we are causing security investigations to be made with the object of pursuing the instigators of this reprehensible conspiracy. With the object in view we are anxious to receive reliable information bearing on the subject, and we will willingly pay the substantial reward named above to anyone giving information which will lead to punishment of the offenders.'
'The Football Kings'

The advert rocked the soccer world and the Football League immediately set up a three-man inquiry which began its investigations in Manchester on 10 May. Betting on football matches was common practice in those days but what was unusual was betting on a correct result and the heavy sums of money laid on a 2 – 0 result for United at seven to one had given the game away. The commission continued meeting throughout the autumn, interviewing players and club officials and delivered its final verdict just two days before Christmas. Its conclusions were damning proving that 'a considerable sum of money changed hands by betting on the match and...some of the players profited thereby'. Eight players were named and 'suspended from taking part in football or football management, and shall not be allowed to enter any football ground in future'. Four players from each club were banned for life. There were also 'grave suspicions' that others were involved but nothing could be proven. It seemed that under pressure of questioning one of the Liverpool players finally cracked, revealing the whole shabby tale of coniving with United players in a Manchester pub and carefully laying bets around the country. In his evidence to the commission, the referee described the game as 'the most extraordinary match I have ever officiated in'.

The Liverpool culprits were Jackie Sheldon who as a former Manchester United player was reckoned to have been a central figure in 'squaring' the United players; Bob Purcell who had been poached from Queens Park in 1911 in an illegal deal which led to Liverpool being fined £250; Tommy Miller, the former Motherwell, Third Lanark and Hamilton Academicals player; and Tom Fairfoul another Scot. Between them they were estimated to be worth £2,000. Of the four United players banned – Turnbull, Whalley, West and Look, only Enoch 'Knocker' West had actually played in the game and for the remainder of his life, he maintained his

innocence. His suspension was finally lifted in 1945 but by then he was too bitter to even attend a game, let alone play one. John McKenna was deeply upset and although only four of the Liverpool team had been banned, most knew about the deal with Pagnam and Ephraim Longworth both warning the others against their actions.

At the end of the War the four Liverpool players had their sentences generously lifted by the Football League who presumably reckoned that four years of fighting should be rewarded in some way. Given McKenna's earlier distress however, it was surprising that three of the players, Sheldon, Purcell and Miller, should ever be selected to play for Liverpool again. Purcell only played two games but Sheldon made a further seventy-two appearances playing on until 1921 when he retired after breaking a leg. Tommy Miller was even capped by Scotland and after a couple more seasons at Anfield was transferred to, of all clubs, Manchester United.

From left to right, Jackie Sheldon, Tom Fairfoul and Tom Miller, three of the four Liverpool culprits found guilty by the Football League for fixing the game with Manchester United. Sheldon, the former United right winger was reckoned to be the central figure and along with the other Liverpool and four United players was banned from football for life. After the War, however, the Football League lifted the ban as a token of gratitude for their part in fighting during the War.

For the most part the soccer played between 1915 and 1919 was meaningless. The Football League had been disbanded and regional leagues set up in replacement. Liverpool and Everton found themselves in a Lancashire League and although they were playing thirty matches a season, key players were absent and there was generally little interest. For the record Liverpool were fourth in 1916, winners in 1917, second in 1918 and third in 1919.

Tom Watson who had served Liverpool as secretary and manager for almost twenty years bowed out in 1915 but not before he had made another crucial signing, that of Harry Chambers. Chambers arrived at Anfield a skinny young lad but once he began playing serious soccer after the War he matured into a fine inside forward and was rewarded with ten England caps. Watson was succeeded by David Ashworth. 'Honest' John McKenna still remained at the helm although he had handed over the chairmanship to W.R. Williams. By now McKenna had become a hugely respected figure in footballing circles and was President of the Football League, a post he held for twenty-six years.

When football made its welcome return to England in 1919, the shape of the Liverpool team was changing. Kenny Campbell remained in goal but it would not be long before Elisha Scott was challenging for the position. The new lad Chambers was soon drafted into the side while Longworth, Tom Lucas and Don McKinlay were still at the back with Sheldon, Miller, Pearson and Lacey continuing up front. Another new name was Bromilow. On the day War ended Tom Bromilow, a Liverpool

schoolboy had knocked on the door at Anfield requesting a trial. He was offered one and immediately signed by the club. He was small and slim with hardly the physique of a defender but he quickly slotted into the left half spot and began to demonstrate a new understanding of half back play. He was a fine distributor of the ball who could pick out players thirty yards away and timed his tackles with perfect precision. Between 1921 and 1926 he won five England caps. Walter Wadsworth, a half back also joined the club along with Jock McNab and Dick Forshaw.

For much of their first season back in football Liverpool were uninspiring. As 1920 broke they hovered in the lower half of the table and seemed to have settled for a fruitless season. In the match programme against Preston the editor cuttingly remarked that 'the quality of the football we have witnessed from our favourites has been of a decidedly streaky character'. Perhaps his words did the trick because within the next six weeks Liverpool notched up seven successive victories and jumped to fourth in the table, a position they hung on to until the end of the season. King George V became the first reigning monarch to watch a League game that season when he saw Manchester City beat Liverpool at Hyde Road.

Liverpool began the 1920−21 season encouragingly and were in fourth place when Everton visited Anfield on a gloriously sunny day late in the autumn. Everton, however, arrived as League leaders and a classic derby was in prospect. Fifty thousand turned up, each paying

H. CHAMBERS.

DONALD McKINLAY · LIVERPOOL

T. G. BROMILOW

T. LUCAS

their one shilling admission and saw Everton play with all the style and polish that one had come to expect, while Liverpool set about their job in a businesslike way. Chambers played his heart out and Forshaw grabbed the winning goal for the Reds just before half-time. The *Liverpool Football Echo* reported that 'the Kop rocked with the convulsion of a volcano'. A week later they crossed Stanley Park for the return match and before another crowd of 50,000 trounced Everton 3 – 0, knocking them from their perch at the top of the table. Everton never really recovered all season and finished well down the League while Liverpool clung to their fourth place. They may not have been champions but they were beginning to show some promise. The following season that promise came to fruition.

Liverpool began the 1921 – 22 season with a 3 – 0 defeat before 40,000 spectators at Roker Park, Charlie Buchan scoring Sunderland's second goal and inspiring them to a fine win. Liverpool took their revenge by two goals to one on the Wearsiders at Anfield a few weeks later before another big crowd and another virtuoso performance from Buchan. From this shaky start they went fifteen games before losing away to another north-east side, Middlesbrough. A week before they had hammered the Boro' 4 – 0 at Anfield. Manchester City with Meredith as ever chewing on his toothpick, were disposed of by four goals to two after City had made a spirited fightback from a two goal deficit. Liverpool had now jumped to fifth position in the table and after a trip to London where they took in a music hall, saw the sights and beat Chelsea 1 – 0, they moved into fourth slot. Both derby matches were drawn one goal each.

By New Year there was talk of a possible championship and when they routed Sunderland by five goals to nil in a first round FA Cup replay, there was even mention of the double. In the next round they drew West Bromwich at home and before a big crowd lost by the only goal. It was probably just as well as it enabled the Reds to concentrate on the League. By the spring, Liverpool were clear favourites but then in the final run-in they dramatically lost three of their last four games against Oldham, Cardiff and West Brom. Having just lost to West Bromwich at home they then had to face them in a return match at the Hawthorns but won comfortably 4 – 1 to capture their third League title. They topped the League six points clear of their nearest rivals Tottenham. Of the forty-two games played they had won twenty-two, drawn thirteen and lost seven conceding thirty-six goals. Again, it was the strength of their defence which was the key to their success and at the heart of it was Elisha Scott, the giant Irish goalkeeper. Up front Harold Chambers with nineteen

goals and Dick Forshaw with seventeen had helped Liverpool to a tally of sixty-three goals. At the club's Annual General Meeting the Liverpool chairman pointedly remarked with more than a passing glance towards Goodison Park that 'I believe that it is in blending, not in paying, that a club succeeds.' Only Longworth and Hopkins had cost Liverpool appreciable transfer fees.

The following season Liverpool fared even better. They began temperamentally winning their opening game against Arsenal at Anfield 5 – 2, then losing to Sunderland and Arsenal away before winning the next four games. After slipping against Burnley they faced an

The legendary Elisha Scott was the finest goalkeeper of his era. Capped 31 times by Ireland, he made over 450 appearances for Liverpool.

LIVERPOOL
FOOTBALL CLUB.
LEAGUE CHAMPIONS

ABOVE Elisha Scott saves an Arsenal penalty, January 1923.
LEFT Trainer Charlie Wilson shows off the First Division trophy in 1922 with Andy McGuigan.

improving Everton at Anfield and before an ecstatic crowd trounced their rivals 5−1. A week later they went to Goodison and won 1−0, signalling to the rest of the League that they were after the title again. Into the spring it looked as if a skilful Sunderland side might offer some serious challenge but when Liverpool beat the Wembley-heading Bolton Wanderers 3−0 at Anfield they went four points ahead of Sunderland. At that game a fire broke out in the Anfield Road grandstand shortly after half-time which the Kop comics reckoned had something to do with Hopkins having just scored his very first goal for Liverpool before the break. Fortunately, nobody was injured although smoke drifting across the pitch almost brought the game to a halt. Two weeks later Manchester City beat Liverpool and the gap narrowed.

Then on 14 April, while Sunderland were beating Burnley, Liverpool could only draw with an improving Huddersfield Town led by Clem Stephenson who were on the verge of a first ever hat-trick of championships. The gap was now down to one point and a week later Huddersfield were the opposition again in the final match of the season at Anfield. Herbert Chapman had not long been managing the Yorkshire team but even in that short time had instilled into them qualities of resistance and team play. Led by Alex Jackson, they shot into an early lead through a lucky goal and before a

40,000 crowd battled as Liverpool surged on their goalmouth. Then in the seventy-third minute Chambers brought the roar from the Kop that Anfield had been hoping for when he hit the equaliser. A few minutes later the results board showed that Sunderland had been beaten by Burnley and there was now no doubt about the destination of the League Championship. Once Sunderland had finished their programme, Liverpool were champions by a clear six points.

This time their record was incomparable. They had won twenty-six of their forty-two games, drawn eight and lost eight. But it was their goal statistics which told the true story. Only thirty-one goals had been conceded over the entire season. No First Division club had ever conceded so few goals over thirty-eight games, let alone forty-two. Again it was Elisha Scott who had kept up the shutters in the Liverpool goalmouth. In the eighty-one games which Scott had played over the two seasons, he had conceded just sixty-three goals, setting standards that future Anfield goalkeepers would find difficult to emulate. Chambers and Forshaw were again the goalscoring heroes with the bustling bow-legged Chambers hitting twenty-two goals. In the Cup Liverpool began well and raised hopes of a double with wins over Arsenal and Wolves but then faltered surprisingly at home to Sheffield United.

Over the two seasons the Liverpool side barely changed and the team pinned on the noticeboard in the dressing-room each week usually read: Scott, Longworth, McKinlay, McNab, Wadsworth, Bromilow, Lacey, Forshaw, Shone, Chambers and Hopkins.

DEPRESSION

Liverpool set out the following season hopeful of a hat-trick of championship wins but it was not to be. For the remainder of the inter-war years they achieved little. Instead, it was Everton, with the Birkenhead-born William Ralph Dean leading their attack, who became champions in 1928, 1932 and 1939. Along with Arsenal and Huddersfield Town they were to dominate English football during the inter-war years. Perhaps if Liverpool's scouting network had concentrated on Merseyside, rather than north of the border, Dean might have left Tranmere for Liverpool instead. Even in the Cup Liverpool showed little endeavour while Everton went on to lift it in 1933. The main problem was often a lack of goals with only forty-nine scored in 1923–24 when they also failed to hit the net in fifteen games.

Perhaps it had something to do with David Ashworth's decision to resign as manager after his two title wins. He moved on, to the surprise of most, to Oldham Athletic who had just been relegated to Division Two but had little success there. In truth Liverpool's failure on the field probably had more to do with an ageing team. Some had been playing since before the Great War and even Elisha Scott had been around in 1912. Throughout the years of success Liverpool had stood by the same team, making as few switches as possible and there was still a reluctance to introduce new faces. Some changes, however, were made behind the scenes. Matt McQueen who had played for Liverpool during the 1890s was appointed manager, R.L. Martindale became chairman and George Patterson secretary. When McQueen lost a leg in an accident in 1928 he resigned and Patterson took over as manager. McQueen was later made a director and set a precedent of being player, manager and director which Bob Paisley would emulate in later years. John McKenna was still there in the background but was growing old and in March 1936 died at the age of eighty-one after serving Liverpool generously for forty years. At his funeral his coffin, like that of John Houlding before him, was carried by three Liverpool players and three from Everton and a commemorative plaque to him still stands in the foyer of the club. He had been a director of Liverpool for more than thirty years, a member of the FA Council since 1905, a former President of the Football League and a vice-President of the Football Association.

There also had to be changes on the field. Liverpool, perhaps learning from their failure to land Dean, were now looking not just to Scotland but overseas as well and particularly to South Africa. Arthur Riley, touring Britain as goalkeeper of the national South African amateur team in 1925, caught the club's eye and was persuaded to remain behind. Before he progressed to the first team he was forced to spend a lengthy apprenticeship enviously watching the veteran Scott. When Scott did eventually step down in 1935 he had played 428 games for Liverpool between 1912 and 1934, and it was not a case of retiring when he did go. Instead, he returned to Belfast Celtic in Ireland and played on for a few more years. In all he won thirty Irish international caps, the last of those with Belfast Celtic in 1936. His international career had spanned sixteen years, even longer than his famour predecessor, Sam Hardy.

Another South African and one of the club's finest ever goalscorers, Gordon Hodgson, arrived in 1926. He combined his football with playing cricket for Lancashire and in 1930–31 set a club record of thirty-six goals in a season that was to stand until Roger Hunt hit forty-one goals in 1962. Other Springboks included Jimmy Gray, Leslie Carr, Bob Priday, Dirk Kemp, Hugh Gerhadi, Denny van den Berg and Berry Nieuwenhuys, all recommended by the club's agent in South Africa. Nieuwenhuys or 'Nivvy' as he was known joined Liverpool in 1933 as a winger and played until 1947, totalling 239 League appearances.

Another remarkable figure at Anfield was the Reverend James Jackson. A full back, he joined Liverpool from Aberdeen, playing football primarily to finance his ambition to become a minister of the church. While still playing for Liverpool he served at the Shaw Street Church and as an elder of Rankin Memorial Church. When his playing days were over he read for a degree in Greek and Philosophy at Cambridge and was ordained in 1933. After ministering in the Isle of Man he returned to Liverpool where he continued to serve the church for many years. The fans knew him fondly as 'Parson' Jackson. In the dressing-room he was a vigorous opponent of alcohol and gambling but on the field was as tough as the next man. He was always a fine sportsman who could play in any position and captained the team

RIGHT TOP Three Liverpool South African players – Gordon Hodgson (left) and Ted Parry from the 1920s; and (inset) Berry Nieuwenhuys, an Anfielder from 1933-47.
BOTTOM The Liverpool captain, the Rev James Jackson (left) at Highbury in October 1928.

WILLS'S CIGARETTES

B. NIEUWENHUYS (LIVERPOOL)

many times. He was also one of the first footballers to have his own newspaper column, writing for the *Liverpool Weekly Post* regularly from 1928.

Tom Bradshaw, Scotland's centre half for the famous 'Wembley Wizards' who had beaten England 5–1, moved to Liverpool from Bury in 1930 for £8,000, the fourth highest fee that had ever been paid. Known as 'Tiny' the 6 feet 3 inches defender towered above his teammates.

In a desperate bid to shore up their defence the club signed the two regular England full backs, Tom Cooper from Derby County for £6,000 and Ernie Blenkinsop from Sheffield Wednesday. Between them they had forty-one England caps but once at Liverpool were never

to play for their country again. Another ex-England forward, Tom Johnson came from Barrow in 1935 but so many former internationals seemed to suggest that Liverpool were guilty of signing players with a glittering history rather than a future. Sadly this showed in their play. One player who could not be accused of having no future was the young Scot, Matt Busby. He was signed

BELOW Gordon Hodgson watches Dick Edmed (obscured by post) scoring the first of Liverpool's four goals against Aston Villa at Anfield in January 1929.

CARRERAS CIGARETTES

E. BLENKINSOP
LIVERPOOL (1ST DIVISION)

T. COOPER

FOOTBALL - T. BRADSHAW, LIVERPOOL

from Manchester City in 1935 having just won a Cup winners medal and played over a hundred games for the Anfielders before war broke out. He was later offered a job coaching at Liverpool but had already given a verbal commitment to Manchester United. Otherwise he might have been manager at Anfield rather than Old Trafford.

Throughout the years of the Depression Liverpool hovered in the mid-table. They rarely looked relegation material, nor prospective champions. Indeed their best season before the War was in 1925 when they finished fourth. In 1927–28 with the offside law changed they hit eighty-four goals yet only managed three away wins. One of these was at Villa Park where the former Partick inside forward, Jimmy McDougall dropped back to left half to replace the injured captain Don McKinlay. He played so well that he retained his place for a decade and eventually won three Scottish caps. Playing for Scotland against Italy in Rome in 1931 he was presented with a bouquet by the Italian dictator Mussolini. Along with Bradshaw and Busby, he formed a remarkable Scottish half back line for much of the late thirties. Helped by 'Demon' Devlin, Liverpool scored twenty-eight goals in their first seven home games but when Devlin was transferred to Hearts just before Christmas, the goals dried up. A record 56,447 watched the Anfield derby with Dixie Dean scoring a hat-trick in a 3–3 draw and the season closed with Harry Chambers leaving for West Brom and the rebuilding of the Spion Kop.

In the next season Liverpool scored ninety goals with Gordon Hodgson hitting thirty but it was still not enough for them to finish any higher than fifth. In an effort to guarantee even more goals the directors signed Jimmy Smith from Ayr United the following season. Smith had scored the British record of sixty-six goals during 1927–28 and went on to notch up twenty-three goals in his first season but surprisingly the team managed only sixty-three goals all season. The next season Hodgson scored thirty-six goals yet was only fifth in the Division One marksmen as Liverpool rattled in eighty-five goals. The goalscoring was complimented by some heavy defeats including a 7–0 drubbing at West Ham. The highlight of the 1931–32 season was the third round Cup defeat of prospective champions, Everton. Despite Dean scoring in the first minute, the Reds went on to win 2–1 before 57,000 spectators. The season however ended on a disastrous note as Bolton gave Liverpool their biggest ever thrashing by eight goals to one.

RIGHT Sam English joined Liverpool from Glasgow Rangers after being involved in the tragic accident that led to the death of Celtic goalkeeper, John Thomson.

The Liverpool defenders Tom Cooper and Tom Bradshaw (white shirts) watch Fred Hobson save from Charlton Athletic's Prior in 1936.

In October 1932 Liverpool hammered Everton at Anfield by seven goals to four with Barton scoring a hat-trick while Dixie Dean hit a couple for the Blues. It was the identical Everton team which would soon win the FA Cup. Three years later they handed Everton an even bigger drubbing when they trounced them 6−0. Howe was the hero that day hitting four with Hodgson adding a couple.

Prior to the opening of the 1933−34 season, Liverpool signed the Irish international, Sammy English from Glasgow Rangers. English who had set a club scoring record for Rangers of forty-four League goals in 1931−32 had also been the central figure in one of soccer's most tragic accidents when John Thomson, the Celtic and Scotland goalkeeper died from a fractured skull after diving in at the Irishman's feet. Blamed by many supporters for Thomson's death, English was continually barracked by Scottish football crowds and left Rangers for the sanctity of England. In his first season at Liverpool he scored eighteen goals but departed a year later, distressed at the heckling he was receiving even from the English soccer crowds.

In the FA Cup Liverpool were drawn away to Tranmere but, given the enormous interest in the game, Tranmere agreed to transfer the venue to Anfield and a record gate of 61,036 paid £4,000 to watch Liverpool win 3−1. However, there were more heavy defeats with both Arsenal and Huddersfield putting eight goals past Liverpool but following the 6−0 hammering of Everton in 1935, Liverpool hit seven against Grimsby at Anfield and five against West Brom a week later. Shortly after this Gordon Hodgson left Liverpool for Aston Villa having scored 233 goals in 358 League games over ten years. Ted Harthill was bought as a replacement but after only two months went to Bristol Rovers in exchange for Phil Taylor.

Jim Harley, a former winner of the Powderhall professional sprint title arrived in 1937 as a full back and in the same year Liverpool signed Ted Harston from Mansfield. Much was expected of Harston who had been the League's leading goalscorer the season before with fifty-five goals, but he was a grave disappointment and after just five games it was clear that he was not First Division standard.

For a brief spell in October 1938 it looked as if war had been averted and a crowd of 60,000 at Goodison for the derby celebrated Chamberlain's return from Munich by singing the National Anthem. Everton won 2−1 and went on to win the championship with Liverpool finishing eleventh. They had won fourteen games, drawn fourteen and lost fourteen with Fagan, Nivvy and Taylor joint top scorers with fourteen goals each.

6
WARTIME HEROES AND PEACETIME CHAMPIONS

The 1939–40 season was a mere three fixtures old when World War Two intervened and the footballing authorities called a halt to the professional game. The relaxed attitude of the early days of the First World War was far removed from the autumn of 1939, everyone knowing instinctively that this war would be a long and strenuous struggle. Nevertheless, football did continue but the early introduction of conscription forced it onto a totally different basis. The old league system was scrapped with regional leagues set up and guesting allowed. It was a hotch-potch of a system with constant changes to the rules and structure in order to satisfy Government orders on travelling, crowd control, absenteeism and air raids.

Within a month of the outbreak of war a regional system of ten leagues had been organised with Liverpool joining the West League where they played twenty-two games and finished in second place behind Stoke. In October they were beaten 4–1 by Everton, the local press reporting 'some differences of opinion among spectators'. Liverpool also met with trouble from the authorities when Peter Doherty, the Irish international visited their dressing-room at Blackpool to chat with some of his footballing colleagues. The club immediately enlisted his services and dropped Ainsley of Leeds who was supposed to be guesting for them. This, of course, meant that Ainsley's journey had been wasted when he could have been better employed and Liverpool were severely reprimanded by the RAF for not playing him when they had sought his release. The club were forced to apologise to the RAF and it was a lesson which did not go unnoticed among the other league clubs.

The guesting system was introduced in order to minimise travelling and allow players to compete for the club nearest their battalion or squadron. It led to an unusual mixture with some of the lesser clubs in the Third Division boasting First Division stars in their line-ups. Even Liverpool managed to attract a few star names with goalkeepers Frank Swift and Sam Bartram donning the green jersey on a number of occasions. The Everton and England international Cliff Britton also made a number of guest appearances for his rivals, as did Stan Cullis and Don Welsh. And during the 1941–42 season a certain W. Shankly played one game for Liverpool.

Billy Liddell, an eighteen-year-old winger from Dunfermline, who had signed for Liverpool in July 1938, made his debut for the Reds in their 7–1 defeat of Crewe on 1 January, 1940. A week later he scored a hat-trick when Manchester City, despite the presence of Frank Swift in goal, were thrashed 7–3. Another future star to make his debut that year was Tom Finney who played his first game at Anfield for Preston North End and although the eighteen-year-old scored, he still finished up on the losing side.

For the 1940–41 season there were two leagues. Liverpool competed in the North and ended the season in sixteenth place after thirty-seven games, behind the likes of Chesterfield, Halifax and New Brighton. Since teams could not always play the same number of fixtures, league positions were decided on goal average alone. For the remainder of the War years the season was divided into two with one championship decided before Christmas and a second beginning in the New Year. In the second half of the 1942–43 season Liverpool were champions, collecting thirty-two points from twenty games but generally they performed rather unspectacularly throughout the War. With signs of an end to hostilities on the horizon, the league reverted to a more identifiable pattern for 1945–46 and wages were increased. There were two top leagues, North and South, with Liverpool competing in the North and finishing in eleventh spot after the normal forty-two games.

Perhaps Liverpool's failure on the footballing field had much to do with their commendable war record off it. They were the first club to join the Territorials and some seventy-six players saw active service, one of the highest in the Football League. Tragically, Tom Cooper, their England international full back was killed in June 1940 when his army motorcycle was in collision with a bus. Another full back, Ted Spicer was also wounded in 1945 but recovered to play for many years after the War. A Lieutenant in the Marines, Spicer had the honour of personally capturing a German NCO and must have been even more pleased with himself when he discovered that his prisoner was a German football international. But there was also a rather shady affair concerning Liverpool's captain Berry Nieuwenhuys. Nivvy spent much of the War working as a driller as well as either playing for Liverpool or guesting elsewhere. His crime was to demand more than the regulation £2 a game and he was exposed after he had written to one club setting out his terms. It was almost certainly not uncommon among players but Nivvy was unfortunate to be caught

Cyril Done joined Liverpool in 1939 playing most of his football during the War.

Liverpool toured America and Canada during the summer and went on a goalscoring spree but nobody attached too much importance to the results. It was really just a generous opportunity for players and management to get to know each other again after the disturbances of the War years.

The season began well with an undeserved one nil win at Sheffield United followed by a storming 7–4 home victory in the third game of the season against a Chelsea side led by Tommy Lawton with goals shared by Jones, Fagan, Roberston and Liddell. The Scottish winger, making his home debut having missed the second game through injury, scored twice with one of them a brilliant individual goal.

Then in the fourth game of the season they surprisingly lost 5–0 away to Manchester United in a game played at Maine Road due to bomb damage at Old Trafford. The club officials panicked thinking that this might herald the end of goals and dashed anxiously to Tyneside where they offered Newcastle United £12,500 for Albert Stubbins. The record fee raised more than a few eyebrows in post-war austerity Britain but at least it signalled that football was back to normal. There was just one problem. Everton had made a similar offer and Stubbins could not decide which of the Merseyside clubs he preferred. So he tossed a coin and Liverpool won. Panic or not on the part of Liverpool's manager George Kay, it turned out to be a wise move for Stubbins was a proven goalscorer having netted 244 goals for United. Over the next six years he was to do a similar job for Liverpool hitting seventy-seven goals, a strike rate of one every two games. Alongside Stubbins was the emerging Billy Liddell. The twenty-four-year-old Scotsman who had joined Liverpool from Lochgelly Viollet in 1938, had been quietly demonstrating his talents during the War years and had already snapped up eight Scottish caps from wartime internationals. But now his stage was bigger and his public grander.

With Stubbins, Jack Balmer and Liddell in attack, Liverpool struck mercilessly. First Grimsby were hit for six away and then four were knocked in at Huddersfield. In November the Liverpool-born Balmer set a record by striking three successive hat-tricks and then in early December the unexpected happened again when Wolves came to Anfield and won 5–1. Having shot to the top of the League Liverpool now stumbled nervously, losing to Chelsea, Everton, Stoke, Sheffield United and Bolton before the coldest January in decades was out.

With the Cup underway Liverpool travelled to Walsall thankful that they were only up against a Third Division side but must have wondered what had happened when Walsall took the lead. Liverpool equalised only for

and was suspended for life. However, like those players suspended during the First World War, Nivvy's sentence was later revoked and he continued to play for Liverpool until after the War. On the brighter side Liverpool had the best of the Merseyside derbies and Cyril Done twice scored forty goals in a season. They also made one of the most astonishing signings in the history of the game when Joe Louis, the World Heavyweight Boxing Champion on a promotional visit to England in 1944, signed on the dotted line to join the Reds. It was all done for fun but at least Liverpool could boast that the Brown Bomber was on their books.

When the War ended in 1945 the nation gradually began the return to normal life. Industry switched from producing tanks, guns and planes to once again manufacturing consumer goods and building homes. The armed forces started the steady trek back from Europe and the Far East and the country looked forward to new prosperity and the prospect of more leisure and sport. By September 1946 everyone was eager and anxious for the restart of League football.

ABOVE Prolific goalscorer Albert Stubbins challenges Leslie Compton at Highbury in 1949.
RIGHT Billy Liddell turns the Arsenal defence.
BELOW Jack Balmer was the first player to score three hat-tricks in consecutive League games in 1946-47.

Walsall to strike again. Now was the time for strong hearts and fortunately Liverpool had them as they romped to a spirited 5 – 2 victory that must have helped restore some confidence. In the next round they were drawn at home to First Division Grimsby seeing them off comfortably by two clear goals. Round five brought Derby County to Anfield with Jack Balmer scoring the only goal. In the quarter-finals Liverpool faced Second Division Birmingham, Stubbins helping them to a 4 – 1 win and a place in the semi-finals with a hat-trick. At this stage it looked as if there might be a chance of the double although Liverpool's semi-final opponents, Burnley had in 1914 snatched the Cup from the Reds when it was within their grasp. Liverpool longed for revenge but before a packed house at Maine Road went down to a disappointing 1 – 0 defeat.

At least the League was still within reach but with five of their last seven games away from home it would require a mammoth effort. They began well beating Sunderland at home and then travelled to Aston Villa where they had a well deserved 2 – 1 win. Another home victory against fellow title contenders Manchester United was followed by an away win at Charlton. Then they stumbled at Brentford only managing a draw. In the next game at Highbury they defeated Arsenal 2 – 1 and now faced second placed Wolves who likewise needed to win this game to bring the title back to Molineux. Even if Liverpool did win they would still have to wait until Stoke City, the only other team capable of winning the League, had completed their season at Sheffield United. It could hardly have been a more exciting climax to a season which because of the atrocious winter had been extended into June. Liverpool scored early on through Balmer and went two up before the interval but in the second half Wolves pulled one back and threw everything they had at Liverpool. But the former Wolves goalkeeper, Sidlow and his defence held steady to clinch victory for the Reds. Liverpool now had an agonising fortnight to wait and on the evening Stoke and Sheffield met, the Reds found themselves playing Everton at Anfield in the Liverpool Senior Cup Final. Liverpool and Everton kicked off fifteen minutes later with the Liverpool players hardly able to concentrate during the final twenty minutes, and just before full-time the announcement at last came over on the loudspeakers that Sheffield had beaten Stoke. Liverpool had won their fifth championship. Anfield erupted and at the final whistle the Kop swarmed on to the pitch to lift the players shoulder-high. In all the excitement it was almost forgotten that Liverpool had just won another trophy as they had beaten Everton by two goals to one. What a night!

LEFT Bob Paisley made 278 appearances for the Reds.
ABOVE Eddie Spicer (left), Willie Fagan and (inset) Laurie Hughes, were important members of the Liverpool side in the 1940s.

Since losing to Everton in late January Liverpool had played eight games, winning six and drawing just two. At the centre of that defence was a twenty-eight-year-old Geordie by the name of Bob Paisley. He had joined Liverpool from the amateur cup winning side Bishop Auckland in 1939, played a few games in the War years and then established himself in the championship winning team with thirty-three appearances. He was a wing half, determined and consistent rather than skilful or brash. Alongside him was a former Bristol Rovers player, Phil Taylor who would also go on to manage Liverpool and Laurie Hughes who had arrived from Merseyside neighbours Tranmere Rovers mid-way through the War. He would later be England's centre half in their first World Cup Finals appearance in Brazil.

Unusually for Liverpool, there were a couple of Welsh internationals in the team with goalkeeper Cyril Sidlow and right back Ray Lambert. It was a tenacious side, a neat combination of solidity in defence and skill and goalscoring ability up front. Stubbins was the leading goalscorer with twenty-six goals making his record fee worth every penny. Captaining the side was Willie Fagan who had joined Liverpool as a nineteen-year-old in 1938. He had arrived via Celtic and Preston where he played alongside Bill Shankly. The Liverpool squad that season was made up of Sidlow, Lambert, Harley, Ramsden, Taylor, Jones, Hughes, Paisley, Watkinson, Balmer, Stubbins, Done, Fagan, Liddell.

With such a strong squad it was all the more surprising that over the next few seasons the team should drop disappointingly into mid-table. Perhaps in that season of 1946–47 this particular Liverpool side reached its zenith. Many of the players had been around since before the War and in the succeeding years would become just a little leg weary for championship chasing.

FA Cup Final 1950 Liverpool v Arsenal

The 1949–50 season found Liverpool making only their second appearance in a Cup final and their first at Wembley. The close season had again been spent in America and Canada with little activity in the transfer market and the break must have done the players some good for they started the season in fine form. By the end of the year they were top of the table, two points ahead of Manchester United and had gone nineteen matches before their first defeat. The pundits on the Kop were beginning to fancy Liverpool's chances for another League title.

The Cup campaign began nervously with Liverpool only managing a goalless draw away to Second Division Blackburn but once on the Anfield turf they were disposed of by the odd goal in three. The fourth round found Exeter City making the long trek to Merseyside only to be sent back on the next train to continue their lowly sojourn near the bottom of the Third Division South. In the fifth round Liverpool travelled the short

distance down the East Lancs road to Stockport and came away with a comfortable 2–1 win. So far the opposition had been stubborn rather than tough but all that was to change when Liverpool drew Blackpool for the quarter-finals. At least it was a home draw and the indomitable Stanley Matthews was injured. It was a hard game with Liverpool made to fight every inch of the way. Willie Fagan put the Reds ahead, only for the England centre forward Stan Mortenson to equalise from the penalty spot after Laurie Hughes had handled the ball. Then late in the second half with Billy Liddell craftily switching wings, the Scotsman put Liverpool into the semi-finals. It was Liverpool's second semi-final appearance since the war.

Everton were also having a good Cup run and when they beat Derby County to reach the semis as well, the whole of Merseyside was talking about a Liverpool–Everton final. Never before had the two clubs met in the final of any major competition. But as luck would have it the two teams came out of the hat together and the venue was Maine Road. Liverpool's winning rhythm in the League meanwhile was temporarily halted. They began to lose matches and by the time the semi-final arrived on 25 March all hope of topping the League had disappeared.

With Hughes injured Liverpool brought Jones into what was otherwise their regular side. Although both clubs were desperate to represent the city at Wembley, all reports spoke highly of the two teams' sportsmanship with the *Liverpool Daily Post* calling it 'the finest of all city inter-club matches'. Watched before a crowd of 73,000 Bob Paisley put Liverpool ahead in the first half with a perfectly judged lob and in the second Billy Liddell squeezed the ball through the Everton defence to score the goal that took the Reds to their first Wembley appearance. For the final, the new manager made just one change. It was a change which has been recalled and reported on many times since. With Hughes fit again, the man to be dropped was not Jones but Bob Paisley. In later years Paisley would tell of the heartbreak of not being chosen but at least in making crucial team decisions he would be able to tell unlucky players that he understood how they felt. Throughout his career Paisley would be dogged by bad luck in the FA Cup. He would never win a Cup winners medal or manage a victorious Cup side.

LEFT Liverpool's Cyril Sidlow saves as the Reds beat Sunderland 4-2 in August 1949. He was one of the first goalkeepers to regularly throw the ball to a colleague instead of booting it downfield. He would play almost 150 games before moving to New Brighton in 1952.

Liverpool's opponents at Wembley were Arsenal who had won one post-war title and been in contention on most other occasions. They boasted a team of star-studded names such as Joe Mercer, Wally Barnes, George Swindin and the cricketer Denis Compton, who planned the Wembley game as his final match before retiring. Joe Mercer who hailed from Merseyside and still lived there regularly trained at Anfield. However, with a Cup final in prospect Liverpool had been left with a problem. Rather than prohibit him from the club's training ground they agreed to let him continue training but down the other end of the pitch, by himself.

The two captains, Phil Taylor and Joe Mercer led the teams on to a Wembley turf which had been drenched in

Liverpool Sidlow, Lambert, Spicer, Taylor (capt), Hughes, Jones, Payne, Baron, Stubbins, Fagan, Liddell.

Arsenal Swindin, Scott, Barnes, Forbes, Compton L., Mercer (capt), Cox, Logie, Goring, Lewis, Compton D.

a sudden downpour shortly before kick-off. Liverpool were quick to master the tricky conditions and were looking the more effective side when a perfectly measured through ball from Peter Goring split the Liverpool defence leaving Reg Lewis with the not too difficult task of beating Sidlow in the Liverpool goal. The game was just seventeen minutes old. The goal shook Liverpool who never really recovered and inspired Arsenal to a vintage performance. From that moment on they dominated the game with short accurate passes and skilful dribbling. Lewis also scored Arsenal's second goal and although Liverpool had their chances, even hitting the bar, Arsenal fully deserved their third Cup final victory. And so it was ex-Evertonian Joe Mercer who led his Arsenal team up the steps to collect the Cup. Liverpool could only look on in envy. The *Daily Mail* reckoned Liverpool had been 'outmatched by a better all-round team'. So, Liverpool, fifty-eight years old had still to win the Cup. It was now being joked that the day Liverpool did win the Cup the Liver Birds perched on the Liver Buildings at the Pier Head would up and fly away.

Early in the New Year of 1951, George Kay retired through ill health. Kay who had captained the losing West Ham team in the famous first Wembley Cup final had been managing Liverpool for fifteen years. Into his shoes stepped the former Charlton and England inside left, Don Welsh who had guested for Liverpool during the War. But it was to be a depressing time both for him and the club. From their post-war glory Liverpool slipped further and further down the League. One interesting signing in 1950 was an American, Joe Cadden who had played for Brooklyn Wanderers in a friendly against Liverpool during their second tour of America. The club was impressed by the Scottish-born centre half and brought him back to Anfield but he was never up to First Division standards and after only four appearances moved on to Grimsby and later Accrington Stanley.

The year after their Wembley appearance Liverpool suffered the humiliation of a third round Cup defeat by Division Three's Norwich. However, the following year they attracted a record gate of just over 61,000 to watch their fourth round Cup win over Wolves. These were the years when soccer crowds were at their peak with a Goodison record crowd of 78,299 watching the drawn derby game in 1948. Two years after losing to Norwich the ignominy continued with Third Division North Gateshead knocking them out in the early rounds although Liverpool could claim some excuse in the blanket of fog which covered the North-East. In the same season the Reds narrowly avoided relegation thanks to a scrappy victory over Chelsea in the final match of the season after having led the table in mid-November. Their only consolation was that Everton had been relegated a few seasons before and were still trapped in Division Two.

However, before the struggle could get any easier, it sadly had to get worse. And so it happened that in the 1953–54 season after an Easter game at Highbury when

ABOVE RIGHT The first Liverpool manager to be sacked, Don Welsh was appointed in 1951, only to take Liverpool into the Second Division. He was sacked in 1956.
RIGHT The Liverpool squad sets out on a five mile training run from Anfield as they prepare for the 1957-58 season.

they lost 3−0, Liverpool were relegated to the Second Division after fifty uninterrupted years in the First Division and just to rub salt into their wounds, Everton were promoted back to the First Division. History was repeating itself. As in their first ever season in League football Liverpool would be in the Second Division while Everton gloried in the First. Tragically, in that game at Highbury Joe Mercer broke a leg and was stretchered off, never to return to the football field again. Also that season manager Don Welsh made two signings on Christmas Day, snapping up the Charlton pair Frank Lock and Johnny Evans but as there were no newspapers over the Christmas period, the first the Anfield crowd heard of it was when the teams were announced over the tannoy.

The least said about Liverpool's demise the better and a couple of months into the new season manager Don Welsh accepted his share of the blame by resigning. Into the managerial chair came Phil Taylor. A former Bristol Rovers player, Taylor had joined the Reds in 1936 and captained their 1950 Cup final side. In seven years of First Division football after the war he had made 223 appearances as a half back for the club. Only Hughes and Liddell remained of the post-war squad while younger players like Melia, Moran, Molyneux, Twentyman and A'Court were being steadily introduced. There was hope that after one season in the Second Division Liverpool would by some divine right shoot back into the First. But there was no such divine intervention. Instead Liverpool finished an unflattering eleventh and Anfield sank into a depression. The only consolation that season was a surprising 4−0 win at Goodison in the fourth round of the Cup but all their heartening efforts came to a swift end in the next round when Huddersfield visited Anfield and came away 2−0 winners. The humiliation reached new depths during the season when they were trounced 9−1 by Birmingham City, their biggest ever defeat although Liverpool claimed the pitch was like a frozen ice-rink.

Despite these years in the Second Division Liverpool could still boast one or two players of quality. In June 1956 they signed a promising Scottish goalkeeper from Hibernian called Tommy Younger. While at Hibs Younger had played in the European Cup and so became the first Liverpool player to have appeared in a European competition. He soon succeeded

ABOVE LEFT Jimmy Melia won fame and two England caps as a nippy inside forward, his finest season being 1961-62 when he helped Liverpool take the Division Two title.

the big South African, Doug Rudham as first team choice in the Liverpool goal. The blonde-haired Younger was a great favourite at Anfield with 120 appearances over the next few years and a couple of dozen Scottish caps. Another international was the Liverpool-born Alan A'Court, a nippy outside left who came to Anfield as an eighteen-year-old in 1952. Over the next twelve years he played 354 times for the Reds scoring sixty-one goals before moving to Tranmere. In 1958 he was awarded the first one of his five England caps. One home-bred favourite then, and still, was Ronnie Moran. He had joined the club in January 1952 after being recommended by a postman who delivered the mail to the home of one of Liverpool's directors. He made his first appearance against Derby County in a Division One game just ten months after signing and went on to play 343 games. A hard, uncomprising left back, he joined the coaching staff in 1964 when his playing days were over and has been a vital component of Liverpool's success ever since. Another teammate, at the time, who was later to become distinguished coach was Jimmy Melia. Like A'Court and Moran he was a Liverpool lad who had joined the club in 1954. An inside left he stayed until 1963 making 268 appearances, scoring seventy-nine goals and winning two England caps before moving on to a succession of clubs. The former England international wing half, Jimmy Wheeler arrived from Bolton Wanderers in 1956 and although he helped prop up Liverpool's ailing defence he failed to impress the England manager, Walter Winterbottom again. Another major signing was Geoff Twentyman from Carlisle United who made 170 appearances at left half.

But the one player who stood out above all others was Billy Liddell. Without him Liverpool might have plummeted even further and certainly their gates would have fallen considerably. Although some of his best years were during and immediately after the War, he was still scheming his way down the left wing and terrorising defences well into the 1950s and played his last game for Liverpool in 1960, twenty-two years after he had signed

for them. It was Matt Busby, then playing for Liverpool who had tipped off manager George Kay in 1938 about the young lad playing for Lochgelly Viollet. In all, Liddell made 495 League appearances and scored 216 goals. He won twenty-eight Scottish caps and eight wartime caps as well as playing for Great Britain against the Rest of Europe in 1947. He took forty-four penalties, scoring from thirty-six of them and missing five of them in front of the Kop. During the 1950s he almost signed for a South American club when he was offered £2,000 to go to Colombia. He was without a doubt one of the finest players to ever wear a Liverpool shirt and is still a regular supporter at Anfield.

Yet despite these signings and internationals Liverpool made little headway in their struggle to escape Division Two. Every season they made the running at the top of the table and looked certain for promotion only to collapse, usually over the Easter period, narrowly missing out on promotion. In successive seasons they finished third, third, fourth and fourth. But the most humiliating defeat for Liverpool came in January 1959 in the third round of the FA Cup when they were drawn away to the non-league side, Worcester City. The game was postponed from the traditional Saturday until the Thursday because of the atrocious arctic-like weather and was a disaster for Liverpool who went down 2−1, causing the biggest upset in the club's history. It was the first Cup-tie that Billy Liddell had missed since the War, having been dropped in favour of Louis Bimpson. This was almost the last straw for the Liverpool directors but they decided to take no action for the moment. The 1959−60 season began promisingly but soon took a turn for the worst and just a few days after Liverpool had lost 5−4 at Swansea they met behind the locked doors of the old boardroom and agreed that something drastic had to be done. Manager Phil Taylor was tired and weary after his years at the helm and it was amicably agreed on the Tuesday evening of 12 November that they should part company. There was little need for the directors to advertise the post as they knew precisely who they wanted for their next manager.

OPPOSITE PAGE Billy Liddell, one of the finest wingers to ever play for Liverpool. Although Liddell joined Liverpool shortly before the war, he did not make his football league debut until August 1946. By then, he was a regular Scottish international. On his Anfield debut he scored twice as Liverpool trounced Chelsea 7-4. In all he would play 495 times for Liverpool between 1946 and 1961, scoring 216 goals and would be capped 28 times by his country. OVERLEAF The team that Shankly inherited. When the new

manager arrived at Anfield, he discovered an overstaffed squad of players, lacking ambition and determination. Within a year twenty-four players had left the club. Back row (left to right): Jones, Lawrence, Younger, Rudham, Molyneux. Second row: Parry, Bimpson, Arnell, Byrne, Moran, Hughes. Third row: Nicholson, Morris, Wilkinson, Best, Murdoch, Campbell, Twentyman, Smith, White. Front row: Morrissey, Liddell, Saunders, Wheeler, Melia, A'Court, Harrower.

8

A MAN CALLED SHANKLY

1959 – 60

There had been whispers circulating Merseyside for a month predicting Phil Taylor's departure, the rumour adding that there was little doubt who would succeed him – Bill Shankly, the manager of Huddersfield Town. The *Liverpool Echo* had his name top of their list but also reckoned the club were thinking about Harry Catterick, Jimmy Hagan and Jimmy Murphy. Even Billy Liddell was said to be under consideration along with two other backroom boys, Reuben Bennett and interestingly, Bob Paisley. Shankly had applied once before for the manager's job at Anfield when Phil Taylor was selected but this time it was the club which approached him.

Liverpool chairman Tom Williams and director, Harry Latham had travelled over the Pennines to Huddersfield in mid-October to watch Town taking on Cardiff City in a Division Two match. It was not the game they had come to see. After the match, the two approached Shankly and asked him bluntly if he would like to manage Liverpool. Although he was inclined to accept immediately he bided his time until Taylor had formally resigned. Three weeks later on Tuesday 1 December 1959, following a board meeting, forty-six-year-old Bill Shankly was appointed manager of Liverpool with an annual salary of £2,500.

William Shankly had been born in 1913 in the coalmining village of Glenbuck, a stone's throw away from the racecourse at Ayr. One of ten children, he was brought up with coalmining and football in his blood, all five sons later playing professional soccer. He was spotted playing football while still a teenager and was snapped up by Carlisle United where he spent a frustrating season in the reserves. In 1933 Preston North End, then struggling in the Second Division, signed him and he began a long association with the north Lancashire club as their right half. He played in two successive Cup finals helping Preston to a win in 1938 and in the same year won the first of his five Scottish caps. But war interrupted his career, stealing him from what might have been a distinguished international spell. He played after the War for a few years and even captained Preston but then in 1949 he was offered the manager's job back at Carlisle. He leaped at the opportunity and after a short spell on the Borders moved to Grimsby, Workington and Huddersfield in fairly quick succession, learning the managerial ropes on the way. When he arrived at Anfield, however, it was with potential rather than reputation. What he found was hardly to his liking. He later wrote that 'the ground was an eyesore. It needed renovating and cleaning up. It was not good enough for the public of Liverpool and the team was not good enough for the public of Liverpool.'

But he did start on one positive note. He told the backroom staff that the new manager would not be introducing any new assistants. He would be loyal to those already on the staff but in return expected loyalty from them. It was a valuable beginning and a lesson that has carried on through the years. Changes among the backroom staff may not have been necessary but after Liverpool's first game when Cardiff City won 4–0 it was quickly apparent that changes on the field were vital. Shankly jotted down the names of twenty-four of the club's long list of players and within a year all twenty-four had moved on. New blood was needed and the *Liverpool Echo* was soon speculating that Dennis Law might be the first signing from his old club but Law's price was already escalating way out of Liverpool's reach. Instead Shankly tried first to sign Jack Charlton from Leeds United but Leeds wanted more than the £18,000 Liverpool were prepared to pay.

Results picked up in the New Year with only one defeat in ten matches and the team slowly began to climb from mid-table towards the top. They also had a fine run at the end of the season but with Aston Villa and Cardiff so far ahead there was never any chance of promotion. Instead they finished third yet again, eight points behind the Welshmen. The attack had knocked in a creditable ninety goals, thanks mainly to a young lad called Roger Hunt who had just been introduced to League football. He scored twenty-one goals but the main problem lay with the defence which had conceded sixty-six goals. It was clear where the first priority lay in the transfer market. In the Cup they faced Leyton Orient in the opening round and comfortably beat them 2–1 only to draw glamorous Manchester United at Anfield in the next round. United won by three goals to one but Liverpool put up a spirited performance against Matt Busby's side. Seventeen-year-old Ian Callaghan was plucked from among the club's apprentices and thrown into the Second Division performing well enough to hang on to his place for the next eighteen years. But these were only just the beginnings. There was still much more to do and it would take more than a season or two before the rich promise could be fulfilled.

1960 – 61

Rebuilding continued into the following season although Shankly's most important forays into the transfer market were yet to come. By now he had sized up the job, knew that it was not easy but relished the challenge and the potential.

In August 1960 he quietly made one signing which was to reap dividends. He had known Gordon Milne since he was a child, having played with his father, Jimmy at Preston. Shankly and Milne had been neighbours and the Liverpool manager had watched the young child over the years, following his career with interest even after leaving Deepdale. The boy had now developed into a tough, combative, wing half itching for first team football. Shankly had no hesitations about the lad's prospects and paid Preston £12,000 for his services. It was money well spent as Milne developed into one of the finest half backs Anfield had seen for many years. Another youngster coming more into the reckoning was Gerry Byrne. With Ronnie Moran firmly entrenched in the left back position, Byrne had few opportunities to break into the first team. He made his debut in late 1957 but soon shuffled back to reserve team football, only reappearing in the Second Division when Moran was injured. When Shankly arrived a frustrated Bryne was on the transfer list but under the new manager the twenty-two-year-old was given his chance and soon established his place automatically in the back two never to reappear on the transfer list. Shankly simply shifted the more adaptable Moran to right back and allowed Byrne the freedom of the left back spot. In a more publicised deal Shankly signed Kevin Lewis, the small Sheffield United winger who went on to make seventy-one appearances, scoring thirty-nine goals including the goal which clinched promotion. After three seasons Lewis moved on to Huddersfield. Tommy Leishman also arrived from Scotland, making over a hundred appearances during the next three years.

Rebuilding the team could not take place overnight. Shankly knew that and fortunately so too did the club's directors. But sadly, the fans did not share their optimism as gates slumped to below 30,000. It was another season of frustration with Liverpool again finishing in third place behind Alf Ramsey's Ipswich and Sheffield United, missing promotion by six points. In

LEFT Shankly's arrival heralded changes on and off the field.
ABOVE RIGHT One of Liverpool's greatest goalscorers, Roger Hunt joined the Reds in 1959 and in a career spanning 484 games, he scored 285 goals.
BOTTOM RIGHT Full back Gerry Byrne was on the verge of leaving Anfield when Shankly arrived.

the seven years since they had been relegated Liverpool had been third on four occasions and fourth twice, so perhaps it was hardly surprising that their supporters should begin to lose patience. There had been little at home over the season to excite them with two defeats and five draws – results which cost Liverpool the chance of promotion – but they did manage to score an impressive total of eighty-seven goals. The young Roger Hunt, now playing regularly in the first team notched up fifteen in thirty-two matches, while alongside him in the number nine shirt Dave Hickson struck twenty-one goals.

Hickson had arrived at Anfield in a headline-hitting transfer from Everton shortly before Shankly's arrival. The powerfully-built, blonde-haired centre forward who looked an older version of Hunt had been born on Merseyside and signed for Everton as a nineteen-year-old in 1948. In the mid-fifties he moved on to Aston Villa and then Huddersfield Town before returning to Everton. Then in a dispute over pay the Goodison favourite sensationally transferred his allegiance across Stanley Park to Anfield. In the sixty matches he played in a red shirt he scored thirty-six goals which for a player supposedly at the tail-end of his career was a more than useful tally. But Hickson was never really a Shankly favourite and the new manager was intent on searching for a younger, more scheming centre forward who could both score goals and create them.

There was little for the Liverpool faithful to cheer about in the Cup as well. After a rousing 3–2 home victory against Third Division Coventry, the Reds faced

another Second Division sleeping giant, Sunderland but went down by two goals to nil. They also made their first appearance in the newly-created Football League Cup going out in the third round to Second Division rivals, Southampton. It would be another six years before Liverpool would again bother entering the unpopular competition and a great deal longer before the new trophy would appear in the Anfield boardroom.

1961 – 62

The break Shankly had been waiting for came one Sunday morning towards the end of the season when he picked up his newspaper and read that Ian St John, the Motherwell centre forward was seeking a move. Shankly had been keeping tabs on St John and another young Scotsman, Ron Yeats of Dundee United for some time and had even tried to sign them when he was with Huddersfield. He kept his interest in the two players when he arrived at Anfield but was never able to persuade the Liverpool board to dig deep enough into its coffers to set up a deal. Now that St John was available it was time for the board to back the man they had hired.

Shankly was a very different kind of manager to any the directors had previously encountered. He had joined Anfield on the strict understanding that he and he alone would choose the team and was one of the new emerging breed of managers, paid to deliver results, provide the odd quip for the press and present the public image of the club. Alf Ramsey, Don Revie, Harry Catterick and Matt Busby were all of the same mould, stamping their personalties on their teams during the late fifties and sixties. To the directors' credit they agreed to back Shankly's judgements, thanks mainly to Eric Sawyer a recent recruit to the board. Sawyer insisted that if Liverpool were ever to be a great club again, then it had to think big. His argument won the day and go-ahead was given. Within twenty-four hours of reading that headline in the Sunday paper, Shankly had dashed to Motherwell and fixed the deal that brought Ian St John to Anfield. It cost the club £37,500 but a week later when St John made his debut against Everton in a Liverpool Senior Cup game he paid off the first instalment scoring a hat-trick in Liverpool's 4–3 defeat. It was the biggest transfer deal Liverpool had ever made but it was only one of the pair Shankly had set his heart on. The next stop was Dundee United where he was politely informed that Ron Yeats was not for sale though one of the Dundee directors privately whispered

ABOVE Liverpool captain Ronnie Moran (left) greets new signing from Everton, Dave Hickson.
RIGHT TOP Ian St John, a £35,000 signing from Motherwell.

BOTTOM Ron Yeats receives the Second Division championship trophy from Joe Richards, President of the Football League.

that they would probably let him go for £30,000. Within a couple of days Liverpool had upped their offer and in July a deal was struck bringing the giant Scottish defender to Anfield for precisely £30,000. The importance of these two signings can never be overstated. They added considerably to the jigsaw and although new pieces would be added along the way they were the stars around who the team would buzz and the heroes who would bring the crowds flocking back to Anfield.

With their new recruits, Liverpool began the season in storming form, dropping only one point in their first eleven matches and scoring thirty-one goals while conceding just four. It was the style of champions as they rattled in a total of ninety-nine goals for the season, their highest tally since they were Second Division champions in 1896. Roger Hunt leading the attack hit a club record of forty-one League goals. His partner up front, Ian St John not only helped create a fair share of those but notched up eighteen of his own. On eleven occasions they hit four goals or more and soon had the fans queuing once again outside the Kop for their fortnightly dose of excitement. Liverpool ended the 1961–62 season as champions, eight points ahead of Leyton Orient and had wrapped the title up long before the end of the season. The squad which took the title was: A'Court, Byrne, Callaghan, Furnell, Hunt, Leishman, Lewis, Melia, Milne, Moran, Slater, St John, White and Yeats.

In the FA Cup Liverpool began with a testing game against First Division Chelsea at Anfield but ran out winners by four goals to three, demonstrating that they had a team quite capable of holding its own among the best in the land. In the next round they travelled to Fourth Division Oldham and came home with a 2–1 victory. Shankly's old club, Preston who were slightly lower down the Second Division table from Liverpool, held them to a goalless draw at Anfield in round five and after a further goalless draw at Deepdale, duly knocked the Anfielders out of the Cup at the third attempt. But with the dreaded Easter period looming when Liverpool traditionally caught the jitters, it was probably fortunate that they were out of the Cup. The Second Division championship had been a foregone conclusion for much of the season and was finally clinched on 21 April, 1962 in the pouring rain at Anfield. In the stirring atmosphere reminiscent of the glory days of the early 1920s Liverpool defeated Southampton 2–0 before 40,000 with Kevin Lewis, deputising for the suspended St John, scoring the final goal. Throughout the match the Kop rang to the chanting which had become a feature of home games during the season. At the final whistle

Ron Yeats, the 'Red Colossus' was Shankly's first major signing. At £30,000 he was to prove a bargain.

Liverpool trooped triumphantly down the tunnel but the Kop refused to go home until they reappeared for a lap of honour. With stockings hanging around their ankles and some already half undressed they finally emerged from their dressing-room to acknowledge the cheering supporters and the rhythmical chanting of Liv-er-pool. Nothing quite like it had been seen on Merseyside or for that matter anywhere before. Shankly had unleashed a new phenomenum of crowd fanaticism and passion which would soon become a legend.

Tommy Lawrence was dragged from the obscurity of the 'A' team and thrown into the first team where he remained for the next eight years.

1962 – 63

Ron Yeats was a giant of a centre half, standing 6 feet 2 inches and weighing almost 14½ stone. Shankly described him as a 'Red Colossus' and within three months of his arrival had appointed him team captain, convinced that he would lead Liverpool into the First Division. Born in Aberdeen in 1937, Yeats was snapped up by Dundee United while still a teenager and soon became the talk of the Scottish League for his powerful strength before moving south to Liverpool in his early twenties. For the next ten years Yeats captained Liverpool to successes across the football stadiums of England and Europe, winning two championship medals and having the distinction of being the first Liverpool player to ever lift the FA Cup. It was an eventful career of over 350 games for the Reds but surprisingly his country capped him only twice in 1965 and 1966 against Wales and Italy. With Yeats at the heart of the defence Liverpool were always a formidable proposition as he marshalled his defenders and patrolled the area with all the authority of his size.

Back in the First Division after eight years Liverpool began like the strangers they were, losing to Blackpool before a welcoming 51,000 at Anfield and then away at Blackburn before scraping a draw with Manchester City. The results did improve as the team gradually adapted its tactics and strengths to suit the higher division. Training was improved with an emphasis on stamina while skills were developed at the club's much improved

training ground at Melwood. Liverpool's tenth game of the 1962 – 63 season at Everton in September provided their first real test of credibility. The two clubs had not met in the League since January 1951 and nearly 73,000 crammed into Goodison to watch the occasion. It was a thrilling match and almost certainly the noisiest ever heard in the country up to then as the innovative chanting of the Liverpool supporters was copied by the Evertonians, shaking the rafters high around the Everton stands. Nerves must have got the better of Liverpool as they almost went a goal down in the first minute after Furnell had dropped the ball. Fortunately the referee spotted an infringement but it was not much longer before Roy Vernon put Everton ahead through a penalty. Shortly before the interval Lewis, deputising for the injured St John, hit a lucky equaliser but Everton went ahead again in the second half when Johnny Morrisey netted against his old club. Then with seconds remaining, Roger Hunt grabbed a late equaliser to give Liverpool a satisfying draw. At the end of the season Liverpool could look back on the match with even more satisfaction as their neighbours had topped the League by six points to win the championship from Tottenham Hotspur. And in the return game at Anfield shortly before Easter the two teams played out another draw before a massive audience of 56,000.

During the previous season Jimmy Furnell, the former Burnley goalkeeper had taken over from Bert Slater as Liverpool's regular 'keeper only to hit a bad patch during the autumn, typified by the derby game. Shankly decided on a switch and introduced another Scotsman into the team, Tommy Lawrence. Lawrence had been at Anfield for five years, languishing in the 'A' team when

Shankly arrived but was soon promoted to the reserves. Now he was given his opportunity and seizing it held on to the green jersey for the next eight years.

As results improved and their confidence boosted, Liverpool began a steady climb up the table with a fine unbeaten run which came to an end in March, lifting them to fourth position. It also coincided with an exciting campaign in the FA Cup taking the Reds to their first semi-final since 1950. After disposing of Wrexham, Liverpool contested an epic struggle with Burnley and following a draw at Turf Moor defeated the Lancashire side before 58,000, Anfield's highest gate of the season. In the fifth round they visited Arsenal and came away with a much-applauded 2 – 1 win before taking on West Ham at Anfield. A goal by Hunt nine minutes from time won the tie for them and a place in the semi-final. Their opponents, Leicester were highly rated by Shankly who reckoned them to be the only team that season to have taught Liverpool anything. They had beaten the Reds 3 – 0 at Filbert Street and 2 – 0 at Anfield and in the semi-final at Hillsborough notched up a hat-trick of wins defeating Liverpool by a single goal scored in the first half. In the second half Liverpool bombarded the Leicester goal but Gordon Banks was equal to everything and Leicester won the coveted trip to Wembley.

The semi-final came just as Liverpool hit a poor run. Tottenham came to Anfield and went two goals up but a spirited Liverpool pulled them back and eventually won a storming match by five goals to two. But when the Reds journeyed to White Hart Lane a few days later for the return match, they were thrashed 7 – 2. It was Liverpool's worst defeat in years and with further dismal results Liverpool's promising season petered out. They finally finished eighth in the table, seventeen points behind champions Everton with Roger Hunt leading goalscorer again with twenty-four League goals plus a couple in the Cup.

Besides Tommy Lawrence, Shankly introduced one other new face to the side. In search of a creative wing half he travelled once more to Scotland and signed the Glasgow Rangers half back, Willie Stevenson. Having won a cup and championship medal with Rangers, Stevenson had emigrated to Australia earlier in the year but returned a few months later and was snapped up by the vigilant Liverpool manager. Liverpool now boasted four Scotsmen in their side, a fact which would have brought a knowing smile to John McKenna's face. One of those Scotsmen, Ian St John struck nineteen goals over the season and was duly awarded with further Scottish caps while Tommy Lawrence donned the yellow Scottish goalkeeper's jersey for the first of

ABOVE Ian Callaghan became the only player to span the years in the Second Division to being European champions. RIGHT Peter Thompson won fame as a fiery left winger.

his three international appearances. Meanwhile Englishmen Melia, Byrne, Milne and Hunt were all capped by their country and with Alan A'Court already having played for England Liverpool began to take on the look of a star-studded side.

1963 – 64

Shankly's jigsaw was almost complete although the team still lacked some width and pace. Callaghan was making penetrating runs down the right but the club's regular

left winger, Alan A'Court was now almost thirty and beginning to lose speed. The player Shankly wanted was Peter Thompson of Preston, who was also catching the eye of a number of other First Division clubs. But Liverpool were finally beginning to think big and Shankly had little problem in persuading his board to pay a club record fee of £40,000 for the Deepdale man. Thompson played with the style of a new Billy Liddell and when the 1963–64 season kicked off began to excite crowds with his daring runs to the by-line in much the same fashion as his famous Scottish predeccesor had done during the late forties and fifties. The quick burst down the left and the short ball to the near post or the high ball crossed to the far post brought countless goals for the Reds as they attacked the First Division championship.

For far too long Manchester and London had dominated the First Division. Now Merseyside was starting to assert itself. Everton had already won the League but this time it was Liverpool's turn. The season began nervously as the team struggled to find its rhythm. Nine games went by and the Reds had merely nine points to show when they faced the champions Everton at Anfield. This was the game that would prove to be the turning point as Liverpool gave a rousing performance to run out 2–1 winners, their first League victory against the Blues since September 1950. With their confidence boosted the Reds went on to amass forty-seven points from a possible sixty over the next thirty games. At home six goals were emphatically knocked passed Ipswich, Sheffield United, Stoke and Wolves while five went passed Aston Villa and Arsenal. In the 5–0 defeat of Arsenal Peter Thompson, speeding

skilfully towards the Gunners' goal struck two memorable thunderous shots from the edge of the penalty area into the back of the Arsenal net, beating the former Liverpool goalkeeper Jim Furnell. Three wins over the Easter period guaranteed Liverpool their sixth championship as they pulled away from the chasing pack to finish four points ahead of Manchester United. In all, Liverpool hit a remarkable sixty goals at home with Roger Hunt again leading the rampage with a season's total of thirty-one League goals. The crowds swooped on Anfield to join in the excitement with gates averaging almost 50,000 and television. latching on as well, carrying the now familiar chants and songs of the Kop into millions more homes.

But while the Reds were forging ahead in the race for the League, their FA Cup campaign ended abruptly. In the third round they knocked five goals past Derby County at Anfield and after a surprising goalless home draw against Port Vale, won the replay by two goals to one. In the fifth round they came away from a difficult game at Highbury with a commendable 1–0 victory then drew lowly Second Division Swansea at Anfield for the quarter-finals. It looked a walkover with some of the more hopeful fans and pundits already fantasising about Wembley's twin towers and a possible double. But it was not to be as struggling Swansea bravely, though perhaps luckily, held out before a packed Kop. The Welshmen won by two goals to one but that never stopped Shankly arguing that 'the score should have been 15–0 to Liverpool'.

Liverpool are First Division champions again as Ron Yeats and Willie Stevenson lead the lap of honour.

MERSEYSIDE RULES

1964 – 65

The mid-sixties were the years of the Beatles as a string of their hits rocketed to the top of the pop charts. On their fourth close season tour of America the Liverpool team had even starred in the Ed Sullivan show and to celebrate the times, the Kop adopted 'You'll Never Walk Alone' as their anthem. Merseybeat, Mersey comedy and Mersey football were the vogue of the period. If ever the moment was right for winning their first FA Cup, it had to be the 1964 – 65 season.

The League Championship also entitled Liverpool to a crack at the European Cup, something Shankly was relishing. Liverpol had never been a club for pursuing competition with continental clubs. They had made regular trips abroad, more often than not to America during the close season, but had rarely invited European teams to Anfield for the occasional friendly. Saabrucken had visited for the 1951 Jubilee and FC Austria had played at Anfield during 1934 but unlike other First Division clubs such as Wolves, Chelsea and Arsenal, Liverpool had not invited the famous Hungarian, Russian and Italian teams to their ground during the fifties. British fortunes in the European Cup had generally been miserable. The Football League had even vetoed Chelsea's entry into the first competition in 1956 although the more progressive Scottish FA sanctioned Hibernian's admission and saw the Scottish champions reach the semi-finals. In 1957 and 1958 Manchester United reached successive semi-finals but since then English clubs had experienced little success. Liverpool's European campaign kicked off in August 1964 in Reykavik, where they comfortably put five goals past the Icelandic champions. In the second leg a crowd of 32,000 turned up to cheer them to a 6 – 1 win and a place in the next round. With most of the minnows disposed of, the opposition became tougher with Liverpool facing the Belgian champions, Anderlecht, a side overflowing with internationals. For the first leg at Anfield, Shankly introduced a nineteen-year-old local lad called Tommy Smith. A half back, Smith had made his debut in May when the honours had been safely secured and had enjoyed a couple of games early in the new season only to return to the reserves. Smith's moment had now arrived and he battled away at the back to help Liverpool take a useful three goal lead to the Belgians. The return fixture packed Anderlecht's stadium but the 50,000 crowd hardly bothered the Reds as they ran out 1 – 0 winners.

The gruelling travel of European football made life in the Football League all the harder and as champions, Liverpool had become the team everyone wanted to beat. Five of their eight opening games in the 1964 – 65 season were lost before they began to rediscover the style of the previous season. Even then they only managed to string a couple of wins together before stumbling again to take a mere three points out of the next six matches. At Christmas the results steadily improved, just in time for the third round of the FA Cup in the New Year. Drawn away to mid-table West Bromwich Albion, Liverpool came away from the Hawthorns with a 2 – 1 victory even though Albion missed a penalty, and then faced an easy draw against bottom of the fourth division Stockport County at Anfield. But easy it was not as Stockport gamely fought out a 1 – 1 draw and with luck might have caused an FA Cup upset to rank with Worcester City's defeat of the Reds back in 1959. In the replay before a packed Edgeley Park, Liverpool squeezed a 2 – 0 win thanks to a couple of goals from Roger Hunt. Their reward was an away tie at Bolton, then pushing for promotion to the First Division. In the event, Liverpool won 1 – 0 before 57,000 Bolton's biggest gate in years only to draw their bogey team Leicester City for the quarter-finals.

Tommy Smith made his League debut in 1963 and went on to play more than 600 games over the next fifteen years.

Before that game could take place, Liverpool had another quarter-final appointment, this time in the European Cup with the German champions, Cologne. The first leg in Germany was a tough affair with neither side conceding much and predictably ending in a goalless draw. In early March the Germans arrived on Merseyside for the second leg and as Anfield began to fill, the cold weather turned to snow and a blizzard struck the city. Within an hour the pitch was covered with a couple of inches of snow and the two teams emerged from the tunnel to total confusion. Watching the Cologne players attempting to knock the ball about, the referee rightly decided that play was impossible and called the game off. The Cologne team and officials reacted angrily but failed to change the referee's mind. The game was finally played a fortnight later and was just as bruising as the first encounter with both defences reluctant to give an inch and after 180 minutes neither side had a goal to show for their endeavours. With Liverpool's fixture list piling up, a replay was the last thing they wanted but they had no choice but to travel to Rotterdam for a third meeting. Before an astonishingly large crowd of over 50,000 for a game on a neutral ground, the goals finally arrived with Liverpool taking a

two goal lead only to surrender it for another draw. The two teams went into extra time but finished still level at two goals apiece. The rules now specified that the game should be decided on the toss of a coin but even now the nightmare continued as the coin stuck in the mud and had to be tossed again. Finally, after 300 minutes of football Yeats and Smith leaped into the air and Liverpool were into the semi-final, only the second English team to have reached that stage of the competition. And when the draw for the semi-final was made, it pitted Liverpool against the mighty Inter Milan, champions of Italy, Europe and the World.

Since returning to the First Division, Leicester City had become something of a bogey team for Liverpool with the Reds managing to lose six times and win only once in their seven engagements so that there was a certain apprehension about their quarter-final meeting at Filbert Street. With England's Gordon Banks in brilliant form, Leicester kept Liverpool at bay and might well have snatched a winner but the Reds held out for a goalless draw. In the replay, Banks barricaded the Kop

Ian St John is cheered by fans after beating Chelsea 2-0 in the FA Cup semi-final in March 1965.

goal as Liverpool bombarded him from all angles but in the end he could not get his fingertips to a Roger Hunt shot and Liverpool were into their third semi-final since the War. The jinx had been broken. The semi-final against Chelsea turned out to be a much easier proposition than had been imagined. Managed by another Preston North End Scot, Tommy Docherty, the young side were having a promising season, chasing Manchester United and Leeds for the title. The two teams had not as yet met in the League but before a crowd of almost 68,000 at Villa Park, Liverpool showed the Londoners who were the masters with a Willie Stevenson penalty and a Peter Thompson goal putting them into their third FA Cup final. By the time Cup final day arrived Liverpool had ended the season in seventh place with Manchester United taking the title on goal average from Leeds. And it was Leeds who Liverpool faced at Wembley. The Yorkshire team, managed by the former Manchester City centre forward Don Revie were in their first season back in Division One and out to avenge their narrow title miss.

FA Cup Final 1965 Liverpool v Leeds United

When Liverpool were beaten in their first FA Cup final appearance against Burnley, it was the former Everton player, Freeman who scored the game's only goal and destroyed their dreams. In their second final appearance, it was another former Everton man, Joe Mercer who inspired Arsenal to a famous victory and now in their third final as the two teams marched on to the luscious Wembley turf, Leeds were led out ominously by another former Everton player, Bobby Collins.

Leeds were a team of budding stars that in time would become household names: Bremner, Giles, Hunter, Charlton, Reaney and Sprake were all making their debuts in a Wembley final as were Liverpool's emerging talents. Just days before the final Gordon Milne was injured and Shankly was forced to bring Geoff Strong, the former Arsenal half back into the side. Tommy Smith was now a regular fixture in defence with another young Liverpool lad, Chris Lawler as full back. Lawler had made his first appearance in a red shirt in 1962 but it was not until 1965 that he laid permanent claim to it. Smith and Lawler would play together in the Liverpool defence for the next ten years forming a partnership that was rarely prised apart. For a Cup final day it was unusually grey and damp but the Liverpool fans more than made up for the miserable weather as they transported the Kop and its songs to Wembley. The old stadium had heard nothing like it.

The game itself was a largely dour affair with the country's two best defences determined not to give anything away. With five minutes gone Gerry Byrne and Bobby Collins collided unfortunately breaking the Liverpool man's collar bone. Substitutes were not allowed and Byrne was still anxious to carry on. After treatment Shankly and Paisley agreed to let him continue, not wanting to reveal the extent of the damage by the Leeds player. It was a brave decision by Byrne and he played on as if nothing had happened, tackling just as sternly while still passing accurately. Like Bert Trautman, the Manchester City goalkeeper who almost ten years before him had played through a Wembley final with a broken neck, Byrne would always be remembered for his fortitude for the rest of his career. The towering giants, Charlton and Yeats dominated at either end while the small men Collins and St John beavered to find a way past them. Chances were few and far between and at ninety minutes neither side had found the net. It was eighteen years since a Cup final had gone into extra time but within three minutes of kicking off again Willie Stevens had slipped a ball down the left wing to Gerry Byrne who instead of shooting from the narrow angle crossed to Roger Hunt. The England man made no mistake. Wembley erupted and a wave of red spread across the terraces. But it was shortlived. Eight minutes later Billy Bremner latched on to a Charlton header in the penalty area and slammed the ball home for the equaliser. Suddenly the game had come to life as tired legs created open spaces and gaping opportunities.

Then in the second half of extra-time the ill luck that had dogged Liverpool for seventy-two years of Cup football was wiped away as Ian Callaghan crossed a magnificent ball towards the oncoming St John. It was at an awkward height but the Scottish international launched himself at the ball and sent his diving header straight to the back of the Leeds net. It was Ian St John's greatest moment. Wembley exploded yet again, the name of St John was chanted around the stadium and for five nervous minutes Liverpool held on to win the Cup. When Ron Yeats lifted the trophy for the first time Wembley was a scene of unforgettable emotion. Back in Liverpool the Liver Birds fluttered their wings but thought better of flying away from such an exciting city.

If Gerry Byrne is remembered for his bravery in that final, Ian St John will always be remembered as the man

OVERLEAF LEFT TOP Managers Don Revie (left) and Bill Shankly lead their teams out onto the famous Wembley turf. BOTTOM Ian St John throws himself at the ball to hit Liverpool's winner against Leeds United. RIGHT TOP A dream comes true. Ron Yeats becomes the first Liverpool player to lift the FA Cup. BOTTOM Half a million people welcome Liverpool home.

who won Liverpool's first Cup. He was a player of genuine quality with the skill to beat defenders as well as score goals. He may have been on the short side but could outjump many a tall defender and had a powerful header as well as a fierce shot. He was the favourite of the Kop playing regularly for the Reds until 1970 and a year later moved on to Coventry City before joining Tranmere. In all he played 334 games in Liverpool's number nine shirt, scoring ninety-five goals and won twenty-one Scottish caps. His craft lay in creating goals rather than in scoring them himself and Roger Hunt was always the first to acknowledge that his goalscoring job was made that much easier thanks to the Saint's ability.

When the Reds returned to Liverpool the following evening, nobody could have guessed at the reception. It was estimated that well over half a million people stood in the warm evening sunlight to salute them. As the team coach drove out of Lime Street station to make the short journey to the Town Hall, the noise was phenomenal. For half a mile on either side of the Town Hall the road was jammed with supporters. It was almost certainly the biggest crowd that had ever gathered in the centre of the city and probably in any other city.

Gerry Byrne with his broken collar bone and Gordon Milne parade the FA Cup before Liverpool take on Inter Milan.

Two days later, with priceless timing Liverpool faced Inter Milan in the European Cup semi-final for what was to be the greatest occasion in Anfield's history. With two hours to kick-off the gates of the Kop were firmly locked and 25,000 swayed and sweated for almost four unforgettable hours. Shortly before the teams appeared the Kop were chanting to see the Cup and down in the dressing-rooms Shankly on hearing them decided to play his ace. He would tell Inter Milan to go onto the pitch first and then send the injured Milne and Byrne out to parade the trophy around the ground. The roof would be raised off the Kop, the Italians would take fright and then Liverpool would appear out of the tunnel. It was a brilliant piece of theatre which worked supremely. When the Italians did come out they ran automatically towards the Kop only to turn tail at the reception and retreat towards the Anfield Road. The Cup was duly paraded around the ground with cheers, chants and not a few tears, and as Shankly had reckoned with Italian nerves twitching, it was not long before Roger Hunt had scored against the finest defence in the world. Mazzola pulled one back before Ian Callaghan added a second and St John struck a third. Liverpool had deservedly beaten the world club champions by three goals to one: 'We have been beaten before,' admitted Helenio Herrara, the Inter Milan manager after the match, 'but tonight we were defeated.' A week later Herrara took his revenge at the San Siro stadium. With 90,000 fanatical Inter supporters determined to outdo the hysteria of Anfield, firecrackers, sirens, rockets and smokebombs deafened and lit the Milan night. Within twenty minutes Inter had pulled back the deficit with three hotly-disputed goals. The first was scored from an indirect free kick while the second was kicked out of Tommy Lawrence's hands. It was an evening which taught Liverpool much about European football. Years later the *Sunday Times* uncovered sufficient evidence to suggest, as Bill Shankly had always alleged, that the referee had been bribed. But there was no justice and Internazionale went on to win the European Cup for a second time.

1965 – 66

In spite of their defeat in the final fixture of the season, 1964–65 had been the season of the cups with an inspiring run of sixteen undefeated games before going down to Inter Milan. Matching it in the new season would be difficult but equal it they did.

ABOVE RIGHT Chris Lawler scores against Inter Milan but the goal is disallowed.

BOTTOM RIGHT Ian St John scores Liverpool's final goal in the 3-1 European Cup semi-final victory over Inter Milan.

Victory in the FA Cup had assured Liverpool of a place in Europe's number two cup competition, the Cup Winners Cup and their campaign began not far from where they had left off, back in Northern Italy. This time the venue was Turin where they faced the famous Italian club, Juventus. In a packed Stadio Communale, Liverpool showed that they had learned their lesson well from Inter Milan by holding the deficit to a single goal. These were the tactics of two-legged European football, a draw away from home or at worst a single goal defeat, then put the pressure on in the home second leg. And if you played the first leg at home, then pile up the goals ready for the onslaught away. Back at Anfield on a chilly

October evening in front of 51,000 Liverpool ran the Italians ragged and there was never any doubt about who would be going into the draw for the next round. With the players and the Kop beginning to enjoy these European evenings, Chris Lawler came cantering out of defence to score one of his typically adventurist goals while Geoff Strong added a second. In the next round Liverpool started with a home tie against Standard Liege of Belgium whose seven internationals turned out to be no match for a slick Liverpool who won by three goals to one. In the second leg Liverpool won 2 – 1 and went into the third round against the Hungarian army side, Honved. Back in 1954 Honved had delighted British football fans with their stunning skills against Wolves when Puskas, Bozsik, Kocsis and Czibor had demonstrated why Hungarian football was the finest in the world. But all that was a decade ago and Honved were no longer quite the force in European football. In Budapest, Liverpool hung on for a goalless draw and then at Anfield backed by 55,600, the Reds won by two goals to nil. When the draw was made for the semi-finals Liverpool pulled out the plum tie with a fixture against Glasgow Celtic.

In the League meanwhile, Liverpool got off to a reasonable start lying sixth in early October but by the time December 1965 had arrived they had stormed to the top of the table. Five goals each were netted against West Ham, Everton, Northampton Town and Blackburn Rovers. With the World Cup looming Roger Hunt was clearly out to impress the England manager, Alf Ramsay and was tormenting defences up and down the land. Once Liverpool were leading the field there was no stopping them and as Easter approached the rest of the pack was falling behind. In the FA Cup, however, disaster struck at the first hurdle when Tommy Docherty's Chelsea visited Anfield keen to avenge their semi-final defeat of the previous season and went away clutching a 2 – 1 victory.

Liverpool arrived at Parkhead for their European semi-final minus Roger Hunt and before 70,000 fanatical Celtic supporters grimly hung on as the Scots tore at them. Before long Lennox had put Celtic into a one goal lead but despite a constant barrage of shots and pressure

Ian St John shows his delight after Geoff Strong scores against Glasgow Celtic in the Cup Winners Cup semi-final.

the Liverpool defence luckily held out to keep the score down to a single goal. The second leg was another of the great European evenings. Liverpool needed two goals to win the tie but with a Celtic side boasting Gemmell, Murdoch, McNeill, Lennox and Bertie Auld they would be no pushovers. Liverpool attacked from the whistle, hitting the bar early on but despite the constant pressure could not find the equaliser and the two teams went into half-time with the Reds still a goal down on aggregate. Kicking towards the Kop after the interval Liverpool peppered Ronnie Simpson's goal with shots. Then in the sixtieth minute the Reds were awarded a free kick just outside the Celtic penalty area and Tommy Smith stepped up to take it. Placing the ball very deliberately, he drove his twenty-five yard kick through the wall of players into the back of the net, sending the Kop wild with delight. The versatile Geoff Strong had again stepped in for the injured Hunt but had ripped a cartilage shortly before half-time and spent most of the second half limping but he never gave up the battle. Five minutes after Smith's equaliser, Callaghan raced down the right and centred a high ball into the penalty area where Geoff Strong, shrugging off the pain, rose to meet the ball and sent a thundering header into the net. With Liverpool now leading, Celtic attacked even more vigorously and with just a minute to go Bobby Lennox hooked the ball into the Liverpool goal but was ruled offside. The Celtic fans, massed at the Anfield Road end, were furious and a barrage of bottles were hurled on to the pitch but the goal still did not count and Liverpool went on to the final.

Ron Yeats always rated the game as Geoff Strong's finest moment but a week later the former Arsenal man was wheeled into hospital for surgery on his injured knee. Strong was often underrated but his loyalty was never in doubt. During most of his six years at Anfield he could only sneak into the first team when someone was injured but he did manage 150 appearances, scoring thirty goals and never complained or angrily slapped in transfer requests. He quietly got on with his job standing in for strikers, defenders or midfielders. He was a vital cog in the Anfield machinery and should not go unmentioned.

On the last day of April 1966, Liverpool entertained Chelsea at Anfield needing just one point to clinch the League title. As the two teams ran out into the brilliant sunshine the London side formed a tunnel and applauded the Reds on to the field. It was almost as if

RIGHT Geoff Strong, a fine utility player who never managed to secure a permanent first team place but was nevertheless a vital squad member.

61

they had conceded defeat before the contest began but once into the match they certainly tried to deprive Liverpool of their triumph. In the end it took a little luck as Hunt's shot bounced off Bonetti for Liverpool's opening goal. Chelsea pulled one back but it was Hunt again who sealed the championship for the Reds, their seventh title win. For the final fifteen minutes, the Kop celebrated in style with a repertoire of improvisations from 'Show Them The Way To Go Home' to 'London Bridge Is Falling Down'.

Before the season ended, Liverpool had another important date in Glasgow, this time at Hampden Park against Borrusia Dortmund in the final of the European Cup Winners Cup. The German side had reached the final with victories over Atletico Madrid and West Ham United and in Siggy Held had one of the most feared strikers in Europe. From the start it seemed that the gods were against Liverpool. The weather was atrocious with torrential rain the entire day, almost flooding Hampden and turning the open terraces into a waterfall. What should have been a packed house of over 100,000 only attracted a gate of 41,000. It was one of those nights

Gerry Byrne, hero of Liverpool's Cup final victory over Leeds United when he played most of the 120 minutes with a broken collar bone, made a total of 329 appearances for the club, joining the coaching staff in 1969.

when nothing would go right. Borussia opened the scoring just after half-time but Liverpool kept plugging away and in the sixty-eighth minute Peter Thompson, taking a pass from Smith, began one of his exciting runs down the right towards the by-line before slipping the ball to Hunt to slam into the back of the German net. With Liverpool now oozing confidence, they piled on the pressure but with just seconds of normal time remaining Hunt missed the opportunity of the evening when he hesitated in front of the goal. Liverpool's name was clearly never meant to be inscribed on the trophy and in extra time, Borussia stole a winner. Although they did not know it then there would come a day when Liverpool would reap their revenge on the German Bundesliga.

St John throws up his hands as Borussia Dortmund's Tilkowski steals the ball from his feet and the Germans hang on to win the European Cup Winners Cup 2-1 in extra time.

However, with the title secured by six points from Leeds United, Liverpool could look forward to European soccer again the following season. At home they had scored fifty-two goals and lost only two games while Roger Hunt ended the season with thirty League goals and was the club's top marksman for the fifth successive year. But for the Liverpool number eight there would be more drama before the summer was out.

NEW RECRUITS

1966 – 67

The glorious summer of 1966 will always be remembered for England's World Cup triumph with Liverpool playing their part in the famous victory. Three Liverpool players joined the England squad when the season was over: Gerry Byrne, Ian Callaghan and Roger Hunt though only Callaghan and Hunt actually played, with Callaghan making just one appearance. Roger Hunt was centre forward in all six of England's games, scoring three goals and playing a major part in their victory. That summer the Liverpool man was probably at the zenith of his career. He had joined the Reds in 1959 as a nineteen-year-old shortly after finishing his national service. Within weeks he had made his first team debut scoring in Liverpool's 2 – 0 win over Scunthorpe in a Second Division game and continued to wear the number eight shirt for the next ten years. He played 401 games for Liverpool, scoring 245 goals and netted a club record of forty-one League goals in the 1961 – 62 season. Despite his phenomenal goalscoring rate he was still much criticised, particularly outside Liverpool. He was never really popular with England fans but Alf Ramsey was astute enough to understand and acknowledge his goalscoring instincts. He was not a skilful player but was quick and sharp and usually in the right place at the right time. He was awarded his first cap against Austria in 1962 and went on to play thirty-four times for his country before leaving Liverpool for Bolton Wanderers in December 1969. He also had the privilege of scoring the first goal on BBC Television's 'Match of the Day' when Liverpool beat Arsenal 3 – 2 and in 1972 just over 56,000 fans came to Anfield for his testimonial to voice their appreciation of one of Liverpool's finest ever goalscorers.

The week before the 1966 – 67 season kicked off, Hunt along with Alan Ball and Ray Wilson of Everton paraded the World Cup, the League trophy and the FA Cup around Goodison when the two Merseyside teams met in the Charity Shield. It was just as well they boasted the silverware as there would not be much to show for a few seasons. The problem was that, like Roger Hunt, many of the players were either at their peak or just past but it would take another season before this became abundantly clear.

Back in the European Cup Liverpool drew the Romanian champions, Petrolul Ploesti in the opening round and at Anfield notched up a two goal lead for their long trip east. But surprisingly, the two goals were not enough as Liverpool crashed to a 3 – 1 defeat and with the away goal rule still to be introduced, the two teams met again in Brussels a week later where Liverpool finished the job with a handsome 2 – 0 win. The next round produced one of the most astonishing games Liverpool had ever played in when they tackled Ajax, the Dutch champions. The Dutch club had not impressed much with their few forays into European soccer and there was little concern around Anfield at the draw. But a closer look at the results of Holland which contained half a dozen Ajax players might have alerted the Reds to the growing threat of Dutch football.

The first leg was played on an early December evening in Amsterdam, not in Ajax's usual ground which had no floodlights but in the handsome Olympic stadium with its 65,000 capacity. The Dutch team had a number of emerging young players who were being steadily groomed by their new manager Rinus Michels. Surendonk, Groot, Nuninga, Keizer and an impetuous youth called Johan Cruyff all lined up against the Reds. But for Liverpool the immediate worry was not the youngsters about to take the field but the weather. Fog had suddenly descended on the Dutch city and visibility was down to about fifty yards. Shankly was not keen on a twenty-four-hour postponement as they had a date with Manchester United on the Saturday but the decision was not in his hands. After an inspection the Italian referee reported that he could not see from one end of the pitch to the other so thought the game ought to be off but the Dutch officials argued that in Holland the criteria was whether one could see the goal from the half-way line and they certainly could. So the game was played. It was a farce with Shankly even walking on to the pitch during the first half and holding a conversation with Willie Stevenson and Geoff Strong without anybody noticing. Ajax took Liverpool apart and as the goal tally increased the score had to be relayed to the Liverpool defenders. At the end of ninety minutes Liverpool had been soundly beaten by five goals to one with Chris Lawler snatching a consolation goal towards the end. It was the biggest defeat Liverpool had suffered for years.

RIGHT Shankly needed only one look at Blackpool's Emlyn Hughes to know that here was a young man who could lead Liverpool to greater glory.

Shankly was still not convinced about the skills of the Dutchmen and predicted victory at Anfield . Such was the power of the man that astonishingly everybody believed him and 50,000 were at Anfield to watch Ajax get their supposed comeuppance. In the event, Liverpool could only manage a 2 – 2 draw as 'the Dutch masters' produced a fine display. Cruyff scored twice and Liverpool might have snatched a win as Peter Thompson hit the post three times in the final ten minutes. Ajax were applauded off the field for they had given notice that an outstanding team was in the making.

Liverpool's season stumbled on and although they finished fifth in the League they never seriously challenged for the title. In the Cup they finally overcame a gutsy challenge from Third Division Watford after a goalless draw at Vicarage Road. In the next round they faced Aston Villa at home and were lucky to sneak a one goal win. But their luck did not hold out much longer as they drew neighbours Everton at Goodison for the fifth round tie. It was not a memorable match, Everton beating the Reds by a single goal in a rugged contest where there was far too much at stake for either side to feel free enough to display their obvious talents. However, the game was memorable for one thing. A giant television screen was erected at Anfield and with the game televised live, more than 100,000 were able to watch. Shortly before that match Liverpool dipped into the transfer market and signed a promising teenager from Blackpool for a club record fee of £65,000. Emlyn Hughes had been catching the eye of a number of managers but Shankly was quickest off the mark and the

new recruit made his debut against Stoke City impressing the Kop with his enthusiasm and energy.

1967 – 68

Two other players arrived at Anfield for the 1967 – 68 season. One was Tony Hateley, the tall Chelsea centre forward whose fee of £96,000 was a club record and a young goalkeeper, Ray Clemence from Scunthorpe who cost just £18,000; two players from either end of the financial spectrum, it was ironic that their footballing fortunes at Anfield should be the opposite of their price tags. Gordon Milne and Willie Stevenson both waved goodbye to Anfield after long service with Milne moving to Blackpool, having played 234 games for the Reds and scored seventeen goals. An intelligent wing half, he had played a vital role over the years, initiating attacks and shoring up the defence with thoughtful composure. He was awarded fourteen England caps, his first in 1963 and later that year played for England against the Rest of the World at Wembley. Willie Stevenson, after 188 games for the Reds moved on to Stoke City before eventually winding-up, like so many Merseyside players, at Tranmere. Despite his creative skills and delightful passing, he was never capped by his country and must go down as one of the finest uncapped Scots since the War. Tommy Smith and Emlyn Hughes took their places at the back to form a new solid line of resistance.

Ray Clemence, another snippet at £18,000 from Scunthorpe continued the long line of outstanding Liverpool goalkeepers.

PREVIOUS PAGE TOP Shankly salutes the Kop after Liverpool's League Championship win, 1972-73 season.

BOTTOM Ray Kennedy flanked by Phil Neal and Phil Thompson ponders the next move.

RIGHT Ian St John.

BELOW John Toshack.

FAR RIGHT Kevin Keegan.

ABOVE Ian Callaghan.

RIGHT Emlyn Hughes.

FAR RIGHT Steve Heighway in full flight.

ABOVE Terry McDermott, Phil Neal and Kenny Dalglish with the European Cup after their 1-0 victory against Bruges.

RIGHT Supersub David Fairclough.

FAR RIGHT Ray Clemence.

OVERLEAF Alan Kennedy.

Tony Hateley was soon off the mark carrying out the job he had been bought for. Against Newcastle in the third game of the season he hit a hat-trick as the Reds romped to a 6 – 0 victory but the early promise was never really fulfilled and a year later he was transferred to Coventry after just forty-three games and seventeen goals. But he did score a couple of vital goals against Malmo in the Inter-Cities Fairs Cup. Liverpool's fifth position in the League the previous season entitled them to entry into what was generally regarded as the least glamorous of the European competitions but which some considered the most difficult to win. Hateley's two goals in Sweden gave Liverpool a comfortable start and a fortnight later at Anfield, Yeats and Hunt completed the job for a 2 – 1 victory. Liverpool now faced the respected German side, Munich but surprisingly trounced them 8 – 0 at Anfield with six players getting on the scoresheet. Despite a couple of big wins, Liverpool's form in the League was paradoxical. By Christmas they were in second place, three points behind Manchester United and although they were steadily winning had only managed to score more than two goals in a League game on three occasions. St John had dropped back into the midfield to accommodate Hateley but the former Chelsea man was not gelling with Hunt. The goals did come a little easier in the second half of the season but they still found it difficult to hit more than a couple a game. With Hunt getting older and Hateley prone to injury, Shankly was beginning to scour the Football League for a formidable striker.

In the third round of the Inter-Cities Cup Liverpool faced the skilful Hungarian side, Ferencvaros and lost by a single goal in Budapest but still held hopes of winning the return leg at Anfield. But the Hungarians turned out to be one of the most impressive sides Liverpool had yet faced and became the first continental team to win at Anfield when they held on for a 1 – 0 victory.

Liverpool were now able to concentrate on the FA Cup and enjoyed a good run which took them to the quarter-finals. They opened their account at Third Division Bournemouth and as tradition would have it came away with a goalless draw to finish the job at Anfield in front of 54,000. The fourth round was a carbon copy as they drew 0 – 0 with another Third Division side, Walsall but this round went one goal better at Anfield, slamming five past the Midlanders. The fifth round produced tougher opponents but another away tie, taking them to White Hart Lane. After ninety minutes the score was one goal each and they returned to Anfield where Liverpool won 2 – 1. Into the quarter-finals with an away game at West Bromwich Albion and holding second spot in the League, there was every possibility of a League and Cup double. For the fourth time Liverpool drew away from home but this time were finally frustrated by West Brom after two replays. West Brom's reward was a Wembley final against Everton which they won in extra time.

After a seven-year pause Liverpool had another crack at the increasingly popular Football League Cup but

Tony Hateley challenges and wins while the ever-alert St John waits for his chance. Liverpool v Munich 1860.

ABOVE Tommy Lawrence dives bravely at the feet of the Ferencvaros centre forward on an ice-bound Hungarian pitch.
LEFT Roger Hunt about to hit the net against Spurs.
OPPOSITE PAGE Shankly with his backroom boys – Bob Paisley, Ronnie Moran, Joe Fagan and Reuben Bennett. The secret of Liverpool's consistent success?

could only draw at home to Bolton before losing at Burden Park. All these extra games had piled the pressure on and any hope of winning the League faded as legs grew weary amid the confusion of fixtures. Manchester City sneaked ahead of Manchester United and Liverpool had to be content with third place, just three points behind the winners. When the number of games was finally totted up, Liverpool had played fifty-nine matches, nine more than City. Without the cluster of fixtures, tiring travel and inevitable injuries Liverpool might have won the League but that was the price they were paying for success.

1968 – 69
Shankly's policy was to rebuild a team before time forced inevitable changes upon him. The process, he argued, should be evolutionary rather than revolutionary. The

history of the Football League is littered with outstanding teams who reached their peak, then faded before anyone though of reconstruction. The secret was to be replacing a player or two each year, a considerably easier job than finding eleven replacements and one which still allowed for continuity.

At the start of the 1968–69 season the Liverpool manager plunged into the transfer market paying Wolverhampton Wanderers £100,000 for the teenage striker Alun Evans. At the time, it was the highest fee ever paid for a teenager and caused a headline or two but Shankly was convinced that Evans had the potential to be a dynamic goalscorer. The young lad began well with a couple of early goals but his career was to sadly take an unexpected turn a few seasons later and finish in disappointment. Gerry Byrne, for so long Liverpool's dependable left back decided to call it a day after recurring injury problems. He had been playing for eleven years, making 273 League appearances and

winning two England caps and although he managed to put through his own net in his first game, he would always be remembered as the man who played on at Wembley with a broken collar bone.

By Liverpool's standards 1968–69 was a poor season with no trophies finding their way to Anfield. Back in the Fairs Cup Liverpool took an early exit when they drew 3–3 on aggregate with the Spanish side, Atletico Bilbao. This time the toss of the coin did not come down in their favour as it had four seasons earlier with Cologne. In the FA Cup Leicester City proved to still hold a spell over the Reds knocking them out at Anfield in the fifth round after Liverpool had drawn at Filbert Street. In the League Cup they went further than ever before beating Sheffield United and Swansea at home before going out to Arsenal at Highbury. This all left Liverpool with less fixture congestion than usual and time to catch their breath in the League. But from the start they always seemed to be trailing in second place,

77

Alun Evans, at £100,000 then the most expensive teenager in British football. But a glittering career was shattered by a cruel blow.

initially to Arsenal and finally to Leeds United who took the title by six points from the Reds. The Leeds team had finally matured and emerged from behind the shadow of Liverpool and over the next five years would be one of their toughest opponents with their clashes guaranteed to pack Elland Road and Anfield.

1969 – 70

Everton proved to be the sternest test for everyone during the 1969 – 70 season even though Arsenal, Leeds,

Liverpool and First Division newcomers, Derby County all fielded unusually skilful teams. The combination of Ball, Kendall, Harvey and Labone with Joe Royle up front was one of the most effective Goodison line-ups for years and although Liverpool finished a creditable fifth, they were still fifteen points behind the Blues who took the title by a clear nine points from Leeds.

Liverpool's Cup fortunes improved marginally with an exciting run in the FA Cup beginning at Coventry with a 1 – 1 draw. In the replay the Reds dismissed the Midlanders at Anfield and then met Wrexham also knocking three goals past them. The fifth round found them at home to the jinxed Leicester City again and when they could only manage a goalless draw it looked as if the Leicester voodoo was working again. But in the replay Liverpool surprised everyone by beating them 2 – 0 to win the right to play lowly Second Division Watford away in the quarter-finals. It should have been a comparatively easy game for the Reds especially as they had already visited Vicarage Road once that season in the League Cup and come away with a 2 – 1 win. But without the injured Peter Thompson and Tommy Smith Liverpool lacked their usual drive and unexpectedly went down by one goal to nil. The game marked a watershed for Liverpool with Shankly deciding that this was the moment to break up the old team and introduce the new blood that would form the basis of the team to stride the seventies.

After their win against Watford in the League Cup the Reds had travelled to Maine Road for the next round where they lost to a Manchester City side now sliding into decline. Contesting the Fairs Cup for the third consecutive year Liverpool faced the Irish part-timers, Dundalk and trounced them 10 – 0, the highest win Anfield had ever witnessed. Only four Liverpool players failed to get on the scoresheet and one of those was the goalkeeper. Another four goals were added in the second leg before Liverpool journeyed, for the first time, to Portugal to play Setubal. The Portuguese turned out to be a far different proposition from the Irishmen, winning the first leg by the only goal of the game. In the second leg Liverpool won by 3 – 2 but with the new away goal rule just introduced, went out of the tournament.

Team changes were beginning to take place. Ray Clemence, the young goalkeeper from Scunthorpe had ousted Tommy Lawrence towards the end of the season and was soon impressing the knowledgeable Koppites. Lawrence had spent eight uninterrupted years guarding the Liverpool goal, clocking up just over 300 games and playing for Scotland on three occasions. He was a safe goalkeeper rather than a spectacular one but nevertheless deserves his place in the archive of memorable Liverpool

’keepers. In the 1968–69 season when Liverpool set a record by conceding only twenty-four goals, Lawrence played his part as much as anyone in keeping the goal tally so low. Shankly's rebuilding took him to Bristol Rovers where he purchased a tall, well-built centre half, not unlike Ron Yeats but by the name of Larry Lloyd and also to Bury for a full back, Alec Lindsay. Meanwhile Roger Hunt, Ian St John and Ron Yeats all disappeared from the first team never to return. It brought to an end a side which for almost ten years had delighted a new generation of Anfield supporters as well as old timers and which had laid the valuable foundations for the future success of the club. They were players who would never be forgotten and who would always be prominent in the annals of the club's history.

Ron Yeats at centre half may have been a stopper but he also netted some vital goals, including this header against Burnley and was virtually unbeatable in the air.

1970 – 71

A new Liverpool team was taking shape with the accent on youth so that by the end of the 1970–71 season the average age of the side was only twenty-two. Given such a young team it was hardly surprising that they should miss out on the silverware once more but as the season progressed there were clear signs that the team was maturing quickly and that its blend of skill and youth would soon bring success.

Steve Heighway was a twenty-two-year-old graduate from Warwick University when he joined the Reds in May 1970. He had played for a couple of years with Skelmersdale United in the Cheshire League where his speed on the wing had impressed Shankly, reminding him of the young Peter Thompson. In what is not generally considered an intellectual man's game, Heighway surprisingly found himself teaming up with another graduate at Anfield, Brian Hall. A midfield player and a graduate from Manchester University, Hall had been on Liverpool's books since the summer of 1968 but had never broken into the first team. Now, with the arrival of Heighway, his opportunity was to come in the new-look Liverpool. Meanwhile other new faces like Clemence, Lloyd and Lindsay had firmly established themselves over the previous season. The Liverpool team of the sixties had now totally disappeared but the team of the seventies was not quite complete. Shankly still yearned for a consistent goalscorer in the mould of Roger Hunt and his search eventually took him one cold November day to Cardiff where he signed a lively six-foot centre forward called John Toshack. The Welshman was only twenty-one but in his brief spell at Cardiff had found the net seventy-five times in 159 outings and had already won half a dozen Welsh caps. He had the makings of an exceptional striker and Cardiff knew it, charging Liverpool £110,000.

In the Fairs Cup, again, Liverpool faced the Hungarians, Ferencvaros, the only European team to have ever won at Anfield up to then but this time the Reds snatched a 1–0 win at home then drew in Hungary. Dinamo Bucharest, the opposition in the second round were dismissed 4–1 on aggregate to award Liverpool with an attractive tie against the Scottish side Hibernian. Toshack in his first European game scored the only goal in Edinburgh while Heighway and Phil Boersma added a couple at Anfield. Steve Heighway had made his debut at Tottenham in early October and in his second game against Burnley found the net and set Anfield buzzing with his talents. Within weeks he had taken the First Division by storm and was the most talked about young player for years. He had the rare and delightful ability to beat players, skipping around them before sprinting towards the by-line and pushing over delicate crosses. When Toshack with his thunderous

LEFT TOP University graduate Steve Heighway who set Anfield alight in 1970 with his dazzling sprints down the left wing.
BOTTOM John Toshack was an expensive buy from Cardiff who after a hesitant start eventually struck up a goalscoring partnership with Kevin Keegan. He totalled ninety-five goals in 236 appearances.

strength and skill in the air teamed up with him, they made a formidable duo.

Bayern Munich were the opposition in the quarter-finals arriving at Anfield with a glittering team boasting names such as Sepp Maier, Georg Schwarzenbeck, Franz Beckenbauer, Gerd Muller and Uli Hoeness. It was the heart of West Germany's national side which had just dumped England despairingly out of the World Cup and which had gone on to take third place themselves. Over the next four years, these five players would win a World Cup for Germany and three European Cups for Bayern. But as part of the maturing process they had first of all to beat the Anfielders. In one of the finest games seen at Anfield for some years, Liverpool dismissed Bayern by three goals to nil as young Alun Evans played the game of his life to score a hat-trick. It was a phenomenal display by the blonde-haired striker as he powered towards goal time and again before unleashing his fearsome shot. It illustrated the potential talent of the former Wolves player which was sadly never fully realised at Anfield. Returning to the Midlands one weekend, Evans was attacked in a night club and his face smashed open with a glass, causing serious injury and scarring him badly. He was out of the side for weeks, losing confidence and becoming prone to injury. Eventually after seventy-seven games and twenty-one goals with Liverpool, Shankly let him go to Aston Villa but it was a tragic story which underlines the vacillations of football.

A 1–1 draw in Munich put Liverpool into the semi-finals against Don Revie's Leeds but the Yorkshiremen were at the height of their powers and sneaked a 1–0 win at Anfield. The second leg was a goalless draw and Liverpool had failed in Europe again. In the League Liverpool chased hard but far too many draws – ten before the end of the year – kept them adrift of Arsenal and Leeds. In the FA Cup a goal by John McLaughlin against Aldershot was enough to put them into round four where they faced Swansea. The Welshmen went down by three goals to nil and Southampton were next to lose by a single goal. In the quarter-finals luck gave them yet another home tie against Tottenham but the Londoners held out before the highest gate of the season for a goalless draw. Liverpool looked to be on their way out as they made the trip to London with fixtures at home and in Europe beginning to pile up. But before another huge gate Steve Heighway mesmerised the Spurs defence to put Liverpool into the semi-final and just ninety minutes away from a trip to Wembley.

Everton who had been League champions the previous season had also been steaming along well in the Cup and had battled their way into the semi-final with a 5–0 win over Colchester. All Merseyside hoped that the draw would keep the two apart but instead they were pitted against each other at Old Trafford. Liverpool had already beaten their rivals in an exciting game at Anfield in November when they fought back after trailing 2−0 to win by three goals to two and had held Everton to a draw at Goodison. It augured well for the Anfielders and that was precisely how it turned out with Evans and Hall scoring in the second half after Liverpool had gone into the interval a goal down. Liverpool were in their fourth Cup final but found themselves playing Arsenal who had not only beaten them in the 1950 final but who on the Monday of Cup final week defeated their North London

RIGHT Tommy Smith, a fearless defender known as the 'hard man' of football.
BELOW Alec Lindsay beats Arsenal's Ray Kennedy but the Gunners win the day with their 2-1 Cup final victory.

rivals Tottenham to clinch the League title. A win over Liverpool would mean the double for Arsenal, making them only the second team to achieve it that century.

FA Cup Final 1971 Liverpool v Arsenal

Sitting high up in the vast Wembley stands watching enviously as Liverpool took the field for their fourth FA Cup Final was a young man who had just been signed by Bill Shankly. As yet he had made no appearances for his new club but within a year he would explode on the English First Division scene to become its greatest talent. The nineteen-year-old lad had made only a handful of appearances for Scunthorpe United before signing for Liverpool but had deeply impressed one man, Andy Beattie. Shankly had hired Beattie who he knew well from his Preston and Huddersfield days, as a part-time scout and as soon as he arrived he tipped Shankly off about the enthusiastic eighteen-year-old. Shankly watched him, as did all of the backroom staff and just a few weeks before the Cup final, the club paid Scunthorpe United £35,000 for the young lad, Kevin Keegan.

8 May, 1971 was a glorious hot summer's day of typical Cup final weather and a shirt-sleeved crowd of 100,000 basked in the breathtaking atmosphere of Wembley. Most of them seemed to be supporting the North Londoners who flooded from their homes along the North Circular Road and down Wembley Way and by full-time would have drowned the Mersey cheers with their Arsenal chants. In the first ninety minutes neither side seemed willing to give an inch with both defences on top. Forwards struggled to find space and it was hardly surprising that when ninety minutes were up there was still deadlock with no score. It had not been the most

exciting of games but once the two sides kicked into extra time the match sprang dramatically into life. Within two minutes the long-legged Steve Heighway had danced past the Arsenal defence to shoot Liverpool ahead. If only he had done it three minutes earlier the celebrations would have been well underway. But even now the party was short-lived as Eddie Kelly poked home a messy equaliser for Arsenal. The deadlock continued into the second half of extra time before the string-haired Charlie George, with his stockings hanging carelessly around his ankles, hit a right foot shot just wide of Ray Clemence. There was no stopping the Gunners now even though Liverpool battled until the last moment and the Arsenal jinx lived on.

Liverpool might have lost the Cup final but they were still a young side in transition and had finished fifth in the League as well as reaching the semi-finals of a European competition. They had played sixty-two games over the season, losing only eleven and had conceded just twenty-four goals in the League, fewer than any other team. Up in the stands young Kevin Keegan was heartbroken as he trooped down to see his new teammates. Shankly took one look at him and thought: 'Here's a character and he's not even playing.' The next time Liverpool came to Wembley Keegan would be playing and this time they would not lose.

Liverpool Clemence, Lawler, Smith, Lloyd, Lindsay, Callaghan, Hall, Hughes, Evans (Thompson), Toshack, Heighway.

Arsenal Wilson, Rice, McLintock, Simpson, McNab, George, Storey (Kelly), Graham, Radford, Kennedy, Armstrong.

A SUPERSTAR ARRIVES

1971 – 72

Kevin Keegan made his First Division debut in Liverpool's opening game of the 1971 – 72 season against Nottingham Forest at Anfield, scoring in their 3 – 1 win. He was an inspiration from the start, wearing the number seven shirt and playing as a scheming midfielder. He would happily retreat deep into his own defence in search of the ball, carrying it upfield into the heart of the attack always dashing and searching for open spaces or prepared to take on defenders. Only 5 feet 8 inches, he could outjump many a defence and his strength made him a difficult man to shake off the ball as he bounced up from hard tackles. He could twist and turn a defence and never seemed to tire, always running until the final whistle. Within weeks of his debut it was clear that Shankly had discovered a star of the highest quality. Eventually he would weld a unique partnership with the towering Toshack that would threaten every defence in Europe bringing them a bagful of goals each season.

'I'll head the ball down to you and you make sure you put it away'. Toshack and Keegan – the partnership that ruled.

However, Keegan's first season at Anfield was not a memorable one for the club as trophies eluded them for yet another year. It was a season when bad luck would haunt the Reds through every competition. In the League Cup Liverpool still could not progress beyond the fourth round as they faltered at West Ham after a couple of fine wins against Hull and Southampton. In the FA Cup Liverpool unluckily drew Leeds United after dismissing Second Division Oxford in their opening tie. Leeds travelled to Anfield and left with a goalless draw before disposing of the Reds in Yorkshire. In Europe, Liverpool were back in the Cup Winners Cup, the trophy they had almost lifted in 1966. In the

first round they were drawn against the Swiss Cup winners, Servette and were surprisingly beaten 2–1 and in danger of being dumped at the first stage. But back at Anfield Hughes and Heighway combined to give them a 2–0 win and a place in round two. Bad fortune again intervened as Liverpool drew their Fairs Cup semi-final opponents of the previous year, Bayern Munich. The Germans were now maturing rapidly into one of the finest teams in Europe having added a sturdy, young full back, Paul Breitner to their ranks and held Liverpool to a goalless draw at Anfield before beating them soundly 3–1 in Munich.

In the League Liverpool made a poor opening loosing four games by mid-September and then getting bogged down in a series of draws. The New Year kicked off with Liverpool well down the table after six defeats and six draws. On 1 January Leeds United came over the

Jackie Charlton of Leeds United challenges Ray Clemence and Emlyn Hughes in one of the many momentous clashes between the two sides during the 1960s.

Pennines to Anfield and won 2 – 0 and a week later went to Leicester only to lose again. Over the Christmas period they had failed to score in five games but just as Liverpool's season seemed to have totally floundered they rediscovered their style and scoring form. They dramatically strung together an astonishing run of fifteen games without defeat, drawing only two of those and swept up the table to challenge Leeds and Derby County. In the penultimate game of the season Liverpool faced an away match with title-chasing Derby County, now managed by the former Sunderland centre forward, Brian Clough. Both sides desperately needed to win if they were to lift the title and just when Liverpool most needed their luck, it deserted them as Derby crept home by a single goal. It put Derby one point ahead of the field but their season was over and while Leeds still had a game at Wolves and Liverpool a game at Arsenal, Brian Clough confidently took his team off for a well deserved holiday to Majorca to await events.

The mathematics were complicated. Leeds needed only a draw to win the title but if they lost, the title would go to either Derby or Liverpool depending on whether Liverpool could defeat Arsenal. Put another way, if Leeds lost and Liverpool won, then Liverpool would be champions. Thousands of Liverpool supporters descended on Highbury fearful that Arsenal were not Liverpool's favourite team. With hundreds glued to their transistor radios at Highbury's famous Clock End, the unexpected news came over that Leeds were losing by two goals to one and the roar went up with the Liverpool fans chanting the score to the players. Liverpool were drawing 0 – 0 and were pressing strongly towards their fans packing the Clock End goal but as the precious minutes ticked away the desperately needed goal would not come. Then in the final minute in a goalmouth scramble, Toshack hooked the ball over the line for what looked like the goal to clinch the title but the linesman's flag was raised and it was disallowed amidst a sea of Liverpool protests. Luck was not on Liverpool's side and they had to be content with third place. The title went to Derby and Liverpool must have cursed their failure to score in those five games over Christmas.

The Liverpool team for the seventies had now taken shape with the arrival of Keegan adding a touch of the unpredictable. The little man netted nine goals and won an England Under-23 cap. International honours were also poured on most of his teammates. Ray Clemence joined Keegan in the Under-23 side while Chris Lawler progressed from the Under-23s to the full England side winning the first of his four caps. Tommy Smith had won his one, and surprisingly only, England cap the

previous season and Larry Lloyd was also settling into the England side. Emlyn Hughes was already challenging Sam Hardy's record as the most capped Englishman in the club's history while Ian Callaghan had fallen out of favour after his 1966 World Cup exploits but would reappear in an England shirt later in the seventies. When England tackled Wales at Wembley in May 1971 there were four Liverpool players in the England team. Although Steve Heighway had not lived in Ireland since he was a child he had opted to play for Eire and perhaps missed out on a more distinguished international career with England. And finally, John Toshack was still regularly knocking them in for Wales and on his way to becoming one of the most capped Welshmen and highest goalscorers in Welsh history.

1972 – 73
Since Willie Stevenson had left Anfield for Stoke in 1967 Liverpool had lacked a half back with his creative qualities so in July 1972 Shankly enlisted the services of Peter Cormack from Nottingham Forest at a cost of £110,000. A former Hibernian player, Cormack had been capped nine times by Scotland but at the age of twenty-six might have been considered a trifle old by Liverpool standards! With so many versatile players already at Anfield and no apparent gaps, Cormack's transfer raised a few eyebrows but as usual Shankly was astute, knowing that it would keep the pressure on his other players as well as strengthen the squad. Winning titles was no longer a matter of eleven quality players but needed a squad of fifteen or so to cope with the additional rigours of European and League Cup soccer. It was Shankly who established the trend of employing a strong and loyal squad, capable of substituting successfully for injury or loss of form. And the importance of a strong squad had never been emphasised more than in the 1972 – 73 season when Liverpool were successfully challenging on all fronts.

The most disappointing of their campaigns was in the FA Cup where they suffered a relatively early setback in round four going down to Manchester City in a replay at Maine Road. In the League Cup they marched into unknown territory, reaching the fifth round for the first time after beating Carlisle, West Brom and Leeds United, all at the second attempt. In their fifth round tie they could only manage a 1 – 1 draw with Tottenham at Anfield and lost the replay by three goals to one. But Liverpool would have their revenge later in the season.

RIGHT Larry Lloyd beats Ray Kennedy to the ball. The former Bristol Rovers centre half went on to greater glory with Nottingham Forest.

Europe was proving to be considerably more fruitful – and lucrative – as they strode towards the final of the Fairs Cup, now known as the UEFA Cup. In round one they encountered the strong German side Eintracht Frankfurt – though the German side was not quite the force it had been when it had been beaten 7 – 3 by Real Madrid in one of the most memorable European Cup finals of all time. Liverpool won the home leg 2 – 0 with goals from Keegan and Hughes and held on resolutely for a goalless draw in Frankfurt. In the next round they were drawn against AEK Athens who offered little resistance as the Reds knocked up a 6 – 1 aggregate win. Dynamo Berlin were the opposition for the third round and after a goalless first leg were comfortably outplayed at Anfield by three goals to one. Another German side, this time East German, came out of the hat for the quarter-finals but Dynamo Dresden, beaten 2 – 0 at Anfield, also lost 1 – 0 to a Keegan goal in Germany. For the semi-finals Liverpool were to face an English side, Tottenham Hotspur who also happened to have won the UEFA Cup the previous year.

Just over 110,000 watched Liverpool's two opening League games at Anfield as they summarily dismissed Manchester's City and United each by 2 – 0. It was a heartening opening and on 24 September Liverpool climbed into the top spot with a 5 – 0 win over Sheffield United. Two weeks later they were encouraged all the more by a fine 1 – 0 win against Everton with Peter Cormack demonstrating how to score goals as well as create them. Toshack was going through a lean spell and had given way up front to either Cormack or Phil Boersma. The Liverpool-born Boersma had been at the club since 1968 rarely managing to break into the first team but had more success than ever in the 1972 – 73 season playing in nineteen games and scoring five goals. For the remainder of the season it proved difficult to knock Liverpool from their top spot and the title was finally wrapped up on Easter Monday in front of 55,000 at Anfield with old rivals, Leeds United as the victims. Liverpool deservedly won by two goals to nil and it was fitting that the goals should come from Cormack and Keegan. Liverpool had clinched a record eighth title, eventually winding up three points ahead of Arsenal. The Kop roared their praises and Keegan was all set to become a superstar.

In the UEFA Cup semi-final Liverpool met Tottenham at Anfield for the first leg but could only snatch a 1 – 0 win, thanks to Alec Lindsay finding his way into the Spurs' penalty area. But would it be enough, they wondered, as they travelled down to London for the return game. White Hart Lane was no place for feint hearts as the holders struggled to keep a

ABOVE A surprise buy, Peter Cormack gave a skilful touch to Liverpool's midfield in over 160 games.

OPPOSITE PAGE TOP Kevin Keegan slots the ball past the Eintracht Frankfurt goalkeeper to give Liverpool a place in the second round of the UEFA Cup in 1972.

CENTRE A delighted Peter Cormack (left) hammers home Liverpool's second goal as they beat AEK Athens 3-0 in the UEFA Cup.

BOTTOM Chris Lawler, an outstanding example of an attacking full back who netted sixty-one goals in 546 games.

grip on their trophy. Martin Peters opened the account for Spurs but Heighway soon pulled one back before Peters again netted to give Tottenham a 2 – 1 win. Liverpool were beaten but in the event it hardly mattered as Steve Heighway's away goal counted double and Liverpool's reward was a two-legged final against another German side, Borussia Moenchengladbach.

The final was played in May after the League title had been won and tired limbs rested which was just as well for Liverpool had already clocked up sixty-two exhausting games. Borussia vaunted a team full of German internationals such a Netzer, Vogts, Wimmer, Bonhof, Heynckes and Jensen and were rated the strongest in Europe by an admiring Shankly. For the

first game at Anfield the Liverpool manager chose Brian Hall up front instead of Toshack thinking the smaller man might perform better in the wet conditions. But with the score still goalless and the torrential rain falling heavier, the referee decided that conditions were simply too bad to play football and called the game off. For the second time in eight years freak weather had caused the postponement of a European game at Anfield. It was agreed to play the match the following night but the brief half hour of play had given Shankly enough clues to plot Borussia's downfall. The German defence looked flat-footed and unable to cope with high balls so Shankly switched Hall for Toshack. It did the trick as Liverpool pumped high balls into the German penalty area for Toshack to flick on to Keegan. Larry Lloyd was also there to lend his height and bagged one goal while Keegan netted the other two in a 3 − 0 victory that looked secure enough to lift the trophy. But the return game was not quite so simple as another torrential rainstorm struck during the first half. Borussia had to attack and on the slippery surface had the Liverpool defence twisting and sliding as they skilfully pressed forward. They scored twice but their early exertions in the rain had tired them and Liverpool held out to win their first European trophy 3 − 2 on aggregate.

Liverpool had become the first Football League club to pick up a European trophy and the League title in the same season. They had played sixty-four games with Keegan scoring twenty-two goals in all competitions and Toshack seventeen and had lost only eleven games. The only major loss was Peter Thompson who after ten years of patrolling the left wing called it a day and moved on to Bolton Wanderers. He had played 318 games, scoring forty-two goals and had delighted Anfield with his daring runs and skilful touches. He was awarded sixteen England caps between 1964 and 1970 but did not find favour in Ramsey's wingless England team winning most of his caps before the World Cup victory.

1973 − 74

Throughout the 1972 − 73 season Liverpool had used only sixteen players although even this was two more than they had employed during the entire 1965 − 66 season. Liverpool's ability to name an unchanged team so regularly was crucial to their cup-winning exploits. Rarely have Liverpool players suffered severe fractures and few have been forced to endure long lay-offs. This has not been luck but rather a combination of skills in

Shankly, man of the people, acknowledges another championship victory with his fans on the Kop.

treating injuries and a style of play which avoids more rugged physical contact. The credit in treating injuries has to go largely to Bob Paisley who over the years kept a detailed file on every conceivable injury and the required treatment. It has been alleged that Shankly and his backroom staff would not talk to players who feigned injury or malingered on the treatment bench and although there may be an ounce of truth to this, they never cold-shouldered any player with a genuine injury. No doubt the threat of another player stepping into your first team position also encouraged some to shake off injuries rather quicker than might normally have been expected. And it was the case with a number of regular first team players that once they had lost their spot through injury it was either never regained or took a further first team injury to allow them back. Liverpool's style of play has also encouraged the early release of the ball before bone-crushing tackles arrive while a steady build-up through passing rather than attempting to run at opponents also lessens the risk of injury. Liverpool players have also been chosen carefully and signed only after a rigorous medical. In Shankly's time two England internationals, Freddie Hill of Bolton and Frank Worthington of Leicester, were both rejected after failing medicals.

The 1973–74 season began and ended with the same squad although there was still confusion about who was playing in the striker's role alongside Keegan. Alun Evans had been relegated to the reserves while Toshack played in less than half the season's League games and had to be content with continuing to share the role with Brian Hall and Phil Boersma. Eventually, however, he would stake his claim and the goals which had been slow to come since his transfer would return.

The UEFA Cup competition had to make do without the holders, Liverpool who as League champions naturally enough elected to enter the European Cup for the third time. In the first round they travelled to the tiny Duchy of Luxembourg to challenge, Jeunesse Esch but found the part-timers in a stubborn mood as they held out for a 1–1 draw. Back at Anfield Liverpool were confident of an easy win but were made to fight all the way, eventually succeeding by two goals to nil with one of those an own goal. The next tie pitted Liverpool against the highly-rated Yugoslavian champions, Red Star with the first leg to be played in Belgrade. With seven of their players in the country's international squad, Red Star were formidable opposition and on a bitterly cold East European night soon shot into the lead adding another early goal in the second half. The warning signals flashed for Liverpool who looked to be in serious danger of elimination but a Chris Lawler goal,

his sixtieth for Liverpool, gave them renewed hope for the return leg. Liverpool were quietly confident but a fortnight later Red Star turned up at Anfield and, encouraged to attack by their manager Miljan Miljanic, played with some considerable style to outsmart Liverpool by two goals to one. A disappointed Liverpool were out of the European Cup and would now have to concentrate on the domestic competitions.

The League Cup eluded Liverpool yet again though they equalled their best run, struggling through to the fifth round before Wolves dismissed them at Molineux. The tale still lingered that Liverpool were not interested in the tournament and were always glad to see the back of it so that they could focus their efforts on more important competitions. With the League Cup and the European Cup out of the way all that remained were the League and the FA Cup.

Liverpool began their League programme with early defeats at Coventry and Derby while Leeds United began in devastating form, taking twenty-three points from a possible twenty-six to shoot to the top of the table. Leeds barely flinched all season but Liverpool kept plugging away and gradually reduced the gap. But, surprisingly for the Reds, their end of season form was poor with only one win in the last eight matches. Nine points had been dropped and Leeds captured the title by five points with Liverpool in second place.

Towards the end of April, Ian Callaghan set a new milestone when he overtook Billy Liddell's record 492 appearances. Like Liddell, the 5 feet 7 inches Liverpudlian had been a loyal and uncomplaining servant of the club. Signed for the usual £10 signing on fee, he made his debut six days after his eighteenth birthday against Bristol Rovers in a Second Division fixture. He began as a skilful right-winger and for a number of years complimented the left side attacks of Peter Thompson before switching in later years to a midfield role. Alf Ramsey capped him twice with one of his appearances against France during the World Cup Finals of 1966 but he had to wait another eleven years for his next two caps, turning out against Luxembourg at the grand old age of thirty-five. He was later to appear in the European Cup winning side and was the only player to have spanned the years from the Second Division to the European triumph. He lost his place a little later and was given a free transfer to Swansea, helping them win promotion to Division Two. In all, he played 636 League games for the Reds, scoring forty-nine goals and was the Football Writers' Player of the Year in 1974. He collected eleven medals with Liverpool, including five championship medals and in 1976 was awarded the OBE.

Doncaster Rovers were lying ninety-first in the Football League when they huddled around their radios to hear the live broadcast for the third round draw of the Cup. And when their number came out of the hat they were not sure whether to cheer or cry for they had been drawn against Liverpool at Anfield. They made the journey across the icey Pennines in early January and were determined to go back with something. As it was they almost returned with Liverpool's scalps causing one of the biggest upsets of the day with their 2−2 draw. With just twenty-four minutes remaining Doncaster were leading by two goals to one and ironically it was the Doncaster-born Keegan who equalised to save Liverpool's embarrassment. Liverpool did not make the same mistake twice and in front of Doncaster's biggest gate for years ended the Yorkshiremen's dreams with a 2−0 victory.

Round four and Liverpool faced a Carlisle United side who were challenging for promotion from the Second Division in what was clearly a set test for the northern club. Already there was a buzz about the city that this was going to be Liverpool's year but when Carlisle scraped a goalless draw in front of 47,000 there must have been some nagging doubts. But at Brunton Park, Liverpool again worked the trick with Boersma and Toshack giving them a 2−0 win. Ipswich Town were the opposition at Anfield for the fifth round but presented few problems as Liverpool ran out 2−0 winners. Through to the quarter-finals and Liverpool faced an away game to Second Division Bristol City where John Toshack scored the only goal. Liverpool were now at the penultimate hurdle, the semi-finals and out of the hat came their old foes, Leicester City. The first match before 60,000 at Old Trafford ended in a goalless draw and it looked like the Leicester voodoo was at it again. However, in the replay the following week at Villa Park, Liverpool swept Leicester aside by three

goals to one and were into their fifth FA Cup final thanks in part to a memorable goal from Toshack that had Wembley stamped all over it.

FA Cup Final 1974 Liverpool v Newcastle United

Liverpool's Wembley opponents, Newcastle United were making a record eleventh appearance in an FA Cup final and were one short of a record number of wins. The north-easterners turned up at Wembley not only with a Cup-fighting pedigree finer than Liverpool's but with the backing of supporters every bit as fanatical. They also had a few players quite capable of destroying the Anfield dreams. Striker Malcolm Macdonald was an England regular and one of the most dangerous finishers in the game while Ian McFaul, David Craig, Bobby Moncur, Tommy Cassidy and Jim Smith were all internationals. They also fielded two youngsters called Terry McDermott and Alan Kennedy who in time would both find their way to Anfield. The Geordies would be no pushover and Malcolm Macdonald had been boasting since the semi-final about what he was going to do to Liverpool's supposed invincible defence.

Larry Lloyd, at the heart of that defence had taken a bad knock earlier in the year and into his boots had stepped a twenty-year-old local lad, Phil Thompson. A tall, gangling, youth with match-stick legs who weighed not much over 10 stones, he hardly looked an adequate replacement for the broad-shouldered, strong-limbed Lloyd. But Thompson was skilful, determined and above all a battler who in later years would captain not only his club but his country as well. The versatile Tommy Smith had also slotted into the right back

In the 1974 Cup final Liverpool overpowered Newcastle to win by three goals to nil. It was Kevin Keegan with this first goal who began the rot.

ABOVE Keegan and Lindsay share their moment of glory.
LEFT TOP Liverpool's third goal scored by Keegan after a spectacular inter change of passes clinches Liverpool's second FA Cup victory.
BOTTOM Emlyn Hughes proudly displays the cup.

position with the unlucky Chris Lawler pushed into the reserves and now close to ending his footballing career at Anfield. Up front Phil Boersma was the unfortunate player left out with Toshack pulling on the striker's jersey. Emlyn Hughes led Liverpool onto the pitch and into a cacophony of noise from the Geordie and Scouse fans that rang around the arena. The first half promised much but never quite delivered. Newcastle looked impressive early on but could never find the well-marked Macdonald who was gradually being blotted out of the game by the novice, Phil Thompson. Shortly before the interval Terry Hibbitt tore a knee and never really recovered and when the half-time whistle went Liverpool were just about ahead on points.

In the second half Liverpool's slow domination turned to superiority when first Lindsay scored only to be ruled offside in the fifty-first minute and then Keegan stabbed home a Tommy Smith cross in the fifty-eighth minute to make it 1-0. A quarter of an hour later and Liverpool took a firmer grip on the cup when Steve Heighway scored from a Toshack backheader. Liverpool now gave an appreciative Wembley crowd a display of footballing skills as they knocked the ball from wing to wing and frequently strung together a dozen passes or more. Newcastle were simply outplayed as Liverpool oozed confidence. The final goal was scored fittingly by Keegan with just a couple of minutes remaining after

Tommy Smith had swapped the neatest of exchanges before crossing for Keegan to tuck away. Some thirteen passes between the red-shirted Liverpool players had created the third goal that deservedly took the FA Cup back to Anfield for the second time in their history.

As Emlyn Hughes strode up the thirty-nine steps to the Royal Box to receive the trophy a security guard, not recognising Phil Thompson stopped him from joining in the party, while down on the pitch with fans kneeling at Shankly's feet another security man tried to usher Liverpool's trainer, Bob Paisley away. But neither of them needed to worry as their faces would soon become familiar enough to the stadium's security staff. The *Sunday People* described the game as 'the most one sided final since 1960' while the Liverpool manager told their reporter that Liverpool 'were the best team in England and probably in the world'. After the adulation on the pitch Shankly returned to the dressing-room and sat quietly in the corner while around him players cracked open the champagne. Sitting there buried in his own thoughts he made a decision that was to rock the football world. Liverpool travelled back to Merseyside the following day to the traditional reception. A quarter of a million lined the streets of the city to cheer them home. Shankly was their god but none of them knew that his days at Anfield were quickly drawing to an end.

Liverpool Clemence, Smith, Thompson, Hughes, Lindsay, Hall, Callaghan, Cormack, Keegan, Toshack, Heighway.
Newcastle United McFaul, Clark, Howard, Moncur, Kennedy, Smith (Gibb), McDermott, Cassidy, Macdonald, Tudor, Hibbitt.

1974 – 75

On 12 July, 1974 Shankly called a press conference at Anfield to introduce his latest signing, Ray Kennedy of Arsenal. There had been little hint that the Highbury striker was a Shankly target and at £200,000 was their most expensive buy. But there was even less hint of what was about to follow. Having introduced the big Arsenal man to the assembled press corp, John Smith the Liverpool chairman read out a short prepared statement. 'It is with great regret,' he began 'that as chairman of the board I have to inform you that Mr Shankly has intimated to us that he wishes to retire from League football.' There was a stunned silence. Was this another Shankly joke? No, it was true. He was tired and had decided to quit while still on top. There had been no dispute with the club; on the contrary, they had offered him a new contract at whatever salary he wanted and had spent the past few weeks trying to disuade him. The news shocked the football world and within the hour was the talking point in every office, factory floor and pub on Merseyside.

Shankly had become a living legend, creating one of the greatest clubs in the history of English soccer and known throughout the football fraternity for his famous quips to the press. 'Some people think football is a matter of life and death.' he once joked, adding, 'it's much more serious than that.' On another occasion during a team talk, he dismissed the Manchester United opposition which contained three of the finest players in the world, by telling his own players that one of them had a dicey leg, the other was too old and the third was rubbish. Of course, he never really meant it but it psyched his own players into believing they could beat United. It was a sad day when he left Anfield and even sadder when bitterness crept in over the next few years. He was lost with time on his hands and wondered why nobody at Anfield consulted him when he still had so much to offer. No directorship came his way and invitations to away games were infrequent. But it was a dilemma for the club. On the one hand they did not want to inhibit the new manager in the way that Matt Busby had continued to dominate affairs at Old Trafford while on the other hand nobody at the club wanted to deny Shankly his rewards.

If Shankly's retirement brought sadness, then his death seven years later brought tears. He had been taken ill late in September 1981 and rushed to hospital but nobody suspected that it was quite so serious. The whole city was stunned when it heard on 29 September that Shankly was dead. Everyone had assumed that the man was immortal and as with John Lennon's death there was a deep sense of personal loss. Both men, in their own way, had made Liverpool an exciting and exhilarating city during the sixties. The tributes poured in from every corner of the footballing globe and his supporters, dressed in their red and white colours turned out in their thousands to wave their final farewells and stood silently on the Kop to pay their lasting tribute. Once asked what was the most enjoyable aspect of football, he replied, 'making the people happy'. There can be no finer epitaph for Bill Shankly, the man who truly created Liverpool Football Club.

Shankly had urged the club to look no further than the famous bootroom where the backroom staff gathered for their cups of tea and footballing talk for his successor. The press naturally enough speculated mentioning names such as Malcolm Allison and Brian Clough but there was never any danger that an outsider would be appointed. Bob Paisley was the obvious choice and with commendable decorum the board met and promoted Shankly's right-hand-man to the job. The other bootroom boys Joe Fagan, Reuben Bennett, Ronnie Moran, Roy Evans and Tom Saunders all moved up a notch in the smoothest transition imaginable.

A bemused Brian Hall looks on as an adoring Liverpool fan sinks to his knees before Shankly.

After the events of July, it was never going to be an easy season. Paisley was under enormous pressure from the newspapers, the supporters, the players and the board. They may have wanted him to succeed but every team selection and every result was liable to be closely scrutinised and analysed. Fortunately, the team went seven games before its first defeat and immediately after that, a 2−0 defeat at Maine Road, they knocked up their biggest ever win when they thrashed the Norwegian side, Stromgodset at Anfield by eleven goals to nil in their opening European Cup Winners Cup match. Nine players hit the scoresheet but in the return leg the Reds could only scrape a 1−0 win. In the second round Liverpool tackled the familiar faces of Hungary's Ferencvaros who they had dismissed from the UEFA Cup five years earlier. It was not easy then and was certainly no easier now as the Hungarians went through on the away goal rule after both legs had been drawn.

The Football League Cup proved to be the usual disaster with Liverpool going out disappointingly at home to Middlesbrough by a single goal after having dismissed Brentford and Bristol City *en route*. Life in the FA Cup was also short-lived as the holders fell in the fourth round at Ipswich, having beaten Stoke 2−0 in the previous round. The League title remained wide open until the end of the season and Liverpool were always challenging. In mid-March they were fourth, three points behind Everton with just four points separating the first seven sides. But in the penultimate game of the season at Middlesbrough, Liverpool went down by a single goal and with it their chances of the title vanished. They finished second, two points behind Derby County and although the season was barren as far as trophies were concerned they had successfully overcome the trauma of Shankly's departure.

Paisley quickly demonstrated that he had learned well from Shankly, plunging into the lower Leagues in October 1974 to make his first purchase, a twenty-three-year-old defender from Northampton Town by the name of Phil Neal who cost just £60,000. He probably made only one better purchase in his entire managerial career at Anfield. Neal was soon drafted into the side at the expense of Alec Lindsay and formed a back partnership with Tommy Smith. In November, Paisley again struck gold when he signed Terry McDermott who had played in the Newcastle Cup final team against Liverpool. He, too, was soon in the team although he would take more time to establish his rightful position. Ray Kennedy also had his problems. A leading goalscorer with Arsenal, he could not settle up front at Anfield looking awkward and jaded and drifted into the reserves before Paisley inspiringly played him in the midfield.

On the debit side Larry Lloyd surprised everyone by moving on to Coventry City for a hefty fee and became one of the few Liverpool stars to ever leave the club while still at the height of their career. He had been a dominant presence in the Liverpool defence, playing 150 games. Like an old-fashioned centre half he towered over opposing forwards but won only three England caps. From Coventry he moved to Nottingham Forest where he haunted Liverpool attackers in the many battles the two sides contested in the late seventies. An unhappy John Toshack almost disappeared as well, signing for Leicester City but failed the medical. He returned to Anfield riled and found a new lease of life, suddenly forming a sensational goalscoring partnership with Kevin Keegan that lasted until Keegan's departure. Chris Lawler's career at Anfield was also winding to an end. He had played 406 League games over twelve years, scoring forty-one goals with another twenty goals coming in other competitions. He was a dependable defender, cool under pressure and always looking to make one of his penetrating overlaps down the flanks. He won just four England caps and after a spell at Portsmouth and Stockport County returned to Anfield to join the coaching staff.

1975 − 76

Paisley's confidence was growing. The quiet, almost shy, avuncular figure at the helm had not really wanted the job in the first place but he was never one to shirk his duty. He had served the club loyally from before the War with 252 games in a red shirt and Shankly's success must have owed much to the careful organisation which Paisley calmly brought to the bootroom. Shankly and Paisley both contrasted and complimented each other perfectly.

Liverpool made a moderate start to the 1975−76 season losing their opening match at Queens Park Rangers by two goals to nil. At the time it seemed Liverpool had thrown away a couple of easy points but by the end of the season with QPR challenging for the title, that result took on a different perspective. By mid-October the Reds had won only six of their first dozen games but over the late autumn shifted into a higher gear and by Christmas were heading the table. QPR threatened the entire season and there was never any doubt that one of them would capture the title, the challenge continuing until the final game of the season. QPR had finished their season and topped the League by one point so that Liverpool needed to beat Wolves at Molineux to take the title. At half-time they were a goal down but just when the pressure seemed to be draining

ABOVE Ex-Gunner Ray Kennedy (right) had played against Liverpool at Wembley. He arrived as a striker but found greater success in midfield. He went on to win 17 England caps as well as a host of domestic and European honours with Liverpool.

LEFT Terry McDermott who had also played against Liverpool at Wembley, for Newcastle United, found himself in a red shirt six months later. But it was to be some years before he established himself in Liverpool's first team.

them, they found new stamina with Keegan, Toshack and Ray Kennedy hitting the net for a splendid 3–1 win.

Toshack and Keegan had scored twenty-eight goals between them as their rejuvenated partnership terrorised defences, with the big Welshman scoring sixteen of them. Third down the goalscoring list came a young red-haired lad called David Fairclough. Born in Liverpool, he had supported the Reds from the Kop as a youngster and then joined the club as an apprentice, making his first appearance in 1975. He regularly came on as a substitute and even by April the Liverpool match programme had nicknamed him, 'Supersub'. It was a title that was to remain with him throughout his Anfield career as the tall, awkward-looking striker made a habit of entering the affray as substitute and scoring vital goals. Late in the season he came on as number twelve to score four goals in three games to help the Reds collect six points. Another Liverpool born lad, Jimmy Case was also promoted from the reserves to begin a popular career in Liverpool's midfield. Joey Jones, a £110,000 signing from Wrexham during the close season made his debut and chalked up a dozen appearances before the end of the season.

The FA Cup brought no luck with Liverpool dismissed at Derby after a useful third round win at West Ham while in the League Cup they beat York City away in the opening round only to go out to Burnley in the next round. But in the UEFA Cup luck was on their side as they marched once more, with increasing menace, across Europe. Their campaign began somewhat unsteadily in Edinburgh where Hibernian notched up a goal lead and missed a penalty but back at Anfield with Toshack in devastating form and scoring all three goals, the Reds crept through to the next round 3−2 on aggregate. The second round pitted them against Real Sociedad of Spain who were beaten stylishly in San Sebastian by three goals to one and then trounced at Anfield 6−0. For their next game, Liverpool travelled east to Poland where they clocked up another away win, this time against Slask Wroclaw in temperatures well below freezing, by two goals to one before completing the job at Anfield 3−0. Liverpool were now in the quarter-finals and found themselves back on a plane to face Dynamo Dresden whom they had defeated on the way to their last UEFA Cup triumph. It was a good omen and although they only managed a goalless draw in Dresden, they narrowly won the return leg by two goals to one and were into the semi-finals.

Liverpool could not have hoped for a more testing draw than Barcelona who now boasted Cruyff and Neeskens among their expensive ranks. But in Barcelona's magnificent Nou Camp stadium, packed with 80,000 Basques, the Reds demonstrated their growing maturity and ability to cope with continental tactics and contrasting styles. The Spaniards were

LEFT The Reds win their ninth title after beating Wolves 3-1 at Molineux in May 1976.
BELOW Keegan beats the Bruges goalkeeper from the penalty spot to put Liverpool into an unassailable lead in the first leg of the UEFA Cup final, April 1976.

beaten, much to the disgust of their own supporters by a Toshack goal. In the return leg, before 55,000 at Anfield, Cruyff orchestrated a more confident Barcelona as they deservedly held out for a 1–1 draw. Liverpool were into their third European final where they faced the Belgian side, Bruges with the first leg scheduled for Anfield just a few days before the League title had been wrapped up. Inexperienced though the Belgians were, they quickly went into a two-goal lead, stunning the 56,000 crowd who had confidently come in anticipation of a Liverpool celebration. But they were not to be disappointed as Paisley craftily replaced Toshack with Jimmy Case at half-time and resuscitated Liverpool's ailing attack. The goals arrived quickly after the interval from Kennedy, Case and Keegan and Liverpool journeyed to Belgium clutching a one goal advantage. The second leg was played almost three weeks later and, as at Anfield, Bruges took an early lead from the penalty spot. With the Belgians still merry-making, Liverpool struck back immediately and within four minutes Keegan's bending shot had brought the sides level. Liverpool hung on

David Fairclough heads towards goal as Bruges go down by three goals to two, to give Liverpool their second UEFA Cup.

obstinately but with growing confidence as Bruges faded in the second half. There were no more goals and when the final whistle blew Liverpool had won their second European prize. It was also the second time they had won the League Championship and the UEFA Cup in the same season.

1976 – 77

Liverpool made their traditional close season swoop into the transfer market in August 1976, signing the England international, David Johnson from Ipswich for £200,000. The Liverpool-born Johnson had been on Everton's books for three years before joining Ipswich but his transfer to Liverpool confused many as they totted up the number of strikers already at Anfield. But there was sense to the signing. Unknown to the general public, Kevin Keegan had approached the club expressing his interest in playing abroad and Real Madrid had already made a tempting offer for his services. A deal was struck: if Keegan remained for one more year while the club attempted to win the European Cup, his request to leave would be granted. Johnson had, in fact, been purchased to provide extra firing power when Keegan left and Toshack moved on.

The foray into Europe began at Anfield where the Reds took on the Irish champions, Crusaders. It was the first time they had met an Irish League club in a European tournament and Liverpool schemed and sweated to break down their tight, well-organised defence. In the end it took a Phil Neal penalty and a John Toshack goal to make the scoreline look reasonably respectable and over in Belfast Liverpool fared better hammering five goals past the part-timers. The next round saw Liverpool breaking new frontiers again as they journeyed to the Black Sea to meet the Turkish champions, Trabzonspor. Weary after their long journey and with a bumpy pitch and poor quality match ball to add to their problems, the Reds struggled to find their rhythm. They conceded a hotly-disputed penalty but held on to keep the score down to a single goal.

Over the years the club had studied and smartly learned the lessons of European travel. In the mid-sixties they would fly out by schedule plane a few days beforehand, returning the day after the match but now they flew out by charter the day before the game and returned immediately. This itinerary reduced boredom to a minimum, avoided diet problems and kept the players fresh for the continuing League programme. Shankly and Paisley had also instilled into them a discipline of never retaliating when provoked by continental teams. These were important lessons and without them Liverpool and many another English team would have folded against Trabzonspor. In the return leg, the Turkish champions were overwhelmed by three goals to nil and the Anfielders were into the quarter-finals where they would meet the previous year's finalists, St Etienne.

Liverpool began their League challenge in sparkling form, losing only two of their first sixteen games and by September had already climbed to the top of the table. There were fine wins against Everton at Anfield by three goals to one and a five-goal hammering of Leicester but then shortly before Christmas, Liverpool were astonishingly thrashed by five goals to one at Aston Villa. It was the first time any team had put more than four goals past the Liverpool defence since Ajax. To that date Liverpool had only conceded more than three League goals on seven occasions since their return to the First Division in 1962. The week after their humiliation

After an unhappy start, the former Everton striker David Johnson eventually formed a useful partnership with Dalglish, scoring 78 goals in 174 games.

at Villa Park, Liverpool lost at West Ham by two goals to nil and the prophets of doom began to write the team's obituary. But they bounced back the following week to end 1976 by beating Stoke City 4–0.

The Football League Cup was soon brushed aside when they lost their replay at the Hawthorns after drawing one goal each with West Bromwich at Anfield. But the FA Cup was a far more serious proposition. In their opening game, Liverpool faced Third Division Crystal Palace but could only draw 0–0 at Anfield and it began to look as if this competition might be short-lived as well. Down at Selhurst Park, however, in front of a near record crowd of 43,000 Liverpool dismissed the South Londoners by three goals to two and drew Division Two's Carlisle for the fourth round. They proved to be easier opposition going down 3–0 at Anfield. There were further lower division opponents

103

when Oldham came out of the famous bag for the fifth round but they too went out by three goals to one. The quarter-finals brought Middlesbrough to Anfield with Fairclough and Keegan combining to dismiss them 2−0 but if the draw had been lucky until then, it turned against them in the semi-final when all Merseyside had hoped they would avoid Everton. So, the eighty-year long prospect of an all-Merseyside final disappeared yet again and instead the two lined up against each other at Maine Road in a semi-final for the fourth time. Like most of their previous cup encounters it was a gruelling contest. The first game ended two goals apiece with local players McDermott and Jimmy Case saving their blushes and they returned to Manchester four days later to recommence battle. This time Liverpool's superiority shone through as they hit three goals past their rivals and the Reds were through to their sixth FA Cup final.

Liverpool's European quarter-final encounter with the French champions, St Etienne has to rank as one of the most exciting and memorable occasions in Anfield's long history. It stands alongside the famous semi-final against Inter Milan, the record gate Cup match against Wolves in 1952 and the 7−4 hammering of Everton in February 1933. It was a night nobody present would ever forget. In the first leg the Reds had gone down by a single goal, though with Keegan absent through injury and Toshack straining an achilles tendon during the match, the one goal deficit seemed a good result. Every inch of the Kop was crammed for the return leg and Liverpool quickly latched on to the electrifying atmosphere as Keegan, now recovered from injury, lobbed the ball past the French goalkeeper within two minutes. The scores were level but St Etienne, with their massed French

Liverpool's European Cup quarter-final victory against St Etienne produced some of the most exciting football Anfield has ever seen as the Reds pulled back a goal deficit to win 3-1 on the night.

supporters singing 'Allez Les Verts', powered towards the Liverpool goal forcing Clemence into some of his finest acrobatics. At half-time the two teams left the pitch to a standing ovation but far better was to come. Within six minutes of the interval Bathenay had equalised to put St Etienne ahead on aggregate and Liverpool were back where they had started. Seven minutes later with the Kop amusingly mimicking the French supporters by singing 'Allez Les Rouges', Ray Kennedy struck a second goal but they were still behind to the French away goal. The evening now became frenetic as Liverpool pressed keenly for the winner, the colour and pace of the game leaving a lasting memory. In the seventy-second minute Toshack limped dejectedly off the pitch for David Fairclough to join the affray. The

occasion was heaven sent for 'Supersub' Fairclough who within minutes was tearing at the St Etienne defence. Then with eight minutes remaining, he collected a pass close to the half-way line and ran at the French defence, sprinting forty yards and swaying past two defenders before driving the ball and beating the advancing French goalkeeper, Curkovic. It was one of the finest individual goals Anfield had ever seen and sent the Kop delirious. By the end of the game which Emlyn Hughes later rated as the most exciting match he had ever played in, the entire ground was on its feet cheering and vigorously singing 'Allez Les Rouges'. It was Fairclough's finest moment with the 'Supersub' magic working once more. Although the spindly-legged youth played in more than 150 games for Liverpool and scored fifty-five goals, he never really established himself as a first team regular and always had to live with the substitute tag. But he would never be forgotten for the stunning goal that destroyed St Etienne on a night of Anfield passion.

Keegan puts Liverpool into the lead in the second minute against St Etienne in one of Anfield's most memorable European evenings.

When Liverpool drew Zurich for the semi-final they must have guessed their name was already etched on the trophy. After St Etienne it was an anticlimax and as expected both legs turned out to be relatively easy with Liverpool bringing a 3–1 lead back from Zurich before finishing off the job at Anfield with a handsome 3–0 win. Liverpool were into another final and were only the second Football League club to have reached the last stage of the competition.

The League Championship was wrapped up at Anfield on 14 May, 1977 a week before the FA Cup final as Liverpool clinched the one point they needed against West Ham in a goalless draw. Just over 55,000 saluted Liverpool's tenth championship with more than 10,000 locked out an hour before kick-off. Their final run-in had been remarkable with not one game lost since 22 January until the title had been secured. They had gone sixteen games without defeat to win the championship by one point from Manchester City. Keegan lead the goalscoring list with twelve League goals, followed by Toshack with ten. In all, thirteen Liverpool players had contributed goals during the season, showing the depth of goalscoring strength throughout the team. With the League trophy safely secured and with two finals impending, Liverpool glimpsed the beckoning vision of an astonishing treble.

FA Cup Final 1977 Liverpool v Manchester United
Manchester United had reached the final the hard way with a semi-final victory over Leeds United and under Tommy Docherty's management had moulded together an exciting young team around Steve Coppell, Gordon Hill, Lou Macari, Sammy McIlroy and Jimmy Greenoff; one which was determined to avenge their defeat at Wembley the previous season. Having won the League title on the previous Saturday and played at Bristol City on the Monday evening, Liverpool were now preparing to meet United five days later at Wembley before jetting to Rome for the European Cup final the following Wednesday. Never before had any team won three major trophies in a season. After his dashing exploits against St Etienne, David Fairclough was surprisingly omitted from the Liverpool twelve with Ian Callaghan named as substitute. Toshack was still injured and David Johnson slotted into the striker's role as Liverpool began their assault on a second trophy and a League and Cup double.

The first half swung indecisively with neither side able to capitalise on the broad unmanned acres of Wembley. United's defence, which had conceded sixty-two goals that season, was looking unusually secure while Liverpool with only twenty-three goals conceded, were as solid as ever. Liverpool's midfield looked the more imaginative as Keegan and Kennedy plotted to find gaps but Johnson was never able to turn their gains to any advantage. At the interval the two teams were still level. Within five minutes of the resumption, Liverpool were a goal behind when Stuart Pearson surprised Clemence with a low shot under his body which, on most occasions, the England 'keeper would have stopped. Two minutes later Liverpool were back on level terms as Jimmy Case crisply collected a pass from Joey Jones and sent a thundering shot past Alex Stepney and into the top left corner of the net. The United roar was silenced but not for long as they struck again three minutes later when a misfired ball into the penalty area bounced disastrously off Jimmy Greenhoff's body and into the Liverpool goal. Kennedy twice hit the woodwork and barring that five minute spell of goals Liverpool always looked the better side. However, as Paisley often reminded people, you need a certain amount of luck in football, and on 21 May, 1977 it was in short supply as far as Liverpool were concerned.

Liverpool were dejected. The League and Cup dream had evaporated; so too had the treble. Now they had to pick up their shattered morale as well as their drained and aching bodies and travel to Rome for the most important game in the club's history. As they slumped wearily away from the Wembley arena they learned that their European Cup final opponents, Borussia Moenchengladbach had just drawn with Bayern Munich to capture the Bundesliga title for the third successive year. It had not been Liverpool's day, but before the week was out they would have won even greater glory and would have forgotten their unlucky day at Wembley.

Liverpool Clemence, Neal, Smith, Hughes, Jones, Kennedy, Case, McDermott, Keegan, Johnson (Callaghan), Heighway.

Manchester United Stepney, Nicholl, Greenhoff B., Buchan, Albiston, McIlroy, Macari, Coppell, Pearson, Greenhoff J., Hill.

European Cup Final 1977 Liverpool v Borussia Moenchengladbach

For some, the long march on Rome began at Wembley Way as they sadly trundled towards the stations, motorways and airports for their trans-European trek. Others made for Liverpool to recuperate and revive before heading towards Lime Street and Speke Airport in what was to become the largest transportation of people across Europe since the War. More than 30,000 of them gathered in the vast and vacant spaces of Rome's Olympic stadium as the warm evening sun set over the Eternal City casting long, dancing shadows across the pitch. When Emlyn Hughes led the Liverpool team out into the arena none of the players could believe it. The stadium was awash with red and the unmistakable sound of Liverpool accents. It was as if the Kop had been shifted to Rome. Toshack was passed fit but Paisley decided not to risk him and instead opted for the old man

Ian Callaghan It was to be Kevin Keegan's final appearance as well as for Tommy Smith who had announced his intention to retire. So the scene was suitably set for a drama in the grandest style.

Almost from the kick-off Liverpool seized control, stroking the ball about confidently and thoughtfully. In the twenty-seventh minute Steve Heighway cleverly worked his way towards the edge of the German penalty area before slipping a delicate through ball for Terry McDermott to snap up. Liverpool were a goal ahead but Borussia, with an array of internationals such as Berti Vogts, Rainer Bonhof, Urlich Stielike, Herbert

BELOW Terry McDermott puts Liverpool into an early lead against Borussia Moenchengladbach. Although born on Merseyside, McDermott joined Newcastle United, even playing against Liverpool in the 1974 FA Cup final. Later that year he signed for the Reds in a £170,000 deal.

Wimmer, Jupp Heynckes and the Danish star Allan Simonsen, were a formidable collection and not surprisingly pulled a goal back shortly after the interval. Inspired by Simonsen's stunning goal, the Germans suddenly besieged Liverpool. Clemence stretched to save superbly from Steilike and Liverpool reeled under the intense pressure. For ten minutes Borussia bombarded the Liverpool goal as the Reds' defence hung on. But there was no second goal and Liverpool began to take control once more. In the sixty-fifth minute Steve Heighway forced a corner and sent in a high cross close to the goal. Suddenly, a head appeared above the flailing arms of the Borussia goalkeeper and the stretching necks of his defence and the ball was in the back of the net. Like a 'Roy of the Rovers' script, the head belonged to none other than Tommy Smith. Wembley was forgotten and all the style and arrogance had returned to Liverpool. Keegan was masterminding the proceedings, running his marker Berti Vogts ragged until the famous German defender ran out of tricks and up-ended him as he tore into the penalty area. A calm Phil Neal stepped up and with just seven minutes remaining slammed the spot kick into the net. The English champions were now the European champions. Five hundred million people watching on television throughout the world had seen a magnificent final superbly won by Liverpool.

The Liverpool supporters went wild, turning Rome red with their colours and adding some new arias to the city's operatic repetoire. Some even found the team's

secret celebratory hideout but nobody had the heart to turn them away. So they joined in the fun, scoffed the food and threw a few players into the swimming-pool. It was that kind of night. But Bob Paisley, now the most celebrated manager in the world, never even had a drink. 'I just wanted to stay sober and savour the atmosphere,' he recalled. Just over thirty years previously Paisley had marched on Rome as an unknown private in the British army's liberating force. Now he stood at the head of his own Red army of players and fans who had accompanied him in the triumphant return to Rome to capture the most prized club trophy in world football.

Liverpool Clemence, Jones, Neal, Smith, Kennedy, Hughes, Keegan, Case, Heighway, Callaghan, McDermott.
Borussia Moenchengladbach Kneib, Vogts, Klinkhammer, Wittkamp, Bonhof, Wohlers (Hannes), Simonsen, Wimmer (Kulik), Steilike, Schaeffer, Heynckes.

109

13

GOODBYE KEVIN, HELLO KENNY

1977 – 78

Kevin Keegan joined Hamburg in June 1977 for £500,000 after playing 230 games and scoring sixty-eight goals for the Reds. His move disappointed the Kop, so unfamiliar to the transfer of their stars but Keegan wanted a fresh challenge on the continent and there was little point in the club clinging on to an unhappy player. In his six years at Anfield he had become the biggest name in English football helping Liverpool win the European Cup, two UEFA Cups, the FA Cup and the League three times while helping himself to twenty-eight England caps. He was the pivot around which the team spun, harrying the opposition, creating goals and running until the final whistle. His enthusiasm was infectious and he never gave less than 100 per cent. At Hamburg he was twice named European Player of the Year but returned to England in July 1980 joining Southampton and later Newcastle United. Shankly rated him the finest English player since Tom Finney and few could disagree with him.

The European Cup final was also supposed to be Tommy Smith's final game but overcome with the occasion and his winning goal, he decided on another season and added a further twenty-two League appearances to his total. When he finally did leave Anfield for Swansea City he had played 467 League games for the Reds and scored thirty-seven goals. Known as a 'hard man', Smith's ghost still haunts many a quick-footed forward who shrank at his ferocious tackles. The Argentinian Ossie Ardiles, for one, will never forget his induction into English Football. Once omitted from the team at Highbury, Smith angrily stormed off home but it was all quickly forgotten and he had soon fought his way back. But he rarely complained and over the years was a loyal and professional servant of the club. For a spell he was captain and although he won only one England cap, he was one of the most decorated players in the game with a bagful of medals to prove his worth.

With Keegan gone the search was on for his successor but Paisley had long since decided on his target and a month after transferring Keegan, he dashed to Glasgow to secure the most rewarding transfer deal in the club's history. Kenny Dalglish was twenty-six years old when he joined Liverpool for a record fee of £440,000 and had already made over forty appearances for his country. He had worn the famous green and white hooped shirt of

Celtic on more than 200 occasions, scoring 112 goals and was the most feared striker north of the border. Dalglish joined another young Scot at Anfield who was about to break into the first team. Twenty-two-year-old Alan Hansen had arrived in April 1977 from Partick Thistle for £100,000 and although he managed fifteen appearances over the season, it would be another year or so before he became a regular choice. In January 1978 a third Scot joined them who was to have an equally impressive career at Anfield. He was Graeme Souness, a £350,000 signing from Middlesbrough.

Dalglish fittingly made his debut at Wembley as Liverpool fought out a goalless draw against Manchester United in the Charity Shield, with the Scot showing early signs of his abundant skills. In the first League game of the season at Middlesbrough, he scored within seven minutes and then scored again in his next two games. Liverpool were off to a flying start but so too were newly-promoted Nottingham Forest, now under the guidance of Brian Clough, who by Christmas had galloped into a six-point lead over Liverpool. The Reds probably waved goodbye to their League title in a disastrous six-week spell between January and March, losing four matches, as well as going out of the FA Cup in the opening round away to Chelsea. Their results picked up after Derby County had beaten them 4 – 2 in early March and they proceeded to win nine of their remaining twelve games and drawing the other three, conceding only six goals. But while Liverpool kept on winning so too did Nottingham Forest who finally took the title by seven points from Liverpool in second place.

Forest were to be the scourge of Liverpool that year and for a number of seasons to come, taking over the mantle of Leicester and Arsenal. In the League Cup Liverpool's ten-year barren spell came to a welcome end as they marched towards the final. Chelsea, Derby and Coventry were all dismissed though all three would take their revenge in the League during Liverpool's lean spring. In the quarter-finals Wrexham were beaten 3 – 1 at the Racecourse and Liverpool, for the first time, were into the last four. Arsenal provided the opposition for

RIGHT They said nobody could replace Keegan but they had not reckoned on a young Celtic striker called Kenny Dalglish who arrived at Anfield for a record £440,000 fee.

ABOVE Never one to shirk a tackle, the Liverpool-born Jimmy Case took over from Tommy Smith as Anfield's hard man. Case made over 170 appearances for Liverpool, winning four championship medals and three European Cup winners medals before joining Brighton and Hove Albion in 1981, where he continued to provide the quality that the Liverpool fans had enjoyed.

Liverpool had tasted the glory of winning the European Cup and it had made them thirsty for more. They were now the most feared and respected team on the continent and began their challenge for a second win at Anfield against Dynamo Dresden who had been beaten on the way to their first UEFA Cup triumph. But the East Germans offered little resistance as Liverpool stormed into a 5–1 lead with a new name appearing on the goalsheet, that of Alan Hansen. In the second leg Liverpool surprisingly lost by two goals to one but it hardly mattered as Liverpool were into the last eight. Their quarter-final opponents were Benfica, twice winners of the champions trophy but now without the glittering names of Eusebio, Neto and Augusto. When Liverpool arrived in Portugal, Benfica were prizing a run of forty-six games without defeat and within minutes of the kick-off the Eagles of Lisbon had taken an early lead. But Liverpool, despite the 70,000 crowd and torrential rain, were equal to the occasion with Jimmy Case and Emlyn Hughes ending Benfica's impressive run. The return leg saw Liverpool in supreme form winning by four goals to one and heading into the final four.

As luck would have it, when the semi-finals were drawn, Liverpool were pitted against their old German foes, Borussia Moenchengladbach. They had faced Borussia twice before, once in the UEFA final and in last year's champions final, winning on both occasions but would it be third time lucky for the Germans? Borussia won the first leg by two goals to one, scoring their second goal in the final minute but at Anfield they folded as Liverpool romped home 3–0 winners for a place in their second successive European Cup final. With just one match remaining Liverpool had already clocked up fifty-eight games. Graeme Souness had slotted impressively into the midfield while Kenny Dalglish was proving that there really was life after Keegan. With a season's total of twenty-nine goals, his delightful skills had captured the hearts of the Kop but there was one more special goal to come before the season was officially over.

European Cup Final 1978 Liverpool v FC Bruges
Wembley was the setting for Liverpool's second European Cup final and the Belgian champions, Bruges were the opposition. Bruges had reached the finals by disposing of Panathinaikos, Atletico Madrid and Juventus and were managed by Ernst Happel, the Dutch national coach. They also fielded a team of Danish, Dutch, Austrian and Belgian internationals but their side showed few changes from the one that had been beaten by Liverpool in the UEFA final of 1976. Liverpool

the two-legged semi-final and in the first match at Anfield, Liverpool set up a 2–1 lead, so a goalless draw at Highbury was enough to put them into the final. Nottingham Forest who now boasted Larry Lloyd among their numbers were the opposition in the Wembley final and probably the only team in Europe capable of beating Liverpool at their best. But the final was a dour affair with neither side able to break the deadlock and the two teams met again four days later at Old Trafford. The replay was a livelier contest with John Robertson scoring the only goal from the penalty spot after Phil Thompson had up-ended John O'Hare. The Liverpool players protested vehemently arguing that the incident was outside the area, and this was backed up by the television replay pictures but in the absence of a television screen on the pitch the referee continued pointing to the spot. Luck, it seemed, was still a scarce commodity for Liverpool in the League Cup.

began the game as the hottest favourites in years yet surprisingly showed five changes from the team that had captured the trophy the previous year: Jones, Smith, Keegan, Heighway and Callaghan were all missing from last year's line-up.

Wembley was brimming with what seemed like 90,000 Liverpool supporters though with the unfair allocation of tickets, it was mystery how they managed to acquire them. Bruges, with two key players injured, began defensively, allowing Liverpool to do the attacking. After a sterile first half with Liverpool finding it impossible to capitalise on their superiority, the neutrals in the crowd must have been hoping the second half would bring a more enterprising display from the Belgians. But they began where they had left off, rarely venturing into the Liverpool half and happy to soak up the pressure. Eventually Liverpool had to score and it was Kenny Dalglish, seizing a pass from fellow Scot, Souness on the right side of the penalty area, who finally broke Bruges' iron wall. He sprinted towards the six-yard box, waited for the goalkeeper to advance and then chipped the ball into the net. It was Liverpool's third visit to Wembley that season but only the first time their supporters had been able to cheer a goal. A goal behind, Bruges still showed little inclination to attack and Liverpool were quite content to sit on their one goal lead and lift the trophy for the second successive year, a feat no British team had ever achieved before.

Liverpool Clemence, Neal, Thompson, Hansen, Kennedy, Hughes, Dalglish, Case (Heighway) Fairclough, McDermott, Souness.

FC Bruges Jensen, Bastijns, Maes (Volder), Krieger, Leekens, Cools, De Cubber, Vandereycken, Simoen, Ku (Sanders), Sorensen.

1978 – 79

Towards the end of the 1977 – 78 season John Toshack moved to Fourth Division Swansea City as player-manager after seven years at Anfield. During that time he had played 172 games in the number ten shirt and scored seventy-four goals, as high a goalscoring rate as any of his predecessors. His early years with Liverpool had been mixed as he failed to settle but once he had struck up a partnership with Keegan, the goals flowed. He was broad and strong and one of the deadliest headers of the ball to ever play for the Reds. Capped forty times by Wales, a record for a Liverpool player, he went on to greater glory with Swansea, taking them from the Fourth Division to the top of the First in five years.

The 1978 – 79 season began disastrously for Liverpool

when they drew Nottingham Forest in the first round of the European Cup. It was a game fit for the final with both teams clearly yards ahead of any other side in Europe. The first leg at Forest went the way of Brian Clough's side with newcomer, Gary Birtles and Colin Barrett putting them into a handy 2 – 0 lead. Back at Anfield with the atmosphere well primed there was still every hope that Liverpool could pull off a dramatic victory but fight as they did, the goals simply would not come. They pressed continually hitting the post and the bar but the longer it went on the more it seemed that Forest's name was already engraved on the trophy. The game ended in a goalless draw and Forest went on to lift the Cup but had to admit that Liverpool had given them the toughest game of all.

Liverpool's second disaster was in the League Cup, going out to Second Division Sheffield United by a goal to nil. Sheffield were later relegated to Division Three and Liverpool were out of two cup competitions before September was over. But there was compensation in the League as Liverpool made a storming opening, winning their first six games and not losing until Everton beat them 1 – 0 at Goodison in their twelfth match. The goals flooded in with the highlight a 7 – 0 hammering of Tottenham with a memorable seventh goal from Terry McDermott which many consider the finest goal ever seen at Anfield. Their two games against Norwich produced ten goals with five against Derby and four each against Manchester City and Bolton. The crowds flocked to Anfield to watch the goalspree and with the gate now limited to 52,000 the Kop doors were locked almost every week. Liverpool soon shot to the top of the table and remained there for the rest of the season, losing only one game after 16 December, to win the title by eight points from Nottingham Forest. It was one of their most impressive championships. Just four games were lost and only sixteen goals conceded with Clemence keeping a clean sheet on twenty-seven occasions. It was the finest defensive record in the history of the Football League and one which will probably remain unchallenged. Dalglish topped the scoring list with twenty-one League goals, followed by David Johnson who had now established himself alongside the Scot with sixteen goals. Alan Kennedy who had been bought from Newcastle United for £300,000 in August 1978 had soon settled, securing the left back spot. Fondly known as 'Barney' he would, over the years, score some of Liverpool's most important goals in his daring raids into opposition penalty areas.

In the FA Cup, Liverpool looked set for another trophy reaching the last four without a goal conceded. Southend, Blackburn, Burnley and Ipswich were all disposed of comfortably before they faced Manchester United at Maine Road. The semi-final was a game Liverpool should have won with McDermott missing a penalty and other easy chances muffed. Hansen scored a late equaliser in the thrilling 2−2 draw and with the replay at Goodison, some were already optimistically talking about Wembley and the double. In the event, it was not to be as Jimmy Greenhoff hit a late goal in another exciting and even contest to send United to Wembley.

Of the fifty-two fixtures Liverpool had played during the season, they had been defeated on only seven occasions and had conceded twenty-two goals, keeping thirty-three clean sheets. Only three teams throughout all those games managed to score more than one goal against them. If this was not Liverpool's most outstanding team, then it was certainly their strongest ever defence and probably the finest defence to have ever played in Britain.

1979 − 80

In the summer of 1979 Emlyn Hughes' Anfield career drew to a close with his tranfer to Wolves. At the time of his signing in 1967 he had cost Shankly a record fee of £65,000 but twelve years later, he had repaid that sum many times over. He was the second Liverpool player to captain England, playing in sixty-two internationals and winning more England caps than any other Anfielder. He was an outstanding club captain, always driving his team on through adversity and encouraging them by his example and enthusiasm. But he was also skilful and although he was known as 'crazy horse' brought a vital calm to the heart of his defence. He played 474 League games for Liverpool and scored thirty-five goals, winning just about every honour in the game with them except the League Cup which he promptly won with Wolverhampton Wanderers. A PFA Player of the Year and an OBE, he later tried his hand at football management, but sadly with little success.

Steve Heighway's best days were also over though he continued to make the occasional appearance as substitute before finally leaving for America in April 1981. The galloping winger made 331 League appearances, scoring over fifty goals and on his day was one of the most exciting sights in football as he swerved and swayed towards the by-line. Capped twenty-seven times by Eire while with Liverpool, he stands alongside Peter Thompson and Billy Liddell as one of the finest wingers in the club's post-war history.

The 1979−80 season was almost a repeat of the previous season as Liverpool took an early exit from the European Cup, reached the last four of the FA Cup and

conquered the League. In Europe they faced a Soviet team for the first time when Dinamo Tblisi visited Anfield. The Georgians craftily appeared on the pitch early, cheekily taking up residence in front of the Kop where they spent fifteen minutes stroking the ball from player to player and mesmerising an appreciative Kop with their flowing skills. It was an ominous sign and once play began Liverpool quickly realised that Tblisi would not be the anticipated doddle. With Ray Kennedy absent through injury, Liverpool struggled but goals from David Johnson and Jimmy Case helped them take an undeserved 2−1 lead to Georgia. However, a fortnight later their slender lead was in tatters as Tblisi heaped up a 3−0 win in front of 80,000 supporters. It was a painful disappointment to be dismissed at the first hurdle again after winning the trophy twice in succession but Liverpool had to admit that they were outplayed by a superior team who had inflicted the heaviest European defeat on them since Ajax.

In the now two-legged opening round of the League Cup, Liverpool crossed the Mersey to homely Fourth Division neighbours, Tranmere Rovers and were quite content to bring back a goalless draw to Anfield where they finished off the business with a 4−0 win. Third Division sides Chesterfield and Exeter were easily disposed of before Liverpool beat Norwich at Carrow Road to put them into the last four. Their reward was another tie with Nottingham Forest. At the City Ground Liverpool went down by a single goal but were hopeful of pulling the deficit back in the second leg at Anfield. As usual, Forest proved to be frustratingly unobliging and Liverpool could only earn a draw and were dismissed.

Liverpool's League campaign began where they had left off the previous season. They lost early on at Southampton and again at Forest in September but otherwise ploughed on undefeated until mid-January. It took them until the New Year before they climbed to the top of the table but once there, they could not be shifted. The title was finally clinched against Aston Villa at Anfield with a 4−1 win. Avi Cohen, the Israeli international defender who had signed for the Reds in July 1979 kicked off the afternoon by putting through his own goal and it began to look as if Villa were about to spoil the party for the 51,500 crowd. But Cohen, unruffled by his gaffe, promptly trotted upfield and hammered the ball into the Villa goal for the Reds. Cohen had arrived from Maccabi of Tel Aviv but was unfortunate in joining a club already rich in defenders. Alan Kennedy had established himself at left back while

OPPOSITE PAGE Graeme Souness.

ABOVE Beglin and captain Alan Hansen parade the FA Cup round Wembley, May 1986.

BELOW The trophies where they belong – back home on Merseyside.

OPPOSITE Sammy Lee and Kenny Dalglish celebrate another goal.

ABOVE The double at last.

OPPOSITE Ian Rush.

BELOW Steve Nicol.

LEFT Alan Hansen lifts the League championship trophy to celebrate Liverpool's record 18th title.

PREVIOUS PAGE LEFT John Barnes.

PREVIOUS PAGE RIGHT Anfield and the Kop are covered in flowers as a tribute to the 95 who died at Hillsborough a week before.

BELOW Peter Beardsley.

Skipper Phil Thompson and Ray Kennedy celebrate Liverpool's twelfth League title after beating Aston Villa 4-1.

Alan Hansen had also forced himself into contention and there was no obvious gap for Cohen. Yet, he was a superb player, unflappable and stylish, who at some other time might have become an Anfield regular and a medal winner. As it was he left Liverpool in 1982, returning to the Middle East.

The Reds were challenging on all fronts as they went in search of the FA Cup. They started with a home game against Third Division Grimsby who offered little opposition, going down by five goals to nil but in the fourth round Liverpool faced Nottingham Forest yet again and away as well. Sandwiched in between their two League Cup clashes with Brian Clough's men, Liverpool surprised everyone when Dalglish and McDermott gave them a 2 − 0 victory. Bury, in the next round, were sent packing and Tottenham were their opponents for the sixth round. It was Terry McDermott who struck the winner at White Hart Lane with a thunderous volley that put them into the semi-final against Arsenal.

With Everton also in the semi-final and drawn apart from Liverpool, there was the tantalising prospect of an all-Merseyside final. Liverpool's first encounter with Arsenal at Hillsborough ended in a goalless draw with nobody having yet managed to score against the Reds in five Cup games. Four days later they replayed at Villa Park with Arsenal managing to beat the Liverpool defence but it ended one goal apiece. Their third fixture a fortnight later again finished 1 − 1. Not since Liverpool played Sheffield United in 1899 had a semi-final gone to four games. The marathon finally drew to a close with Arsenal winning the fourth game by a single goal just when it looked as if the two teams would not have sorted it out by Cup final day. In all, 168,000 watched the four games with only five goals scored in 420 minutes of football. Everton also took West Ham United to a replay before losing so that instead of an all-Merseyside final the country faced an all-London encounter. The dream of an all-Merseyside final continued to look like foolish fantasy.

David Johnson again topped the goal charts for the season with twenty-one League goals and six others· while Dalglish netted a total of twenty-one. As the 1979–80 season ended Bob Paisley finally acted on the advice of scout Geoff Twentyman and signed a young striker from Chester City for £300,000, who had made only thirty-three appearances in Division Four. For a striker he was aptly named. He was called Ian Rush.

1980–81

Liverpool's policy of buying young players cheaply from the lower divisions and grooming them in the reserves had long been a hallmark of their style, having been initiated by Shankly and continued under Paisley. Heighway, Clemence, Keegan, Lloyd, Lindsay and Neal were all among those who had come through the ranks. Coupled with this policy the club had encouraged home-grown players like Fairclough, Lawler, Hunt, Thompson, Case, Byrne and Smith who merely cost the standard signing-on fee. Not all made it to the top. Those like Bobby Graham, John McLaughlin, Peter Wall, Roy Evans, Ian Ross, Doug Livermore, Brian Kettle and others never quite established themselves in the first team but were always ready and available. Typical of this policy were two eighteen-year-olds who joined the club during the 1979–80 season: Ronnie Whelan arrived at Anfield from the Irish club, Home Farm for a small fee, making his debut in April 1981 but taking a couple of seasons to fully secure his spot; and Ian Rush. Over the next few seasons Ian Rush would prove to be one of the most astute signings any Liverpool manager ever made and in time he would go on to break not only the club's all time goal-scoring record but help Liverpool to the most successful phase in their history.

1980–81 was a season of draws as Liverpool totted up a total of seventeen drawn fixtures. They lost only eight games, the same as title winners Aston Villa but the draws were vital points dropped and Liverpool finished the season in fifth spot, their lowest position for sixteen years. For the past eight seasons they had never been out of the top two and it was probably the concentration on other trophies that cost them a serious challenge in the League. In January their magnificent record of eighty-five home games without defeat came to an end when, of all teams, bottom club Leicester City won 2–1 at Anfield. There was an early exit in the FA Cup when they visited Goodison Park to tackle Everton in the

fourth round with the Blues coming out on top by two goals to one. But there were still two other competitions to contend.

The League Cup had been in existence for twenty years and still remained the one trophy not to have flattered the Anfield boardroom. What success they had achieved had been in recent years with their lost final against Nottingham Forest. But this season Liverpool would go one better and finally carry the trophy home. After their first fixture, however, this looked unlikely. Away to Fourth Division Bradford City in the two-legged second round they went down by one goal to nil and there must have been further doubts about Liverpool's commitment to the tournament. But back at Anfield, Bradford were put in their rightful place by four goals to nil. Swindon Town came to Merseyside for the third round and were soundly beaten 5–0 before Portsmouth arrived for a similar drubbing. They went out by four goals to one and Liverpool were into the quarter-finals. After another win against Birmingham, Liverpool were rewarded with a semi-final against Manchester City. The first leg at Maine Road went to Liverpool with Ray Kennedy scoring the only goal and in the return leg Dalglish gave Liverpool a draw and a place at Wembley. West Ham United have always been sturdy competitors, determined to play attacking football and at Wembley in the League Cup final against Liverpool proved worthy opponents. Alan Kennedy put Liverpool ahead and with just a minute remaining the score still stood at 1–0. However, West Ham kept battling and were rewarded with a penalty almost on time. The replay went to Villa Park where the pace hotted up, the Hammers shooting into a goal lead. Dalglish equalised and with the Reds piling on the pressure, Hansen snatched the winner and Liverpool had at last lifted the elusive trophy, qualifying them for a place in Europe.

Liverpool travelled to Finland for their opening European Cup encounter to meet Oulun Palloseura and in their friendly ground came away with a 1–1 draw. But it was a different proposition when the Finns visited Anfield and confronted an attack in its full glory. Souness and McDermott each hit hat-tricks while Fairclough, Lee and Ray Kennedy netted another four between them to give Liverpool a resounding 10–1 victory. The Reds travelled north again in the next round, though this time not nearly so far, to tackle Scottish champions, Aberdeen. Alex Ferguson's side were developing a keen reputation with players like Strachan, Rougvie, McLeish and Miller in their ranks but Liverpool showed few signs of being over-awed, beating them 1–0 at Pittodrie. When the Dons travelled to Anfield the gap between English and Scottish soccer was put neatly into perspective as Liverpool romped home 4−0 winners. The Reds were now into the quarter-finals and opened their encounter with CSKA Sofia at Anfield by scoring five goals. Graeme Souness hit his second hat-trick of the competition and there was no doubt that Liverpool were on their way to the semi-finals. A 1−0 victory in Sofia in front of 60,000 enthusiastic Bulgarians secured the spot but there were three other outstanding teams remaining − Real Madrid, Inter Milan and Bayern Munich.

Between them the semi-finalists had won the European Cup on no less than thirteen occasions. Liverpool drew Bayern Munich and at Anfield were surprisingly held to a goalless draw. It looked like the end of another European campaign but in the return leg, Liverpool gave one of their finest displays with reserves Richard Money, Colin Irwin and Howard Gayle entering the affray. Gayle came on as substitute for Dalglish and was ordered to stay on the left wing and simply run at the German defence. Bayern had not reckoned with Gayle, his name not even featuring in their planning. He ran them ragged in the electric atmosphere of Munich's Olympic stadium with Ray Kennedy breaking the deadlock seven minutes from the end. Karl-Heinz Rummenigge equalised in the final minute but it was too late. Liverpool were through to their third European Cup final.

European Cup Final 1981 Liverpool v Real Madrid
It was Real Madrid who won the right to face Liverpool in the 1981 final of the European Cup at the Parcs des Princes in Paris. Six times winners of the trophy and in their ninth final, Real were the most famous club name in soccer who would always be associated with Puskas, Di Stefano, Kopa and Gento. And while Liverpool had some ground to make up before they could join their illustrious company they were desperate to be ranked alongside three-times winners Ajax and Bayern Munich.

The Kop, predictably uprooted itself and, decked in red, moved *en masse* to Paris ready to scale another European summit. But although the occasion was to be memorable the match itself fell way below expectations. The attacking flair of Real was rarely evident while their defence was more prone to ruggedness rather than skilful resistance. And, it has to be said, that Liverpool too barely showed the control and quality which had reaped so many honours over the years. Perhaps the fear in both sides of losing was the crucial factor which made it such a negative game. The battle took place mainly in the midfield between Liverpool hard-man Graeme Souness and Real's Uli Stielike, a battle which was won

convincingly by Souness. Real possibly had the better of the first half but there was little between the two teams at half-time. After the interval, however, Liverpool's stubborn determination began to wear down the famous Spanish side and gaps gradually appeared in the midfield and at the back. But it took until the eighty-second minute before the Reds could capitalise on their progress. Ray Kennedy's throw-in was chested down by Alan Kennedy and the Liverpool back began one of his adventurist runs into the penalty area. He outsprinted Cortes, skipping over his pitiful tackle and from the narrowest of angles fired a stunning shot into the Real net. Liverpool had scored at the decisive moment and with the Kop ecstatic there was no way they would now relinquish their grip on the trophy. They powered at Real in a far more lively finish and Souness might have hit a second but for some fine goalkeeping. Thompson lifted the trophy and Paisley became the only manager to have won three European Cups. Liverpool could now proudly hold their heads high with the best in Europe. The Kop, singing 'Gay Paree, Gay Paree, Gay Paree' marched triumphantly into the Parisian evening and began to paint another European capital red.

Liverpool Clemence, Neal, Kennedy A., Thompson, Kennedy R., Hansen, Dalglish (Case), Lee, Johnson, McDermott, Souness.

Real Madrid Agustin, Garcia Cortes (Pineda), Garcia Navajas, Sabido, Del Bosque, Angel, Camacho, Stielike, Juanito, Santillano, Cunningham.

1981 − 82
Phil Thompson was well on his way to becoming the most honoured footballer in the history of English soccer. Shankly used to joke that he had tossed with a sparrow for a pair of legs and had lost. Yet, despite his apparent physical drawback he was as tough a defender as anyone in Europe. He never shied away from a tackle and brought a sophistication to defending not normally associated with the department. He was capped forty-two times by England and continued playing first team football until 1983 before going to Sheffield United for a short spell.

Ray Kennedy's list of medals was marginally shorter than Thompson's although he could boast League and Cup double medals from his earlier days with Arsenal. His association with Liverpool came to an end in January 1982 when he went off to join the Liverpool veterans at Swansea. If Thompson was whippet-like, then Kennedy was more of a bulldog. He was strong and powerful, could ride tackles and hold the ball while attackers scurried into position. When he arrived at

Bob Paisley with just one of the six League Championship trophies won during his managerial reign.

Anfield he came with the reputation of a striker but had grown weary of the buffeting and punishment and it was Bob Paisley's inspired decision to drop him back into the midfield. It gave him a new lease of life and his determination gave Liverpool a new will. Whenever he lost form or seemed tired, you could be sure the whole team would look lethargic. He played 275 League games for Liverpool, scoring fifty goals and won seventeen England caps.

The team that had won three European Champions trophies was steadily breaking up but the biggest shock of all came during the summer of 1981 when Ray Clemence, still at the peak of his goalkeeping skills was dramatically transferred to Tottenham Hotspur for £300,000. As the last line of resistance, he had saved Liverpool on so many occasions and deserved to be ranked alongside the legendary Hardy and Scott as three of the finest goalkeepers in Liverpool's history. He was capped fifty-nine times while at Anfield but went on to win further honours with England and Tottenham. Into the breach stepped an unusual recruit, a twenty-four-year-old South African goalkeeper. But he was not the first: Arthur Riley had kept goal for Liverpool during the 1920s and was replaced by another South African,

Dirk Kemp while Doug Rudham who kept goal in the 1950s were just three of a number of South Africans to play for Liverpool over the years. Bruce Grobbelaar had joined Liverpool in March 1981 from Vancouver Whitecaps for £250,000. He had played a season with Crewe Alexandra but clearly thought there was no future for him in English soccer until Liverpool stepped in. Although born in South Africa most of his life had been spent in Zimbabwe where he had won international honours. And as the 1981–82 season opened he was sensationally tossed into the inferno of Anfield.

It was not an auspicious start. Liverpool lost the first game 1–0, as well as their fourth and also managed a couple of early draws. The newspapers were soon foolishly heralding the end of Liverpool. Another South African coincidentally joined Liverpool a month after Grobbelaar. He was Craig Johnston who had been born in Johannesburg before emigrating to Australia where he played for Sydney City. From there he had travelled to Britain determined to forge a career for himself in

Dalglish's skill and ability to turn a player made him one of the most dangerous attackers in world football.

League football and had been taken on by Middlesbrough. He was soon given his chance at Anfield after his £500,000 transfer making seventeen appearances during his first season but for several years had difficulty in holding on to the number ten jersey.

Liverpool's League Cup challenge produced the bulk of goals as Exeter City were thrashed 6 − 0 and 5 − 0 in the two legs while in the next round Middlesbrough went down 4 − 1. The fourth round brought Arsenal to Anfield after a goalless draw and they too were finally dealt with by three goals to nil. Barnsley travelled from Yorkshire for the fifth round and returned with a goalless draw and hopes of dismissing Liverpool. But it was not to be as the Reds stepped up a gear at Oakwell to win 3 − 1. The two-legged semi-final threw Liverpool against the consistent Ipswich. At Portman Road, Ian Rush and Terry McDermott gave Liverpool a two-goal cushion and a virtual place in the final while back on Merseyside, Ipswich held the Reds to a 2 − 2 draw and Liverpool were Wembley bound. Tottenham were

Liverpool's opponents in the final and Ray Clemence was the goalkeeper they had to beat in what turned out to be a memorable match. In the eleventh minute of the game, Steve Archibald struck and with Clemence performing majestically in goal, Liverpool were kept at bay. The score remained 1 − 0 with Tottenham matching Liverpool in every department and in the eighty-fifth minute Archibald should have made sure of the game but was thwarted by Souness' goal-line clearance. Then with just two minutes remaining and the Tottenham fans already celebrating their victory, Ronnie Whelan lashed a shot past the helpless Clemence to level the score. Tottenham were stunned and at the final whistle dropped wearily to the floor. Paisley, sensing their tiredness and disappointment dashed on to the pitch and told the Liverpool players not to sit down but to run about looking eager for extra time. It was a brilliant psychological move and with the Liverpool chants still ringing around the stadium from the goal, the Reds keenly set about destroying the Londoners. New boys Ronnie Whelan and Ian Rush finally demolished them to give Liverpool their second League Cup in succession.

The FA Cup was not quite so thrilling as Liverpool tripped up away to Second Division Chelsea in the fifth round by two goals to nil, after beating John Toshack's Swansea 4 − 0 at the Vetch Field and Sunderland 3 − 0 at Roker Park. The European Cup also brought disappointments with fixtures that were almost a repeat of the previous year. The Finns, Oulun Palloseura were the fodder again for the first round, receiving a slightly more respectable drubbing this time by only eight goals to nil. The Dutch champions, AZ'67 Alkmaar were a far different proposition from the last Dutch team Liverpool had faced in the European Cup. Then, they had travelled to Amsterdam to lose 5 − 1 to Ajax but on this occasion David Johnson and Sammy Lee gave them a 2 − 2 draw. In the home leg Liverpool won an exhilarating encounter by three goals to two and went on to a rematch of the previous year's quarter-final against CSKA Sofia. Liverpool had won that by six goals to nil on aggregate and were confident of a place in the semi-finals. As it was they could only squeeze a one goal lead to take to Bulgaria. In Sofia, CSKA won by two goals to nil after extra time and Liverpool found themselves dumped ungraciously out of the Champions Cup. Disappointment in Europe was coupled with a bitter let-down in the World Club Championship, contested by Liverpool for the first time in December 1981. Flamengo of Brazil proved to be a side of flair and skill and disposed of Liverpool in a twenty-minute burst scoring three goals to beat them 3 − 0 in Tokyo. Had the game perhaps been played nearer home instead of a twenty-hour flight away and at a time when the team were playing well and not embroiled in four other competitions, they might have had more success.

The League brought better fortunes after its unpromising opening. At the end of October they were hovering in the lower half of the table with the press gleefully writing the obituaries yet again but the results gradually picked up. As usual, it was Liverpool's final gallop at the end of the season that won the championship. Beaten at home by Brighton who now numbered Jimmy Case among their ranks, on 6 March, they then manufactured eleven successive wins to take the title by four points from Ipswich.

Ian Rush had been introduced into the side late in the previous season and had showed little potential, making seven appearances without scoring. But Paisley did not lose faith. After a short spell back in the reserves he returned to the first team in October with Paisley telling him to be more selfish in front of goal. He was, scoring five goals in his first three games and beginning a goalscoring career that would lead to fame and fortune. He scored seventeen League goals in 1981 − 82, a further thirteen in other games and with Dalglish had formed the most devastating partnership in Liverpool's history.

1982 − 83

The 1982 − 83 season had a familiar ring about it as Liverpool celebrated the same triumphs and suffered similar misfortunes to the previous season. The only new recruit was striker David Hodgson signed from Middlesbrough on the eve of the season for £450,000. He remained for the next three years but never really settled, failing to secure a regular spot in the team and eventually returned north to Sunderland. But there was one unhappy departure, that of manager Bob Paisley who announced that this would be his final season in charge of team affairs. After forty-three years at Anfield, he had decided to retire. He had given dedicated service as player, coach and manager and would be rewarded with a directorship and of course, by the end of the season, with a couple more trophies. He had become not only the most successful manager in the history of English soccer but the most successful in Europe.

Manchester United made the early running in the League but by mid-November Liverpool had asserted themselves at the top of the division and were on course for their fourteenth League title. By early April and with nine games remaining they were sixteen points clear of their nearest rivals, Watford. It was so easy that the Reds eased up and cantered to the finishing line with five defeats and two draws in their last seven games, their worst spell since they had been promoted to Division One. Yet, at the end of the season they still topped the League by eleven points from Watford.

Liverpool began their assault on the FA Cup with an away win at Blackburn before beating Stoke City 2 − 0 at Anfield. The fifth round brought lowly First Division opponents, Brighton who were managed by the former Liverpool inside forward Jimmy Melia, to Anfield for a Sunday match. Unfortunately, the former Liverpool man knew just a little too much about the Reds' tactics and Brighton sneaked a 2 − 1 victory with another former Liverpool player, Jimmy Case striking a late winner.

In the European Cup Liverpool reached the quarter-finals before losing to the Polish champions, Widzew Lodz. In the earlier rounds the Reds had disposed of Ireland's Dundalk by five goals to one on aggregate and had then faced the Finnish champions J K Helsinki who stole a 1 − 0 lead in Finland. Back at Anfield Liverpool overwhelmed them by five goals to nil with Alan Kennedy hitting two. But when it came to Lodz, Liverpool's luck totally deserted them. In the first leg in Poland a couple of disastrous errors by Bruce

RIGHT Bob Paisley carries his last trophy back to the Anfield boardroom, May 1983.

Another Wembley photo. Liverpool win the League Cup, March 1983. Back row (from left): Lawrenson, Fairclough, Hansen, Whelan, Rush, Grobbelaar, Paisley (manager). Front row: Johnston, Dalglish, Neal, Souness, Lee, Kennedy.

Grobbelaar allowed the Poles to strike up a two-goal lead but Bob Paisley remained confident that Liverpool could still squirm through to the semi-finals in the home leg. Instead Lodz strode into a further lead when Souness gave away a penalty and with Liverpool forced to attack, they ended up handing them yet another goal. 4 – 1 down, there was no way Liverpool were going to retrieve the situation but they had a determined try, scoring three goals through Neal, Hodgson and Rush to wind up 3 – 2 winners on the night but losers over the two legs.

Winners of the Milk Cup two years in succession, Liverpool set out on their journey to win it an historic three times with a trip to Ipswich where they beat the East Anglians 2 – 1. They followed that up with a 2 – 0 win at Anfield and then dismissed Rotherham through Craig Johnston's single goal. Another East Anglia team, Norwich, made the long trek to Merseyside for the next round only to return home empty handed after a 2 – 0 defeat. Into the last eight the Reds knocked out West Ham and then faced Burnley in the semi-final. A 3 – 1 win on aggregate and Liverpool were back at Wembley. With Manchester United as their opponents, nobody

Paisley becomes the first manager to ever climb Wembley's famous steps to receive a trophy. No other manager could have better deserved such an accolade.

imagined it was ever going to be an easy game. United stormed into an early lead through Norman Whiteside and hung on desperately for over an hour as Liverpool pressed for an equaliser. When Alan Kennedy on another of his charges scored, it was reminiscent of the previous year's final against Spurs. Similarly, there was never any doubt who would win in extra time as Liverpool heaped on the pressure. David Fairclough entered the arena as substitute and with more care might

have had a sensational extra time hat-trick but it was Ronnie Whelan who fired Liverpool into a winning 2 – 1 lead. At the final whistle, captain Graeme Souness stepped aside and pushed Bob Paisley who had announced his intention to retire at the end of the season, up the steps to receive the trophy. It was the first time a manager had ever climbed the famous Wembley steps to lift a cup and no manager deserved it more. In his nine years at the helm, since Shankly's dramatic retirement, Paisley had won thirteen trophies: three European Cups, six League Championships, three Milk Cups, and one UEFA Cup with only the coveted FA Cup missing from the sideboard. That was his one regret but he would have a hand in its arrival a few years later.

FAGAN TAKES OVER

1983 – 84

As next in line, Joe Fagan took over the controls from Paisley. Although born in Liverpool, Fagan's footballing talents had gone unnoticed by the club and he had wound up down the other end of the East Lancs Road at Manchester City following war service in the navy. A right half, he played at Maine Road between 1946 and 1950 making 148 appearances in the First and Second Divisions and scoring a couple of goals. He even skippered City before a broken leg led to a free transfer to the now defunct Bradford Park Avenue in August 1953. He also enjoyed non-league spells with Nelson, Hyde United and Altrincham before joining Rochdale as team trainer under Harry Catterick. In 1958 he moved to Anfield as assistant trainer and was promoted second-in-command to Paisley when Shankly retired. So, after twenty-six years of backroom service at Anfield and at the age of sixty-two, Joe Fagan found himself manager of Europe's leading football team.

Within twenty-four hours of taking over Fagan had plunged confidently into the transfer market, recruiting Coventry's Scottish Under-21 central defender Gary Gillespie for £325,000. Another of his early decisions was to give the twenty-one-year-old Scotsman Steve Nicol his opportunity. The former Ayr United full back had signed for Liverpool in a £300,000 deal in October 1981 and had spent a couple of years impressing in the reserves. He had already tasted first team soccer with two outings the previous season but now he was promoted to the full squad. Michael Robinson also arrived during the close season in a £200,000 deal with Brighton. In his short career the twenty-four-year-old striker had already cost Preston, Manchester City, Brighton and Liverpool almost £1.5 million.

Only two teams had ever claimed a hat-trick of League Championships: Huddersfield Town and Arsenal. Both had been managed by Herbert Chapman during the 1920s and thirties and the first of those Huddersfield wins in 1924 had ended Liverpool's hopes themselves of a hat-trick of titles. On four occasions Liverpool had stood on the edge of a hat-trick, failing on three of those occasions. Now they were about to succeed with their name finally ranking among the greatest teams in soccer history.

Liverpool climbed to the top of the table in mid-November and barring a short break in March when Manchester United proffered a serious challenge, they remained in the number one spot through to the end of the season. Ian Rush was again the symbol of their success, striking thirty-two League goals with a further thirteen from other matches. The previous season he had hit the net twenty-four times in the League and six times in other games. He had become a phenomenal goalscoring machine and when Liverpool beat Luton Town by six goals to nil in the League, it was Rush who struck five of them. He also hit four against Coventry City and a hat-trick at Aston Villa as Liverpool finally wound up the season three points ahead of Southampton.

Again the FA Cup failed to inspire and after a stunning opening 4 – 0 victory against Kevin Keegan's Newcastle United they faced Brighton again, this time down on the south coast. With the television cameras showing the game live, Souness limped off with a pulled hamstring in the first half and Liverpool collapsed. Brighton scored twice and the Reds had been ditched prematurely out of the cup by a Second Division side in front of millions of viewers. But there were other trophies to be won.

The holders drew Brentford for their opening Milk Cup tie and disposed of them 8 – 1 on aggregate before Third Division Fulham took them to three games until Liverpool went through by a hair's breadth. There was now no doubting Liverpool's commitment to the tournament even though it took a further replay for them to beat Birmingham City. Sheffield Wednesday forced yet another replay in the quarter-finals with Liverpool winning a thrilling match by three goals to nil at Anfield. In the semi-finals the Reds faced Third Division Walsall and received something of a shock at Anfield as the Midlanders gallantly earned a 2 – 2 draw. However, Liverpool recovered their senses for the return leg winning comfortably by two goals to nil. Now into their fourth Milk Cup final their opponents turned out to be none other than neighbours and oldest foes, Everton.

It was the first Wembley clash of the two Merseyside teams and had set the city of Liverpool awash with euphoria. Tickets were impossible to obtain even after 70,000 or more had been distributed between the clubs. The two teams met in the pouring rain of a dismal

RIGHT Phil Neal watched by Craig Johnston shows off the new League Championship trophy. It was Neal's seventh title win, equalling Phil Thompson's record.

March Sunday that did nothing to dampen the spirits of the capacity Wembley crowd. After years of looking jealously over their shoulders at their neighbours, Everton under manager Howard Kendall, were beginning to shape together an impressive squad of players, worthy of challenging Liverpool for the trophy.

Everton began confidently, frightened neither by the occasion nor the reputation of Liverpool and might well have gone ahead when Hansen's clearance looked suspiciously like handball. But the referee judged otherwise and the Reds had a lucky escape. As the game wore on Liverpool gained in composure but, like Everton earlier, were unable to capitalise on it. After ninety minutes neither team had managed a goal and the game slid into extra time with Robinson replacing Craig Johnston. Rush almost put Liverpool ahead within four minutes but Southall, the Everton goalkeeper turned a fierce shot aside and the game slowly petered out into a draw. As the two teams walked a lap of honour together around Wembley, the crowd chanted 'Merseyside, Merseyside' and the scramble was on to find tickets for the replay. Maine Road was the setting for the return and in front of a crowd of 52,000, Everton again started furiously with Grobbelaar sent full stretch to save from Peter Reid. But in the twenty-second minute Graeme Souness settled the issue when he struck a low drive from just outside the penalty area. The ball shot beyond the fingers of the diving Southall and Liverpool had scored the crucial goal. It proved to be the match-winner although both sides went close on a number of occasions, so Liverpool lifted the Milk Cup for a record fourth time.

With two trophies in the bag the Anfielders still had one more pot of gold to chase but they hardly needed reminding that no English team had won three cups in a season. Their first-round opponents in the European Cup were the Danish champions, BK Odense who were outsmarted 1−0 away and 5−0 at home. The second round brought a much tougher challenge from Atletico Bilbao who held Liverpool to a goalless draw at Anfield before surprisingly losing to an Ian Rush goal in northern Spain. Benfica turned up for the quarter-finals and offered a spirited defence at Anfield, losing by the only goal and in front of 70,000 in Lisbon, Liverpool gave one of their finest performances running out 4−1 winners on the night. The Reds were into their fifth Champions Cup semi-final where they faced another team they knew well, Dinamo Bucharest. In the first leg at Anfield, Sammy Lee gave Liverpool a narrow one-goal lead but any fears that it would not be enough were discounted in Romania where Ian Rush scored twice in a magnificent 2−1 victory.

European Cup Final 1984 Liverpool v AS Roma

Liverpool returned to Rome, scene of their first triumph for their fourth European Cup final. It could hardly have been more daunting as their opponents, AS Roma, were playing on their home ground. When the Liverpool fans arrived in the Eternal City, they must have wondered if they were back home judging by the red and yellow colours bedecking the city. The only problem was that they were the colours of Roma and not Liverpool. On their previous visit, Liverpool had won the hearts of the Romans but this time the friendliness was edged with rivalry.

The Olympic Stadium was not a place for weak hearts as smoke bombs, flares, klaxons and flags greeted the local heroes. Even the 20,000 travelling Liverpool fans found themselves outnumbered and outshouted and as many of them would later testify, with more than a dash of hatred and violence. The game may well have been won in the tunnel itself as the Liverpool side, standing alongside Roma and awaiting the signal to take the field, began singing spontaneously. The Roma players looked on in disbelief, their nerves clearly visible to everyone. Liverpool, quickly putting aside any nerves, calmly took control of the early stages and in the fifteenth minute shot into a lucky lead when Phil Neal pounced on a loose ball after the Roma goalkeeper had looked to be fouled by Johnston. Liverpool continued to dictate the pace of the game until almost on the stroke of half-time when Pruzzo headed home a Conti cross of the equaliser. It was just the fillip Roma needed and after the interval they tore at Liverpool but could not snatch a winner. Once Liverpool had soaked up twenty-five minutes of pressure they leisurely regained control but similarly could not score. Extra time brought no recompense and at the end of 120 minutes the two teams faced the unenviable prospect of a dramatic penalty shoot-out.

OPPOSITE PAGE TOP Phil Neal puts Liverpool into an early lead in their 1984 European Cup final against AS Roma. BOTTOM Few football managers receive such adulation from their supporters.

SHANKS MARMALIZED MILAN
PAISLEY MUNCHED THE GLADBACH
NOW
FAGANS MAKING ROMAN RUINS

Given the number of penalties Liverpool had missed during the season, few would have backed them at this stage to win a fourth European Cup. Steve Nicol confidently volunteered to take the first kick just as Phil Neal was assuming the responsibility. But the young Scot blasted his shot over the bar and the odds stacked even higher against Liverpool. Roma did not make the same mistake with their first penalty, nor did Phil Neal with Liverpool's second. Bruno Conti stepped up for the next kick and blazed it over the bar to even the scoreline. Souness, Righetti and Ian Rush all converted their kicks before Graziani slowly placed the ball on the spot. With Bruce Grobbelaar astonishingly clowning around in goal, a genuinely nervous Graziani sent the ball over the bar. Grobbelaar's antics had clearly disturbed the famous Italian international. It now needed only Alan Kennedy to convert his kick and the Cup would be won. With exemplary calm, he strode up, placed the ball, took a few steps back and struck it into the back of the net. He turned and with arms outstretched ran towards his teammates. Alan Kennedy had won the European Cup yet again. Liverpool had overtaken Bayern Munich and Ajax with this, their fourth triumph, and only Real Madrid could now claim to have won more European Cups than Liverpool.

Liverpool Grobbelaar, Neal, Kennedy, Lawrenson, Whelan, Hansen, Dalglish (Robinson), Lee, Rush, Johnston (Nicol), Souness.

AS Roma Tancredi, Nappi, Bonetti, Righetti, Nela, Falcao, Di Bartolomei, Cerezo (Strukelj), Conti, Pruzzo (Chierico), Graziani.

1984 – 85

Having captained Liverpool to three trophies, Graeme Souness decided to try his luck in Italy and during the close season was transferred to Sampdoria, the Genoa club for £500,000. The one-time wayward Scot had been transformed at Anfield into a responsible, creative midfielder who had become one of the prime forces behind Liverpool's success. He won his first cap in 1974

Like many before him, Craig Johnston took time to settle in the Liverpool team but once his place was secure, the Australian began to show the talent and pace that had made him a £½ million player. A strong player whose speed enables him to get past defenders, he is nevertheless brought down in this fierce tackle by Roma's Bonetti.

and by the time he left Liverpool had collected forty Scottish caps and was captain of his country as well. He had played almost 250 League games for Liverpool, scoring thirty-eight goals with a further hundred appearances in other games. The loss of a world-class player like Souness was a blow and unearthing a replacement an unenviable task. The Scottish international, John Wark had joined Liverpool from Ipswich towards the end of the 1983–84 season for £450,000 adding some vital goal-punch to the midfield but he was hardly a replacement for Souness. A more obvious choice was the Danish international, Jan Molby who was signed from Ajax for £200,000 during the close season and later in the year Kevin MacDonald was another expensive purchase from Leicester City. There was an added problem with Kenny Dalglish also entering the final years of his playing career so Paul Walsh, the skilful Luton Town forward was recruited for £900,000.

ABOVE With the score at 1-1 after 120 minutes, Liverpool and Roma are forced into a penalty shoot-out. Alan Kennedy again scores the vital goal that wins Liverpool their fourth European Cup.

RIGHT New boy Paul Walsh demonstrates a few skills to the Manchester United defence in this FA Cup semi-final at Goodison Park, April 1985.

The 1984–85 season was one which Liverpool would want to forget, not simply because they failed to win a trophy for the first time in nine years but for events off the field in what should have been a magnificent climax to the season. Without the presence of the inspiring Souness, the season got off to a wretched start as they lost the Charity Shield at Wembley to Everton by a single goal. Shortly after Everton had again beaten Liverpool towards the end of October in their first victory at Anfield for fifteen years, they slumped to twentieth place in the League and into the relegation zone. The press speculated, yet again, and predicted the end of an era. But there was no panic at Anfield, just a few more cups of tea in the bootroom and a reassertion of confidence in the team. Results picked up and the Reds

began a gradual climb towards the top of the table but too many points had been dropped early on. They still looked a shadow of the team that had captured three trophies the season before and Everton, streaking ahead at the top, were not going to do them any favours by dropping points themselves. Much to Liverpool's credit however, they pulled up to second place by the end of the season but were still thirteen points behind their neighbours and champions.

In the FA Cup the Anfielders went to within a whisker of a Wembley trip, taking Manchester United to a replay in the semi-final. The early rounds brought wins against Aston Villa, Tottenham and a seven-goal hammering of lowly York City. In the quarter-finals they struck four at Barnsley and then faced United at Goodison in one of the most exciting semi-finals for years. With just minutes of normal time remaining Ronnie Whelan hit an equaliser for Liverpool only to see them go behind again in extra time. Then after a slick show of skill from Kenny Dalglish, Paul Walsh snatched another equaliser with only seconds of extra time left. With such luck everyone expected Liverpool to win the replay comfortably and even more so when they went into a lead but United hit back to score twice and win the trip to Wembley.

After winning the Milk Cup four years in a row, Liverpool took an early exit with Spurs prising open their grip on the trophy after they had beaten Stockport County in the opening round.

Phil Neal had succeeded Souness as captain but was clearly in the later stages of his footballing career, as was Dalglish, and now there was talk of Ian Rush following Souness to either Italy or Spain. Younger talent had emerged with both Lawrenson and Nicol, players of the highest quality. Lawrenson was already regarded as the finest defender in the Football League whose perfectly timed tackles had abruptly ended many an attack. Towards the end of the season another young Irish defender, Jim Beglin who had joined Liverpool from Shamrock Rovers was given his first opportunity although he would not secure his spot until the following season.

The European Cup, which would later end in such tragedy, began in Poland with a one-goal win over Lech Poznan and a polished 4 − 0 win at Anfield. Ian Rush single-handedly beat off the challenge of Benfica at Anfield scoring all three goals in Liverpool's 3 − 1 win. In Lisbon, Benfica finally got the better of Liverpool with a 1 − 0 victory but Liverpool were into the last eight. Before the quarter-finals, however, Liverpool had two other continental appointments. The first was for the World Club Championship against Independiente of Buenos Aires. The game was staged in Japan again and with Liverpool still fumbling way below their best, they went down by a single goal. The European Super Cup was played in mid-January but when Liverpool arrived in Turin to face Juventus they found the stadium covered in a thick layer of snow. Reluctant to call the game off given the difficulties the two clubs had encountered in finding a mutually agreeable date, the pitch was cleared and the capacity of the crowd reduced.

But on a treacherous pitch and with Boniek in full flow, Liverpool lost 2 − 0. In the quarter-finals of the European Cup Liverpool faced FK Austria Memphis, winning 5 − 2 on aggregate and then in the semi-finals disposed of the Greek champions, Panathinaikos by four goals to nil at Anfield and by a single goal in Athens to reach their fifth European Cup final.

Liverpool met Juventus in the final of the Champions Cup on a delightfully sunny evening in Brussels. But before the sun had dipped over the stadium wall and before a ball had been kicked, tragedy struck and thirty-nine people lay dead. Rioting between the Juventus supporters and the Liverpool fans who had been allotted the same terracing broke out when so-called Liverpool supporters smashed down the flimsy wire fence segregating them and invaded the Italian sector. Not surprisingly, the Juventus fans fled in fear and in the ensuing crush a wall collapsed adding to the casualties. Most of those dead were Italians and most were crushed under the sheer weight of the panicking crowd. Millions watching on television throughout the world saw the tragedy unfold like a nightmare before their eyes yet, astonishingly, most of the Liverpool supporters on that terrace never knew the extent of the tragedy until considerably later that evening. For almost thirty years Liverpool fans had delighted football crowds throughout Britain and Europe with their good humour and decent behaviour and now they stood condemned before the gaping eyes of the world. The Heysel Stadium was not an adequate venue for a game of such consequence, nor had the police taken sufficient precautions to segregate and control two sets of committed supporters. But even allowing for all that there could be no excuses for what had happened. The final was eventually played but suffice it to record that Liverpool lost to a single goal, a penalty scored by Michel Platini.

A NEW ROLE FOR KENNY

1985–86

As the crowds gathered at Anfield on a bright Saturday afternoon in mid-August, it was not to herald a new season of football but rather to mourn the past season. It was a mere three months since the tragedy of Heysel and had been the most traumatic period to date for the club. An intense debate had swept through Parliament and the media about the problems of football violence while the Merseyside police were conducting a thorough investigation into the riot. Culprits were found and dossiers handed over to the Belgian authorities. In Belgium itself, the Government coming under increasing criticism, had been forced to resign and call a general election. Politicians on Merseyside and in Turin crossed the channel to help heal the wounds and pay their respects but the memories of those who had suffered or lost innocent friends and relations could never be erased. Not surprisingly, the European Football Association took the sternest action possible, banning English clubs from playing in Europe indefinitely and imposed a further ban of three years on Liverpool.

In the match programme for that first game against Arsenal, chairman John Smith warned that 'last season must be the last of its kind – English soccer simply cannot go through another season like it if it is to survive as a sport.' A pull-out page with photographs also carried an appeal from the police to help identify and track down some of the suspects from Heysel. For Joe Fagan, Brussels had been a particularly sad occasion. It was his final game as manager, having announced some weeks earlier his intention to retire at the end of the season when he was sixty-four. He had hoped to bring another European trophy home and bow out in triumph. Instead, he emerged from the debris of Heysel in tears, disillusioned with soccer and its supporters. It was a tragic end to a career which had helped bring so much success to the club and its followers over the years, and his anguish should never be forgotten.

Throughout the summer devoted Liverpool supporters had pledged that they would never go to Anfield again, such was the horror they had experienced in Brussels. But on that first Saturday 38,000 turned up to see the new Liverpool manager, Kenny Dalglish lead his team on to the field. The appointment of Dalglish had come as a genuine surprise to many. Since the retirement of Shankly, new managers had appeared from the backroom staff and it was widely expected that

Ronnie Moran, as next in line, would automatically assume the legacy of manager. In the event, Dalglish's appointment was widely welcomed with those close to the club, as well as the players, applauding it and confirming his qualifications for the job. And, more importantly, Bob Paisley had also been given the job of advising and assisting him. Since Dalglish had joined Liverpool he had developed into one of the most outstanding post-war British players. In November 1983 he scored his 100th League goal for Liverpool becoming

For manager Joe Fagan it should have been the climax of his career. Instead he arrives at Liverpool's Speke Airport for the unhappiest homecoming in the club's history.

After Joe Fagan's sad departure, the Liverpool board surprised the football world by appointing Kenny Dalglish as player-manager.

the first player to ever score 100 goals in the Scottish League and the Football League. In 1986 he notched up another record with his 100th Scottish cap. His skills were breathtaking with his ability to hold the ball and turn before chipping it delicately into the open path of an oncoming player. He had vision and above all consistency and although comparisons are unfair most would agree tht he was the finest player to ever don the red shirt of Liverpool. He could create openings and danger where none seemed to exist and as long as Dalglish was on the field, Liverpool always held a trump card.

The team that kicked off was much the same as the one which had ended the season and it easily disposed of the Gunners by two goals to nil. Within a few weeks, however, the two long-serving defenders Alan Kennedy and Phil Neal had decided to call it a day. Kennedy went back to the north-east and his home club, Sunderland,

having played 352 games for Liverpool during his eight years at the club and winning two England caps. The left back will always be remembered for scoring some fine goals, among them two of the most crucial in the club's history. Phil Neal began the season rejecting one job offer but by November had accepted the player-manager's position at Bolton Wanderers. Neal had been Paisley's first buy from Northampton Town in October 1974 and had proved to be one of the astutest purchases he ever made. For the next eleven years he was Liverpool's regular right back making 641 appearances for the club and winning fifty England caps. He underservedly went into the history books as the only Liverpool captain of recent times not to have lifted a trophy. Nevertheless, he was probably content to leave the club as the highest medal winner in the history of English soccer with eleven medals, seven of those championship medals. He was one of the most creative right backs of the post-war era with so many of Liverpool's attacks stemming from him and was always involved in the action of the game, scoring a total of fifty-eight goals for the club.

Steve McMahon, the former Everton midfielder who had eluded Liverpool two years earlier when he signed for Aston Villa, finally came to Anfield lending some much needed strength to the midfield. With three new players in the side Liverpool did not flow quite so fluidly as in previous years. Manchester United, in a stunning opening to the season, swept to the top of the table with a ten-point lead and as far as the press were concerned the championship was all over. But, just as dramatically, they crashed and by the end of November their lead had been sliced to two points and Liverpool might well have caught them but for dropping two home points to a lively Chelsea side. Dalglish, assuming the manager's responsibility had dropped himself in favour of Paul Walsh and at one stage it looked as if he had quietly retired from playing. Walsh and Rush had been scoring regularly, if not spectacularly, but in December the goals dried up for Rush. In twelve matches he managed just two and Liverpool began to look sluggish. With Molby acting as a sweeper behind the back four, Liverpool were also playing with five men in defence, although normally it was a case of Molby pushing forward as the game progressed so that Liverpool often looked a far better proposition in the second half. Christmas brought little cheer with three draws and two defeats, the most dramatic away to lowly-placed Manchester City and Liverpool slipped to fourth in the table, three points behind Everton.

Liverpool's Cup exploits began at home to Second Division leaders Norwich. There was a feeling about Anfield that this was Liverpool's year and when they ran out 5 − 0 winners the sense of destination increased. In the fourth round Liverpool tackled Chelsea at Stamford Bridge and with the Londoners looking like prospective champions, the road to Wembley suddenly began to look short. An early injury to Kerry Dixon, however, eased Liverpool's worries and before a live television audience they slowly grabbed control of the game winning by two goals to one. The fifth round found the Reds drawn away remarkably to York City who they had played in the fifth round the previous year. At Bootham Crescent, York's picturesque ground, Dalglish at last returned to the side but Liverpool were given a hard time scraping a one-goal draw. The replay at Anfield did not go quite as planned either as plucky York forced Liverpool into extra time before their Third Division legs grew weary and conceded three goals.

In the League, Liverpool faced table-topping Everton at home and were soundly beaten 2 − 0 by the best side seen at Anfield all season. With Everton now stretching their lead to six points and with a game in hand, it looked as if all hopes of the title had disappeared. Liverpool

Steve Nicol, a powerful, young Scottish full-back was a typical bargain purchase from Ayr United, joining the Liverpool squad in 1983.

were also having a good run in the Milk Cup, defeating Oldham and then Manchester United in a titanic struggle at Anfield. In the fifth round they comfortably disposed of Ipswich 3 − 0 and then faced Queens Park Rangers in the semi-final. They lost the first game at Loftus Road by a single goal and were confident of pulling the deficit back at Anfield but instead experienced a nightmare. Not only did they miss a vital penalty but also generously construed two own goals to give QPR a lucky 2 − 2 draw and a place in the final.

In the sixth round of the FA Cup Liverpool tackled Elton John's Watford at home but after a frustrating goalless draw looked to be on their way out. In the replay at Vicarage Road it seemed even more likely with Watford a goal ahead and only minutes left. Then with the final whistle about to be blown, Rush was brought down in the penalty area and Jan Molby hammered home the spot kick. In extra time, Liverpool took charge and to the delight of the 10,000 travelling supporters Rush put them into the semi-final. Rush was back at his goalscoring best and in the semi-final against Southampton at White Hart Lane he underlined his importance with two goals in extra time. With Everton beating Sheffield Wednesday as well, the dream of a Merseyside Cup Final had finally been realised after ninety-three years of FA Cup competition.

Liverpool's two successes of the season had been Craig Johnston and the Dane, Jan Molby. Johnston had been in and out of the team under Fagan but won favour with Dalglish who assured him of his place. Although he had skilful ball control he had rarely scored goals and just as rarely provided the telling pass to create a goal. But Dalglish's faith reaped dividends as Johnston's confidence grew and the goals resulted. Jan Molby had been bought from the Dutch champions, Ajax in August 1984 for £200,000 as a replacement for Souness. In his first game he had shown astonishing skills as he flicked the ball around Anfield but his talents quickly evaporated as the autumn nights drew in and he was relegated to the reserves to 'learn the trade'. When he returned at the start of the new season he was soon displaying his pedigree with balls sprayed around the field with pinpoint accuracy. It was a delight to watch as his passing tore defences apart and his fierce shot ripped towards goal.

Since their League defeat by Everton, Liverpool had strung together a useful run that had taken them nearer the top of the table. Over the Easter period they faltered in a difficult away game at Sheffield Wednesday, managing only a goalless draw but the League was still within their grasp in what had become the tightest championship in years. To have any hope of capturing it, however, they had to win their remaining seven games, five of which were away, and trust that one of their rivals would tumble.

Over the years Liverpool has shown that they are at their best under pressure and the 1985-86 season was to be no exception. While Liverpool forged on undefeated, Everton crashed 1-0 at Oxford United, leaving Liverpool to win their final game of the season against Chelsea. Liverpool had gone fifteen League and Cup games without defeat but there was no denying the enormity of the task at Stamford Bridge. But it was Dalglish who once again proved to be the inspiring difference between the two sides. Early in the first half

Gary Gillespie arrived from Coventry City but with so much talent at Anfield, the young Scotsman took time to secure a regular spot.

Ian Rush, the most lethal striker in European football and possibly the finest goalscorer in Liverpool's history.

he caught a flighted ball on his chest, neatly brought it down and drove home the goal that won Liverpool the championship. It was a fitting finish to a season that had dramatically swung Liverpool's way with the return of their player-manager to the side. Liverpool had won their sixteenth League title, twice as many as their nearest rivals. Now all they had to do was to beat those closest rivals, Everton, in the Cup final to achieve the one double which had so far eluded them.

FA Cup Final 1986 Liverpool v Everton

With the League Championship under their belt, Liverpool returned to London the following week to face their greatest rivals, Everton. For a month the whole of Merseyside had been abuzz with excitement. The city centre had become a confusion of red and blue with market stalls selling flags, rossettes, T-shirts and other souvenirs while the blackmarket price of tickets had been rising astronomically. Outside Wembley it would have cost you £100 for a £6 standing ticket. This was the game

everyone on Merseyside wanted to watch. London was invaded by Scousers. Down the motorway they poured, red scarves and blue hanging out of car and coach windows with dozens of special trains pulling out of Lime Street station. Liverpool's only doubt for the game came at the last moment when Gary Gillespie who had so ably deputised for the injured Mark Lawrenson over the latter weeks went down ill. In some respects it was fortunate, saving Dalglish from a difficult choice, so MacDonald kept his place with McMahon as substitute. And to mark the occasion the cold wet spring weather of the previous week gave way to sunshine and blue skies.

In the opening encounters Liverpool looked more settled while Everton seemed a trifle nervous but a few early sorties by Everton soon instilled some confidence into them. Then just before the half-hour Everton struck when Lineker raced away from Alan Hansen and sent in a low shot which Grobbelaar did well to get to but could only parry away for him to score off the rebound. The goal was just about deserved and sent waves of panic through the Liverpool defence as Everton knocked in high crosses to test the anxious-looking Grobbelaar. While Everton grew more confident, Liverpool became more confused and as the half-time whistle sounded it

145

seemed the Cup and double would elude them yet again.

The break made little difference as Everton attacked the Liverpool goal with increasing pressure. Grobbelaar looked the unhappiest man at Wembley as he dealt with a succession of awkward centres before finally coming almost to blows with Jim Beglin as the Liverpool defence tied itself in knots. Rarely had a Liverpool team looked so rattled. Dalglish screamed at them from the other end of the field but for the moment it seemed to do little good. Jan Molby, suddenly rediscovering the skills which he had been demonstrating all season, held on to a ball from Whelan on the edge of the Everton box following a poor Everton clearance and as their defence surrounded him, he slipped a neat ball through to Ian Rush. The Welshman accepted it gratefully, rounded Mimms and struck the ball perfectly into the back of the net. Wembley erupted. Liverpool had never been beaten when Rush had scored and now nobody expected them to be beaten this time. Five minutes later it was 2—1 as Molby and Rush combined again before feeding the ball to Johnston to hit

ABOVE One of Ian Rush's two goals against Everton in the 1986 FA Cup final — goals which gave Liverpool the double. Rush would go on to score a total of five goals in FA Cup finals with Liverpool as well as breaking the all time individual Cup scoring record.

home from close range. The game had turned dramatically and with just six minutes remaining Ian Rush made sure of the double when he drove Ronnie Whelan's carefully placed chip past Mimms. There was now no way that Everton who had dominated most of the game could come back and Liverpool might have had more but for several squandered chances.

Liverpool had won a memorable final and had achieved the double, becoming only the third team this century to win the League and FA Cup in the same season. Tottenham had done it in the sixties and Arsenal had beaten Liverpool at Wembley in the seventies to achieve it. Now in the eighties it was finally Liverpool's turn. It may not have been the finest team in Liverpool's

ABOVE Kenny Dalglish, Steve Nicol and Craig Johnston with the League Championship trophy and FA Cup.

history but in winning the double they had shown all the qualities which have become associated with the club — resilience, strength of character, determination and a refusal to accept defeat until the final whistle. It was also appropriate that the team of Dalglish, Rush, Hansen, Lawrenson and Nicol should have achieved the honour. It was a side that contained some of the finest players to ever pull on Liverpool shirts and who richly deserved their double honour. In his first season in charge, Dalglish had proved himself to be a manager to be reckoned with. At the end of the game after they had received the cup and run their triumphal lap of honour, the massed Kop remembered the man who had made it all possible as they quietly and movingly sang the name of Shankly.

Liverpool Grobbelaar, Lawrenson, Beglin, Nicol, Whelan, Hansen, Dalglish, Johnston, Rush, Molby, MacDonald.
Everton Mimms, Stevens (Heath), Van den Hauwe, Ratcliffe, Mountfield, Reid, Steven, Lineker, Sharpe, Bracewell, Sheedy.

1986 – 87

After their Double success, the inevitable happened with Ian Rush signing for the Italian champions, Juventus in a £3.2 million deal during the close season. Rush had been stalked by every major European club during the previous season and his two historic goals against Everton at Wembley finally convincing Juventus officials that he was the man to replace their ageing French star Michel Platini. But there was some consolation: Rush would not leave Anfield until the end of the 1986–87 season. Liverpool had just one season to size up and sign a replacement.

The season began where it had ended – against Everton at Wembley – with the traditional showpiece, the Charity Shield. The game ended in a 1–1 draw and gave an early debut to the club's latest signing, Barry Venison as well as reserve goalkeeper Mike Hooper who came on to deputise for the injured Grobbelaar. The former Sunderland defender, Venison, was a surprise buy who arrived at Anfield after writing to every first division club when his contract at Roker Park had come to an end. It was an enterprising move on his part and manager of the year Kenny Dalglish seized the opportunity to sign the young player.

The league campaign began at St James Park and with Hooper continuing to deputise for Grobbelaar, Ian Rush added another two goals to the one he had already netted in the Charity Shield giving Liverpool a comfortable 2–0 victory. After a goalless draw with Manchester City and a 2–1 defeat of Arsenal the Reds found themselves sharing top spot in the first division but then lost 2–1 at Leicester before bouncing back with a 5–2 thrashing of West Ham at Upton Park, thanks to a couple of goals from the manager himself. After beating newly promoted Charlton Athletic, Liverpool went down 2–1 at Southampton where substitute Kevin MacDonald was stretchered off with a broken leg that tragically finished his season after just a couple of games.

Liverpool began their Littlewoods Cup campaign with a visit from third division Fulham. It could have been a tricky encounter but in the first leg at Anfield a small gate of 13,500 marvelled as Liverpool thrashed the Londoners 10–0 to notch up their biggest ever win in domestic football. Their previous best had been a 10–1 defeat of Rotherham in 1896 and had only been bettered by the 11–0 hammering of Strömsgodset in 1974. Steve McMahon helped himself to four goals with Rush and

Mike Hooper, an able deputy in the Liverpool goal.

Wark adding a couple each. Nicol and Whelan were the other scorers. In the return leg at Craven Cottage Liverpool came out 3−2 winners with McMahon scoring yet again.

September ended with Aston Villa clinching a 3−3 draw in the league at Anfield that saw Liverpool slip to fifth place. Liverpool also claimed their first trophy during the month beating Everton in the final of the Screen Super Cup. This was played over two legs and Liverpool won the first game at Anfield 3−1 and then thrashed Everton 4−1 in the return fixture at Goodison with Rush hitting five goals in all.

Steve McMahon, linchpin of the Liverpool midfield.

Meanwhile October brought mixed fortunes. Wimbledon and Oxford were soundly beaten and Tottenham scraped their second successive win at Anfield while Luton surprised everyone by slamming the champions 4 – 1 on their artificial turf at Kenilworth Road. It has often been said that when Liverpool are beaten they promptly demolish the next team they play and this was to prove the case again with Norwich City on the end of a 6 – 2 thrashing the following week. Paul Walsh scored a hat-trick while Rush added a further two goals. With a 3 – 1 win over Queens Park Rangers, Liverpool shot back to the top of the table but slipped after Sheffield Wednesday squeezed a draw in front of the TV cameras at Anfield. A week later at Everton there was another draw and the remainder of 1986 brought defeats by Watford and Manchester United but victories over Coventry, Chelsea and Sheffield Wednesday with a goalless draw at Charlton.

The Littlewoods Cup continued to bring good fortune both for Liverpool and Steve McMahon. Drawn at home to Leicester, McMahon hit another hat-trick, bringing his tally to eight goals in the competition's three games.

Versatile midfielder Nigel Spackman, a £400,000 buy from Chelsea.

In the fourth round they travelled to Coventry where a goalless draw earned them a replay. This time it was Jan Molby who inflicted the damage, scoring an astonishing hat-trick of penalties in a 3 – 1 victory that gave them a plum draw against Everton.

As the New Year dawned three clubs appeared to be in contention for league honours – Arsenal, Everton, and in third place, Liverpool, seven points adrift of the Gunners. Barry Venison and the young Scottish defender, Gary Gillespie had by now become permanent fixtures in the Liverpool defence although Mike Hooper had reverted to life in the Central League. The young Irish defender Jim Beglin had continued to impress and became a regular choice in the right back slot until a severely broken leg curtailed his season. Steve Nicol was also injured shortly before the year was out and was sorely missed for the remainder of the season. To compensate for these injuries Dalglish was forced into the transfer market, searching desperately for a left back. Derek Statham of West Brom looked set to join the champions after terms and a transfer fee had been agreed but then surprisingly failed a medical. Eventually Nigel Spackman, the versatile Chelsea midfielder arrived for a fee of £400,000 making his debut in February against Southampton.

Sammy Lee's fine Liverpool career drew to an end during the early season when he left to join Queens Park Rangers. He had played 295 games for Liverpool since his debut in April 1978, scoring 19 goals and winning 14 England caps. A midfield dynamo, the short stocky Lee was a popular member of the side and had been a valuable asset of the outstanding team that had captured three successive league championships during the early 1980s.

1987 kicked off with a visit to Nottingham Forest, handily placed in fourth spot, and an Ian Rush goal gave Liverpool a precious point and began a sequence of results that would take them through to the end of March before they would lose again. West Ham United, Manchester City and then Newcastle United were all beaten without a goal being conceded before Leicester City were defeated with Rush hitting another hat-trick in an exciting 4 – 3 romp at Anfield. The gap at the top of the table had now narrowed with Everton in pole position and Liverpool three points behind in third place but with a vital game in hand.

The FA Cup proved to be a disaster with the Cup holders eliminated at the first hurdle, beaten 3 – 0 by Luton Town in the second replay after the first two games had ended in goalless draws. After the first draw at Kenilworth Road where no visiting supporters had been allowed, Liverpool looked forward to the replay at Anfield. But they were thwarted at the first attempt as Luton failed to turn up having been stranded in a snow storm. Dalglish fumed as conditions at Anfield were perfect but there was little chance that the Football Association would award the tie to Liverpool. When the replay did take place Alan Hansen and Ian Rush were injured and although they remained on the field Liverpool were unable to capitalise on their dominance as the match petered into another goalless draw. For the second replay Liverpool demanded a neutral venue but Luton would not agree and instead a coin was tossed. Luton won and Liverpool once more were forced to play on Luton's pitch which they so disliked. It all proved too much for the Reds and they slumped out of the Cup in a 3 – 0 defeat. During the tussle with Luton, Alan Irvine and Gary Ablett made their Cup debuts. Irvine, a tall striker from Falkirk looked particularly dangerous with his diagonal runs while Ablett, a home-grown fullback looked impressive and confident as he carried the ball into the opposing half.

Sandwiched in between the epic encounters with Luton was the Littlewoods Cup clash with Everton at Goodison. Just over 53,000 paid to see the season's fifth clash of the Merseyside rivals with more than 230,000 watching the five contests. So far Liverpool had had the best of their encounters with two wins and two draws and on a bitterly cold January night their luck continued to hold. But it was not all fortuitous. The young Irish defender Jim Beglin was carried off with a seriously broken leg after a collision with Gary Stevens. Steve McMahon also limped off with a groin strain and with Everton dominating the early stages of the game, it looked odds on that Liverpool were about to be dismissed. But all the old fighting qualities of Liverpool began to emerge. Perhaps Everton, and in particular Gary Stevens were shocked at the horrendous accident to Beglin because from that moment on Liverpool began to take control. Eventually it was Rush who pounced with only six minutes remaining to break the deadlock and take Liverpool into the semi-finals for the eighth time in ten years.

The young Irish defender Jim Beglin.

Southampton were their opponents for the semi-final with the first leg played at the Dell. But it produced a dour goalless draw which unfortunately would be best remembered for the sending off of Paul Walsh. In the return leg Dalglish appeared and celebrated his 36th birthday by getting on the scoring sheet after Ronnie Whelan had opened the account. Molby added a third and Liverpool were in their sixth Littlewoods Cup final.

Back in the league Aston Villa held Liverpool to a draw at Villa Park during February but the Reds followed that up with wins over Southampton and Luton before they faced Arsenal at Highbury in what promised to be one of the key league contests of the season. By the end of the night an Ian Rush goal had given them a 1 – 0 victory and a six point lead at the top of the table. The prospects for another championship were looking good and after further victories over Oxford United and Queens Park Rangers, Liverpool looked odds-on for the title. But just as suddenly they collapsed.

At the end of January the long search for Rush's successor had ended when John Aldridge of Oxford United joined the Anfield staff in a £750,000 transfer deal. Aldridge, a Liverpool lad, had long dreamed of playing for the champions but as a youngster had escaped the Liverpool talent spotting net. Instead he had wound up at Newport County and after scoring 81 goals in less than six seasons signed for Oxford United, then a third division side. With Aldridge upfront Oxford climbed from the third division to the first with the young striker hitting an impressive 31 goals during his first season in the premier division. Adridge made his debut against Aston Villa but with Rush in such devastating form, he would have to wait until the following season before winning a permanent place in the first team.

In late March Wimbledon paid their first visit to Anfield and astounded everybody by sneaking away with a 2 – 1 win. Meanwhile an Everton victory over Arsenal slashed Liverpool's lead over their neighbours to just three points with the Blues holding a vital two games in hand while Tottenham hovered menacingly behind them. Two weeks later it had changed dramatically as Liverpool lost their third league game in succession, this time at Norwich while Everton, continuing their winning streak, soared ahead. Liverpool had just six games remaining and after beating Nottingham Forest 3 – 0 the title was still within their grasp but two days later at Old Trafford they went down 1 – 0 and as Everton notched up another victory the pendulum swung firmly towards Goodison Park.

John Aldridge with the unenviable task of stepping into Ian Rush's boots.

Ian Rush scores in the Littlewoods Cup final, April 1987

Arsenal were Liverpool's opponents for the Littlewoods Cup final played at Wembley on Sunday 5 April. The two teams had met twice before in Wembley finals – in the 1950 and 1971 Cup finals – and on both occasions Arsenal had emerged triumphant. But when Ian Rush shot Liverpool into a 20 minute lead, it looked as if it might prove third time lucky for Liverpool. After all, Liverpool had never lost when the Welshman scored. Yet it was not to be. Minutes later Charlie Nicholas, once a transfer target for Liverpool, hit a close range shot home for the equaliser. Liverpool continued to play well and dominated the midfield with their accurate passing and strong running. Then just as the game seemed to be moving towards extra time Arsenal introduced substitute Perry Groves and it was his fresh legs and determined sprints down the left flank which were the final undoing of Liverpool. With only seven minutes remaining the young Gunner seized on a pass from Kenny Sansom and cut the ball back for Charlie Nicholas who hit a low shot at goal. Grobbelaar moved swiftly to his left in anticipation but the ball struck Ronnie Whelan and changed

flight leaving the goalkeeper frustratingly stranded as it bobbled into the net. Liverpool had fought valiantly and were undeserved losers and for the first time in 144 games Ian Rush ended up on the losing side after scoring.

By now Tottenham were out of the league race and as Everton visited Anfield in the most crucial game of the season, everyone admitted that a victory for the Blues would virtually gaurantee them the title. But Liverpool were in no mood to let their oldest enemies clinch the championship at Anfield and in a game of breathtaking skill, Steve McMahon gave Liverpool an early lead with a thundering shot. Minutes later Everton were on level terms but just on the stroke of half time, Ian Rush sent the Reds into the dressing room with a slender lead. The second half was as exciting a battle as Anfield had seen all season which ended with Rush rounding off the scoring ten minutes before time to make it 3 – 1. It was his 19th derby goal, equalling the longstanding record of Dixie Dean. Liverpool's victory however made little difference. Everton still led by three points and had a fixture in hand. Liverpool now had only three games remaining and two of those were away from home.

An emotional farewell to Anfield from Ian Rush.

The title turned on the following match as Everton visited Maine Road to face bottom of the table Manchester City. They scraped a lucky draw while Liverpool away at Coventry failed to capitalise on their neighbour's lapse and went down by a single goal. Injuries had taken their toll. Steve Nicol had not played in 1987 while Mark Lawrenson with Achilles tendon problems ended his season in late March and Bruce Grobbelaar injured an arm as the season wound to its important conclusion. On the May Day Bank Holiday the fight for the championship came to an end as Everton travelled to Norwich and won 1 – 0.

On the same afternoon Ian Rush walked out of the tunnel at Anfield for the final time and typically signed off with the only goal of the match against Watford. With just minutes remaining and with the Kop willing the ball into the back of the net, Rush finally latched on to a pass from John Aldridge. As Steve Sherwood the Watford keeper advanced, Rush calmly chose his spot and shot home Liverpool's winner. The 40,000 crowd erupted and when the final whistle blew Rush made an emotional lap of honour around Anfield. But before departing down the tunnel for the final time, he tore off his number nine shirt and raced towards the Kop throwing it to the ecstatic crowd. In the final game of the season he scored yet again as Liverpool drew 3 – 3 with Chelsea at Stamford Bridge to end the season in second place nine points behind their great rivals Everton. It was a season that had promised much but in the end delivered nothing and for Liverpool that was simply not good enough.

17

TRIUMPHANT AGAIN

1987 – 88

With Ian Rush departed for Turin, Liverpool continued the search for new talent. John Aldridge had already been signed but no one man could replace the goalscoring skills of Rush and so Dalglish plunged into the transfer market to purchase the Watford winger John Barnes. Barnes, initially reluctant to join the Reds, eventually signed for a £900,000 fee. Next in line was Peter Beardsley, the Newcastle striker who was setting the first division alight with his breathtaking performances. He had long been a Liverpool target and shortly before the season began the club broke the British transfer record by paying out £1.9 million for his services.

With this fresh array of talent Liverpool began the season with a difficult fixture at Highbury but soon showed that press talk about Rush's departure signalling the end of Liverpool was nonsense. Liverpool won 2 – 1 with a late goal from Nicol adding to Aldridge's earlier strike. This was the first of three away fixtures forced by a collapsed sewer under the Kop and it was not until 12 September that Anfield got its first glimpse of Barnes and Beardsley. By then, Barnes was creating a stir with Liverpool winning 4 – 1 at Coventry and then drawing at West Ham. In their first home game they beat Oxford 2 – 0 and then Charlton 3 – 2 in an exciting tussle. In front of the TV cameras at St James Park they trounced Beardsley's former team-mates 4 – 1 and then hit another four goals against Derby County and Portsmouth that sounded a warning to the rest of the first division. Queens Park Rangers, who had been making the early running in the league, were Anfield's next visitors but were unlucky enough to find Liverpool, and in particular John Barnes, in devastating form. Liverpool struck another four goals with Barnes hitting two and displaying all his considerable skills, scoring his second after winning the ball on the centre line and racing towards the penalty area, swerving past three players before slotting the ball into the net. It was one of the most memorable goals Anfield had seen in years.

That win put Liverpool at the top of the table with games in hand. As if that was not enough Dalglish then demonstrated that he was determined to build the strongest squad possible when he plunged into the transfer market yet again in mid-October, this time to spend £800,000 on the Oxford midfielder Ray Houghton. A week later Houghton took over Johnston's

1988 Footballer of the Year John Barnes.

number nine shirt and helped the Reds to a 1 – 0 win at Luton.

Next in line were two classic confrontations with neighbours Everton. In the Littlewoods Cup Liverpool had made a laboured opening drawing with Blackburn Rovers at Ewood Park before winning the second leg 1 – 0 at Anfield. That gave them a tie against Everton, yet another meeting of the two sides in cup competitons. More than 44,000 were at Anfield for the clash and with Liverpool struggling against a well-drilled Everton defence it took a slice of luck to settle the battle when a Gary Stevens shot was deflected to give the tie to Everton. It was Liverpool's first defeat of the season. Three days later Everton were back at Anfield for a league fixture but this time Liverpool did not make the same mistake with McMahon and Beardsley scoring two splendid goals in a 2 – 0 win.

Liverpool then drew their next three games with Wimbledon, Manchester United and Norwich before another 4 – 0 win over Watford. That was followed by victories over Tottenham, Chelsea, Sheffield Wednesday, Oxford and Newcastle with a draw against Southampton. By the end of the year Liverpool were still in the top spot and had yet to be beaten in the league, having scored 51 goals and conceded only 11. Even at this early stage there was little doubt who would win the title with praise being lavishly heaped on the team. It was said that this was a different Liverpool, not as regimented as past sides but a team with flair, imagination and the confidence to try new ideas. Barnes, soon to become Player of the Year, was a revelation and was drawing crowds wherever he went with his deft touches, turn of pace and exciting dribbling. Houghton had also settled quickly giving more balance to the midfield while providing accurate crosses for the confident John Aldridge. And as the New Year started Peter Beardsley began to show why he was the most expensive footballer in the league.

Although he had only scored four goals at this stage, he scored twice against Coventry in a 4 – 0 win on New Year's Day and was soon regularly on the scoresheet. Arsenal were the next to be beaten, losing 2 – 0 at Anfield, with an audience of 250 million watching live on television throughout Europe. There were further wins over Charlton, Watford, Portsmouth and QPR before they travelled to Derby needing just a draw to equal Leeds' record of 29 unbeaten games from the beginning of a season. Craig Johnston opened the scoring and although Liverpool dominated the match Derby crept back with an equaliser. But Liverpool had matched the record and even further they had won more games, claimed more points and scored more goals than

Ray Houghton, a reliable midfield player.

the famous Leeds side of 1974. There was just one more game to make the record their own but their next league fixture was at Goodison Park.

If any team was capable of beating Liverpool it was Everton and already they had demonstrated how to do it in the Littlewoods Cup. Although there had been much talk of Liverpool going the whole season without a defeat, it was never realistic. They had to have an off day or a day when luck would not go their way and in front of 45,000 at Goodison Wayne Clarke ended Liverpool's magnificent run. Early in the year Liverpool began to encounter injury problems. Mark Lawrenson, after returning from an Achilles tendon problem the previous season, limped off again and never returned. Ronnie Whelan was also injured and did not reappear until the end of the season. Meanwhile Gary Ablett briefly appeared for the injured Gillespie and then took over from Barry Venison when he too was injured, only to be injured himself.

After just over a hundred games in a Liverpool shirt and 42 goals John Wark waved goodbye to Anfield in January and returned to his former club Ipswich. In the last few seasons injury and competition for places had kept the powerful Scot out of the first team but he would always be remembered for the 27 goals he contributed during the 1984 – 85 season. In April Mark Lawrenson accepted the inevitable truth that he would never be fit enough again to play league football and seized the opportunity to join Oxford United as manager. It was a great loss to Liverpool for he had been one of the surest defenders ever to wear the red shirt. There were few finer sights in football than to see the old-fashioned, well-timed tackles of Lawrenson which had been a hallmark of the Liverpool defence since his £900,000 arrival from Brighton in August 1981. He had played 356 games for Liverpool scoring 18 goals. Paul Walsh also decided to try his luck elsewhere and joined Tottenham after a mixed career at Anfield. Injury and the arrival of Barnes, Beardsley, Aldridge and Houghton had severely limited his opportunities. A skilful player, he had promised much on his arrival but somehow never really lived up to his potential though he always remained popular with the Kop and scored 37 goals in 112 appearances.

Liverpool were also going great guns in the FA Cup having reached the semi-final after wins over Stoke, Aston Villa, Everton and Manchester City. In the semi-final they faced Nottingham Forest but the week before that game they also had to face Forest in a league fixture at the City Ground. Brian Clough's young team remained in contention for the title and against a Liverpool side which left Peter Beardsley and Ray Houghton on the bench, showed just why. Liverpool lost 2–1, their second and last league defeat of the season.

A week later they took their revenge in the semi-final and four days after that they faced Forest yet again, this time in the league at Anfield. That night, in front of almost 40,000 Liverpool turned on a performance of such high quality that the press rated them possibly the finest English side since the Spurs double team of 1961. Tom Finney, the former Preston and England winger went further. He reckoned it was the greatest performance he had ever seen anywhere. Aldridge scored twice while Gillespie, Beardsley and Houghton added the others to send the Anfield faithful home mesmerised. A week later Liverpool travelled to Norwich needing a victory to win the title but could only draw and instead their 17th championship was clinched fittingly on a Saturday afternoon at Anfield against Spurs who went down to a Peter Beardsley goal. And there were still four league games remaining. Three of those were drawn but another five goals were slammed in at Hillsborough against Sheffield Wednesday, three of them coming in the last couple of minutes.

At the final count Liverpool had struck four goals or more on a dozen occasions; they had conceded only 24 league goals while scoring 87 and had lost just two games, winning 26 and drawing 12 leaving them with 90 points to equal Everton's record even though they had played two games fewer. Top marksman was John Aldridge with 29 goals while Peter Beardsley hit 18 and John Barnes 17.

Peter Beardsley scoring against Everton, 1 November 1987.

FA Cup Final 1988 Liverpool v Wimbledon

Liverpool reached Wembley the hard way, drawn away from home in every round. They began in early January with a visit to second division Stoke where a goalless draw meant a replay at Anfield. Yet Liverpool might so easily have gone out of the competition at this early stage had Stoke's young substitute Graham Shaw shot more accurately when he burst through unmarked with just three minutes remaining. A fine save by Mike Hooper, deputising for the injured Grobbelaar, however, helped save Liverpool from a shock defeat. In the replay before almost 40,000 at Anfield an early Peter Beardsley goal was just enough for Liverpool to squeeze into the next round where they faced an Aston Villa side challenging for promotion to the first division.

More than 46,000 packed into Villa Park saw the Midlanders begin brightly but Liverpool soaked up the pressure and slowly took command with John Barnes scoring from a rare header and Peter Beardsley adding a second. After two tricky openers Liverpool could have hoped for easier opposition in the fifth round, but instead they drew Everton, yet again, and this time at Goodison Park. Liverpool might have had the best of recent encounters with the Blues but their dismissal from the Littlewoods Cup earlier in the season still rankled and was the only defeat they had suffered to date. It was the seventh meeting of the two sides in various cup competions in four years. Liverpool set out confidently and with almost 50,000 inside Goodison and millions watching on television at home battled against a rugged Everton side set on avenging their defeat in the 1986 Cup final. But with so much at stake it was not a classic contest and in the end one moment of brilliance was the only difference between the old rivals. It came from John Barnes who fired over a cross for Ray Houghton to head home and start talk of Liverpool winning the League and Cup Double.

In the quarter-finals Liverpool faced another second division side, Manchester City, whose talented youngsters had been catching the eye of many first division managers. Some thought they might be the team to upset Liverpool but in the event City were totally overpowered by a breathtaking display of skill. Ray Houghton opened the account shortly before half time after City had held firm for half an hour or more. That goal forced them to commit more men forward and in the second half Liverpool exploited the gaps and inexperience of City's young defenders. Seven minutes into the second half Craig Johnston was upended in the penalty area and Peter Beardsley converted the spot kick. Johnston scored a third himself before John Barnes added a fourth after one of his typically dazzling runs.

Liverpool might well have scored more but had to be content that they had provided a feast of entertainment for the 44,000 crowd and another Sunday afternoon audience at home.

The semi-finals were to be contested by four teams – Nottingham Forest who were serious challengers for the championship, Wimbledon and Luton Town, the team that had knocked Liverpool out of the cup the previous season. Everyone was eagerly anticipating a Forest/Liverpool final but it was not to be as the two were drawn together for the semi-final. Hillsborough was the venue and 51,000 were present to see if Liverpool could take a step nearer a famous second Double. Only a week before their encounter Nottingham Forest had beaten Liverpool in a league fixture at the City Ground that had made Brian Clough's young team favourites for Wembley. But this time Liverpool began at full strength and took an early lead when John Aldridge converted a penalty after Barnes had been tripped in the box. Two minutes into the second half Forest almost equalised when Nigel Clough scraped the crossbar. But once again it was the combination of Beardsley, Barnes and Aldridge that won the day when a neat ball from Beardsley found Barnes working his way down the left flank. Without hesitation the England international chipped over a delicate cross for John Aldridge to meet on the volley. It was to be the goal of the season and took Liverpool a step nearer the Double.

Wimbledon were not a fashionable club. Eleven years previously they had been a non-league side but now they were a first division team at Wembley and with Liverpool having pocketed the league championship the odds were stacked against a Wimbledon victory. Liverpool, at 4–1 on were the hottest Wembley favourites since the War and most expected them to become the first side to clinch the Double twice. The famous boot room however was taking nothing for granted. Only the previous season Wimbledon had made their debut at Anfield and sneaked away with a win and had already forced a draw at Plough Lane and lost narrowly at Anfield that season.

Rarely can any club have taken so few supporters to a Cup final as Wimbledon. With an average home gate of less than 10,000, most of Wimbledon's ticket allocation had found its way to Merseyside and at least 60,000 Liverpool supporters were crammed into the old stadium basking in warm sunshine. Liverpool, with only three players remaining from the 1986 final with Everton, began slowly, content to stroke the ball around in the heat and let the oppositon do the chasing, occasionally increasing the pace when an opening appeared. In the 26th minute Wimbledon's 6ft 4in goalkeeper Dave Beasant saved well from John Aldridge but eight minutes later was beaten as Peter Beardsley, shrugging off a foul, shot firmly into the net. Wembley erupted but referee Brian Hill had already blown his whistle for the foul on Beardsley. It was an astonishing decision which was not approved of on the terraces. Hardly had Liverpool recovered from that shock when Wimbledon struck with Lawrie Sanchez sending a glancing header past Grobbelaar. The unthinkable had happened and Wimbledon were in the lead.

After half time everyone expected Liverpool to reorganise themselves and step up a gear but instead they plodded on unable to fathom Wimbledon or break down their well-drilled defence. Then in the 61st minute an otherwise dull match exploded when John Aldridge was brought down in the penalty area. The referee redeeming his previous mistake pointed to the spot. Aldridge, who had scored from all 11 penalty kicks during the season, calmly stepped up to take his kick and although he drove the ball hard and low, Beasant guessed well and saved magnificently. It was the first penalty miss in Cup final history and Aldridge's first

failure of the season. From that moment on Wimbledon were always going to win the Cup. Liverpool continued to attack but time and again they could not breach Wimbledon's defence which was strung across the field in numbers. Nicol narrowly missed in the dying seconds but it was not to be Liverpool's day. They had failed to win the Cup although they could still proudly point to the League championship and as they left the field at Wembley the chants that rang around the stadium were not for Wimbledon but for Liverpool who had delighted so many millions with their skilful and adventurous football during a memorable season.

Liverpool Grobbelaar, Nicol, Gillespie, Hansen, Ablett, Houghton, Spackman (Molby), McMahon, Barnes, Aldridge (Johnston), Beardsley.
Wimbledon Beasant, Goodyear, Young, Thorn, Phelan, Wise, Jones, Sanchez, Cork (Cunningham), Fashanu, Gibson (Scales).

Dave Beasant saves the penalty from Aldridge in the 1988 FA Cup final against Wimbledon.

1988–89

It was to be the saddest season in the history of Liverpool Football Club. A season everyone would want to forget, but for so many there would be no forgetting. It would be summed up in one word – Hillsborough.

Yet the season could hardly have opened with a bigger and more unexpected delight. Ian Rush was coming back to Anfield. After just one season in Italian football the Welsh striker was being lured back to his natural home. His stay in Italy had not been a happy one. Injuries, acclimatisation, illness, plus the iron defences of Italian league soccer had left Rush short of goals and, with a £3 million price tag around his neck, he had become a costly liability for the Italian club Juventus. On the debit side, Craig Johnston had decided to quit football and return to Australia. The arrival of Ray Houghton had limited his opportunities and he appeared to be growing disillusioned with English football. A lively winger, his pace had often carved unexpected openings for the Reds and, since his £500,000 arrival from Middlesbrough in April 1981, he had made over 260 appearances, scoring a valuable 38 goals.

Robbed of a unique second Double by lowly Wimbledon, Liverpool kicked off their season with some satisfaction by taking revenge on the south London side in the Charity Shield. It was hardly a sparkling contest, but John Aldridge, concerned that he might become surplus to the side's requirements with Rush's return, proved a point by snatching a couple of goals in Liverpool's 2–1 win. A week later at Charlton in the first league game of the season, Aldridge went one better, hitting a hat-trick in Liverpool's 3–0 win. Rush, sitting on the bench, must have wondered if he would ever win back his number nine shirt. A week later at Anfield Rush was again on the bench, but it hardly mattered as Liverpool managed their first home win over Manchester United since 1978, thanks to a Jan Molby penalty. Maximum points so far, but not for long, as Liverpool dropped a couple of points at Aston Villa and then at home to Spurs.

By the end of September, Liverpool's injury list was mounting, with Alan Hansen sidelined for much of the season and now Steve McMahon and John Barnes joining the doctor's queue. Then Bruce Grobbelaar found himself on the treatment bench. Add to that the tragic loss of Mark Lawrenson and Craig Johnston's departure, and the Reds were taking on a very different

appearance from 12 months ago. But at Southampton you would never have realised the backroom crisis, as Peter Beardsley inspired Liverpool to a 3–1 win. But the injury problems were about to take their toll.

In the Littlewoods Cup second round first leg, the Reds struggled to a 1–0 win over lowly Walsall and then a few days later slumped to a 2–1 defeat at home to Newcastle, followed by a 1–0 defeat at Luton. The problem was obvious. Although Barnes had recovered, it was now the turn of Gary Gillespie to limp off injured and he would not return until the spring. Jan Molby was

David Burrows, a £500,000 signing from West Brom.

also taking a short enforced rest, care of HM Prisons. Although Liverpool are not a club to look for excuses, everyone had to admit it was the worst injury crisis anyone at Anfield could remember. To counter the growing problem, Dalglish plunged into the transfer market signing the young West Brom fullback David Burrows for £500,000. But it was still hard going as they managed only a goalless draw at Anfield with Coventry before losing at Nottingham Forest. Three league defeats already and October was not out, but Liverpool would lose only three more games over the next seven months.

The turnaround began at West Ham, with Rush scoring a spectacular goal to help Liverpool to a 2–0 win. A few days later, Arsenal came to Anfield for the third round of the Littlewoods Cup and gave Liverpool a rare footballing lesson. But, although they ought to have won, the Reds snatched a draw. A week later at Highbury, more than 54,000 saw Liverpool give a fighting performance, but still neither team could break the deadlock and a further contest was called for. That came towards the end of November at Villa Park and at last Liverpool began to show their old qualities, finally winning 2–1. In the league, meanwhile, the Reds had notched up a couple of wins and a draw, so when Wimbledon arrived at Anfield everyone expected the Reds to take revenge for that Cup final defeat. But in the last minute, an agonising own goal gave Wimbledon a far from deserved draw. Four days later, Liverpool journeyed to West Ham for their fourth round Littlewoods Cup tie hoping at least for a draw. Instead, they suffered their heaviest defeat in eight years and their biggest cup defeat since the War. They lost 4–1 and the word was out again that Liverpool were there for the taking. They had slumped to fourth in the table, eight points behind surprise leaders Norwich. December seemed to begin on a slightly brighter note, with Jan Molby returning to Anfield after his stint in prison, though his appearances would still be restricted. There was also another tussle with Arsenal, this time in the league, and not surprisingly it ended all square yet again.

The next four weeks brought little luck. Everton snatched a 1–1 draw at Anfield, table-toppers Norwich went one better winning 1–0 and then on New Year's Day, in front of the TV cameras at Old Trafford, United gave Liverpool a 3–1 roasting. After that humiliation, the bootroom door was slammed shut while Dalglish and his staff put their heads together. Although Liverpool were still hanging on to the leaders, they were inconsistent, missing chances and lacking their usual determination. The inquest was to do the trick, as the Reds then went 24 games without defeat.

First to feel Liverpool's sting was Aston Villa, beaten 1–0 at Anfield and then Peter Beardsley's old club Carlisle United were cuffed 3–0 in the third round of the FA Cup. For the next round Liverpool travelled to Millwall where twin strikers John Aldridge and Ian Rush inspired them to a fifth round clash at Hull. Gary Gillespie made a brief return for that match, only to limp off again after ten minutes. Hull battled hard, but in the end Liverpool sneaked a 3–2 win thanks to a couple of goals from John Aldridge.

At the end of February, Liverpool looked to be well out of title contention. They were in eighth place and an astonishing 19 points behind new leaders Arsenal. But, thanks to a 2–0 win over Charlton and a handsome 4–0 victory at Middlesbrough, the table changed dramatically. Arsenal were still top, but Liverpool were

Gary Ablett finally established himself in defence.

gradually closing the gap, now down to ten points. A week later, when John Aldridge helped himself to a hat-trick against Luton in Liverpool's thrilling 5–0 win, it really began to look as if Liverpool might be able to catch the Gunners. The goals were finally beginning to arrive. Against third division Brentford in the FA Cup quarter-finals, Liverpool confidently struck another four and were through to their 17th FA Cup semi-final. Meanwhile, back in the league, the Reds continued to chalk up more victories, this time handing out a lesson to high-fliers Coventry at Highfield Road that narrowed the gap to eight points. Wins followed at Tottenham, at home against Derby, and then at Norwich to make it seven wins in a row.

From Norwich, Liverpool travelled to Dubai to face Celtic in the British Cup. The competition was something of an irrelevance, Liverpool losing 4–2 in a penalty shoot-out. Yet it seemed to do their championship hopes no harm, as they hammered Sheffield Wednesday 5–1 in a morning match at Anfield on Grand National day to go top of the table for the first time that season. But, as expected, by five o'clock Arsenal were again heading the league. Three days later, however, Liverpool climbed above them once more as they beat Millwall 2–1 at the Den. Seventeen games without defeat, nine consecutive wins – and to think, back on New Year's Day they were writing Liverpool off.

Top of the table and in the last four of the Cup, everyone at Anfield was looking forward to the semi-final clash with Nottingham Forest at Hillsborough. It was to be a game everyone would remember for the rest of their lives, though not for reasons to do with football. Everything seemed so normal as the two teams trotted out on to the pitch, began their kick around, and then kicked off, Liverpool defending the Leppings Lane end of the ground where all their fans were massed. Peter Beardsley struck the cross bar and then, six minutes into the game, a policeman ran on to the pitch towards the referee. It was the first indication that a disaster was taking place. Within moments the two teams had been directed off the pitch and, before the eyes of millions, a tragedy began to unfold. At first it seemed that a barrier had collapsed and there had simply been a few injuries, but gradually the full extent of the disaster became apparent. First-aid men rushed towards the Leppings Lane end, makeshift stretchers were carried by fans, and everywhere there was chaos and confusion. By late afternoon the death toll was mounting. Initially it seemed there were just a couple of deaths, then 20-odd. By five o'clock there was talk of more than 50, then almost as suddenly it was over 60. By the time of the early evening news bulletins it was 75. By late that evening it was 94.

The 95th death came a few days later when a 14-year-old boy on a life support machine finally passed away.

The speculation, the investigations and the questions began almost immediately. Someone, it seemed, had tragically opened the gates at the Leppings Lane end of the ground to usher fans into the stadium as quickly as possible. And, in the rush, they had all poured down the tunnel and into an already packed part of the ground. With fences around the perimeter preventing fans from getting on to the pitch, a disaster was inevitable.

The nation was stunned by the immediacy of the tragedy. Millions had watched it unfold on television. And in news bulletins throughout the next few days the same horrifying pictures would be repeated. For the second time in five years, Liverpool Football Club had

Confusion reigns on the Hillsborough pitch in the aftermath of the disaster in which 95 fans died.

been associated with a major tragedy. Nowhere was the disaster more felt than in Liverpool. It seemed that everyone in the city had a relative, a friend, a workmate or a colleague who had been either injured or killed. Everyone on Merseyside who had ever been to a football match recognised just how easily it could have been them.

Within hours the Shankly Gates at Anfield had become a shrine. The following day they were bedecked in flowers, as first hundreds, and then thousands, began to thread their way towards Anfield. Many wanted to lay wreaths on the Kop and the club unhesitatingly threw open the gates. It was a sign for all football fans to come and pay their respects. Within days the Kop and half the ground were covered in flowers. Not only did Liverpool and Everton players join in the homage, but footballers from all around the world came to pay their respects as well as politicians and other dignitaries. Prince Charles

visited, as did Opposition leader Neil Kinnock, while former players John Toshack and Craig Johnston flew in from distant shores. No one who went to Anfield that week will ever forget the sight and the smell of so many flowers, with only the sound of rustling cellophane disturbing the silence. Scarves, hats and rosettes adorned the railings of the Kop and grown men wept openly. It was an astonishing and moving sight. Football might be important to the city of Liverpool, yet suddenly everyone realised just how unimportant it was.

Everyone at the club was distraught, particularly those like John Aldridge and Steve McMahon who had been born and bred in the city. A fund was set up, the club donated generously, the Football Association postponed matches, players attended funerals and helped comfort the bereaved. But life had to go on and, after a respectful period of mourning, football returned to Merseyside.

Liverpool began the road back with a friendly in Glasgow against Celtic in an effort to shake the nightmare of Hillsborough out of their system. More than 60,000 turned up and movingly sang 'You'll Never Walk Alone'. Even Kenny pulled on a red shirt that night, pushing Steve McMahon out of the way to open Liverpool's scoring as they won 4–0. Three days later, Liverpool returned to league soccer, appropriately against Everton at Goodison. It was a tough game that ended in a 0–0 draw, but at least Liverpool were back. On the same day as Liverpool had faced Nottingham Forest at Hillsborough, Everton, in the other FA Cup semi-final, had beaten Norwich to throw up the prospect of an all-Merseyside final. But, first of all, Liverpool had to face Forest once more. That semi-final eventually took place on Sunday 7 May at Old Trafford and, thanks to a couple of goals from John Aldridge, Liverpool went on to beat Forest 3–1 and set up the second all-Merseyside Cup final.

Now Liverpool could briefly concentrate on the league. There were wins over Forest again, Wimbledon, and Queens Park Rangers to keep the Reds breathing down Arsenal's neck. And, as Liverpool set off for Wembley, there were only two more league fixtures left, against West Ham, who faced a drop into the second division if they lost, and then the final game, against leaders Arsenal at Anfield.

FA Cup Final 1989 Liverpool v Everton

Was there ever a Cup final played on a sunnier day? Outside Wembley, thousands basked in the Mediterranean warmth, Liverpool and Everton fans chatting together, lying on the grass verges, buying each other rounds in the pubs. And, as had happened on previous occasions, they made their way towards Wembley sharing cars, coaches and trains without ever a sign of hostility. They marched up Wembley Way, arms round each other, swapping scarves and jokes, wearing both teams' colours. The outcome seemed almost unimportant. It was the occasion that mattered. And, although it may at times have seemed like a family affair, the nation was welcome to share the moment. Three years previously, Liverpool had beaten their old rivals to clinch the Double. Now a unique second Double was on the cards as Liverpool lined up for their ninth FA Cup final. But first of all they had to defeat Everton again.

Inside the stadium, the atmosphere was emotional. Nobody could forget the Hillsborough dead. Wembley's perimeter fencing had been pulled down for the day and there was only the barest sign of segregation. Gerry Marsden led the singing of 'You'll Never Walk Alone' and there was a minute's silence to remember Hillsborough's dead, but once the whistle had sounded the serious business of winning the Cup was quickly underway.

If there were any nerves, they were soon forgotten, with Liverpool off to a flying start, scoring within five minutes. A long ball upfield from Steve Nicol found Steve McMahon bursting through the Everton line. He squared the ball to Aldridge and the tall Liverpool striker pounced to make amends for his penalty miss of Liverpool's last final. Wembley exploded. 1–0 to Liverpool. For the next hour the Reds held the upper hand, neatly playing the ball around but unable to find the net again. It was not until the final 25 minutes of normal time, when Everton brought on Stuart McCall, that the Blues began to make any impression. Then they began to push up, pinning Liverpool into their own half. Yet, with only seconds remaining, it looked as if the Cup was going to Anfield until McCall dramatically swooped on a rebound Grobbelaar had failed to hold. All square, and suddenly we were into extra time.

As if Liverpool had not had a tough enough schedule in recent weeks, they now had to face a further 30 minutes in the sunshine of Wembley. Ian Rush came on for Aldridge and, within minutes of the resumption, Liverpool went ahead again as Rush swept in to break Dixie Dean's long-standing goalscoring record in Merseyside derbies. From a Steve Nicol cross he shielded the ball, then swivelled to fire in a right-foot shot past Southall. But still Everton were not finished. A minute later McCall added a second with a fierce volley from just outside the box and Liverpool had to do it all over again. But, with Ian Rush in your side, you need never fear, especially against Everton. There he was again, on the end of a John Barnes cross, to head Liverpool into the lead: 3–2. There were no more goals in the second period of extra time. Liverpool had won the Cup and, as the final whistle blew, the pitch was invaded by the hundreds who had been sitting around its perimeter, making it impossible for the winners to perform their usual lap of honour. It was the only blemish on a day when Liverpool had clinched the first leg of the Double. They had done it for those who died at Hillsborough. Now all they had to do was beat West Ham and Arsenal in the league to secure the second part.

Liverpool Grobbelaar, Ablett, Staunton (Venison), Nicol, Whelan, Hansen, Beardsley, Aldridge (Rush), Houghton, Barnes, McMahon.
Everton Southall, McDonald, Van Den Hauwe, Ratcliffe, Watson, Bracewell (McCall), Nevin, Steven, Sharp, Cottee, Sheedy (Wilson).

Three days later, Liverpool tackled West Ham at Anfield in a game the Londoners had to win to stay in the first division. But in Liverpool they had met their match. John Aldridge began the rout and, although West Ham equalised, Ray Houghton put Liverpool ahead again. Houghton scored his second, with Barnes and Rush also getting on the scoring sheet in a 5–1 victory. So many goals now meant that Arsenal had to win by two clear goals to steal the championship from Liverpool. Surely even Arsenal could not do that at Anfield. Few teams in the past decade had managed it.

On the Friday evening of 26 May, in front of a massive TV audience and a full house at Anfield, Liverpool and Arsenal took the field to decide the championship. It was Liverpool's third game in six days that had included a two-hour Cup final in the heat of Wembley. So far they had shown few signs of any after-effects following Hillsborough, but there were some who wondered if their nerve might finally crack in this game. Liverpool supporters will need little reminding of what happened that night. It was like a bad dream. The first half ended all square, with Liverpool more than equal to any Arsenal attack. But then in the second half Arsenal opened their

scoring with a controversial goal. An indirect free kick from Nigel Winterburn shot into the net without touching a player. Grobbelaar made no effort to save it; the linesman raised a flag, but the referee reckoned Alan Smith had touched the ball before it went over the line. Liverpool's protests were of no use. Then, with barely seconds to go and well into injury time with the entire ground on its feet roaring Liverpool on to the Double, Michael Thomas found himself racing into the box and with enough space to flick the ball beyond the grasp of Grobbelaar: 2–0 to the Gunners. It was unbelievable. The league championship, after nine months of hard slog, had been decided in the final seconds. It was the most dramatic conclusion to the championship in the history of the Football League. Liverpool had been denied the Double.

In hindsight, had Liverpool not scored so many goals against West Ham they would have been forced to be more adventurous against Arsenal. As it was, they were content to stroke the ball about rather than to go on the offensive. And that had been their undoing. Rarely has Anfield looked so dejected. Fans shook their heads in disbelief, there was a stunned silence from the Kop, though they generously applauded Arsenal as they lifted the trophy. Thousands poured out of Anfield into the night air, barely a word being spoken, wandering off to their cars and buses in disbelief at what they had just seen. They have a word for it in Liverpool. Gobsmacked.

Ian Rush, having come on as a substitute, proved Liverpool's saviour once again as he hit his second goal in the all-Merseyside FA Cup final.

GOALS GALORE

1989–90

After their humiliating defeat by Arsenal on that warm May evening there was only ever going to be one team in the championship race the following season. And that was precisely how it turned out. Liverpool had to restore their pride.

The season began, however, with a couple of notable changes. Out went the tenacious Kevin MacDonald, transferred to Coventry City after just 40 league appearances. His career had been interrupted by injury, as had that of Jim Beglin, who left to join Leeds United. Beglin had made 56 appearances for the Reds, mainly as a fullback, but a horrific broken leg, sustained in a match against Everton, kept him out of action for some time and he never really regained his place. There was just one major signing – Glenn Hysen, the stylish Swedish international defender from the Italian club Fiorentina. Hysen was signed from under the noses of Manchester United and made his first appearance at Wembley in the Charity Shield against Arsenal, where at least there was some compensation for Liverpool as they beat the Gunners 1–0. Hysen, man of the match, was to become a permanent fixture in the Liverpool line-up from the start.

Liverpool opened their league campaign at Anfield by sweeping newly promoted Manchester City aside and then had a couple of draws at Aston Villa and on Luton's plastic before they returned to their winning ways against Derby County. In the second week of September, another side new to the division, Crystal Palace, came to Anfield and left on the wrong end of a nine-goal hammering. The 9–0 scoreline equalled Liverpool's best-ever league victory and ranked as Palace's worst-ever defeat. Steve Nicol claimed two goals, with Hysen, Beardsley, Gillespie, Rush, Barnes, McMahon and Aldridge hitting the others. Aldridge's goal from the penalty spot, with his first kick of the match, was also to be his last for Liverpool. At the end of the game he tearfully threw his red shirt into the Kop and the following day signed for the Spanish club, Real Sociedad. The likeable striker had played 83 league games for Liverpool, scoring a remarkable 50 goals. Wherever he had played, Newport, Oxford and Liverpool, he had found the net, although his goalscoring touch always seemed to desert him when he pulled on the green shirt of Eire. Sadly, the return of Ian Rush made it inevitable that he would eventually be squeezed out of the first team and, although everyone felt sad that he should leave, nobody blamed him and he would always be welcomed back at Anfield.

Although Liverpool had made a stuttering start to their campaign, with three draws in their first six games, they had conceded only two goals. By the end of September, the picture had changed as Liverpool roared to the top of the division. Everton were beaten 3–1 at Goodison and Wigan were knocked out of the Littlewoods Cup. But then in October, after victory over Wimbledon, came one of their heaviest league defeats in years, a 4–1 hammering at Southampton. That was

followed by another defeat, this time at Highbury, where the Gunners knocked Liverpool out of the Littlewoods Cup. But it wasn't all gloom. Spurs were beaten and the Reds still clung to their top spot. In November, however, it began to look as if things might be about to go wrong. Coventry came to Anfield and returned to the Midlands with a surprise 1–0 win, while the following week Queens Park Rangers put three goals past Grobbelaar to chalk up a 3–2 victory at Loftus Road. But, as usual, Liverpool came bouncing back with a win at Millwall and then a 2–1 victory over Arsenal at Anfield that gave some

LEFT Glenn Hysen established himself at the heart of Liverpool's defence.

RIGHT John Aldridge scored yet another goal on his farewell appearance for Liverpool.

deserved satisfaction. Steve McMahon and John Barnes hit the net, Barnes bringing his goal tally to 11.

The month ended with Liverpool visiting bottom-of-the-table Sheffield Wednesday for the first time since the Hillsborough tragedy. It was an emotional evening and, perhaps not surprisingly, Liverpool went down 2–0, though they still found themselves heading the table. Four league defeats already and they had played only 15 games. As usual, the pundits were sharpening their pencils looking for a chink in the Liverpool armour. But Liverpool would defy them by losing only one more league game that season.

December kicked off with a fixture at Maine Road against Manchester City, where Liverpool took full advantage of the managerless club by winning 4–1, with Ian Rush knocking in a couple. Aston Villa, who appeared to be mounting a dangerous challenge for the title, came to Anfield next and proved that they were indeed a serious proposition, sneaking away with a well-earned draw. Another high-flying side, Chelsea, were next but, unlike Villa, their challenge disintegrated in front of their own supporters as they crashed to a 5–2 defeat. Rush hit a couple more, his fourth brace of the season, and seemed at last to be returning to his old goalscoring ways after a first season that had brought only 11 goals. Two days before Christmas, Liverpool's luck against Manchester United was again in short measure, but at least they managed a goalless draw at Anfield before taking revenge against Sheffield Wednesday on Boxing Day. The year ended with Charlton Athletic the victims at Anfield, a win that put Liverpool four points ahead of Aston Villa.

The new decade opened with a couple of draws, against Nottingham Forest where Rush hit another brace and then a goalless draw in the third round of the FA Cup at Swansea. Not that Liverpool played badly that day, it was simply that the Swansea keeper, Lee Bracey, saved them from a hiding. But a few days later, in the replay on Merseyside, there was little he could do as Liverpool stormed to their best-ever Cup win. Back in 1892, in the qualifying rounds of the FA Cup, they had beaten Newtown 9–0. Now, in the FA Cup proper, they slaughtered poor old Swansea 8–0. Ian Rush hit a hat-trick that night, while John Barnes helped himself to a couple. Back in the league, next-to-bottom Luton Town came to Anfield and were within seconds of sneaking away with a win until Steve Nicol hit a last-minute equaliser. Next, Liverpool travelled to Selhurst Park remembering their famous 9–0 victory over Palace earlier in the season. It was not quite so easy this time, though they managed a comfortable 2–0 win.

In the fourth round of the FA Cup, Liverpool faced a tricky tie away to Norwich and, not surprisingly, it ended in a goalless draw. But, in the replay, Liverpool cruised to a 3–1 win once Steve Nicol had given them the edge. In the return derby against Everton, Liverpool were 2–0 up and appeared to be heading for a comfortable victory until Graeme Sharp scored. Then, in a frenetic finish, the Reds found themselves hanging on as Everton desperately pursued an equaliser. But it never came and, with the bad weather causing the postponement of Arsenal and Villa's fixtures, the Reds opened up a three-point gap at the top of the table. The following week they drew 0–0 at Norwich.

In the last 16 of the FA Cup Liverpool faced Southampton and welcomed two old favourites – Jimmy Case and Sammy Lee – back to Anfield, albeit in the colours of the opposition. But after 90 minutes the old boys had to admit that nothing much had changed at Anfield. Liverpool still kept on winning. This time it was thanks to Ian Rush, Steve Nicol and Peter Beardsley in a comprehensive 3–0 win. Liverpool were now into the quarter-finals but found themselves drawn away to Queens Park Rangers, as tricky a tie as imaginable. Earlier in the season they had lost 3–2, but this time it was markedly different. Liverpool controlled the game virtually from the start, twice taking the lead but twice finding it snatched away from them. The game eventually ended all square at two apiece. In the replay Liverpool took an early lead through Peter Beardsley's 16th goal of the season but then seemed to lose interest and finished up hanging on to their one-goal lead as QPR almost snatched a draw.

Meanwhile, in the league Liverpool beat Millwall and then faced Manchester United at Old Trafford in a vital game. Villa had by then edged ahead of Liverpool and defeat at Old Trafford could have severely dented Liverpool's title dreams. But it was not to be. At one point it looked as if the old United jinx would continue, as Ronnie Whelan put into his own net, but John Barnes was there to make amends and rescue the day with a second goal in a superb individual performance. But, three days later, Liverpool went down to their first league defeat of the year when they visited White Hart Lane and lost 1–0. Villa still had their noses in front in the race for the championship, though by now Arsenal were beginning to slip.

March ended with Liverpool regaining their top spot as they beat Southampton 3–2 at Anfield. Pulling on a red shirt for the first time that day as substitute was the Israeli international Ronnie Rosenthal. Signed on loan from the Belgian club Standard Liège, Rosenthal had made a few outings with Luton reserves but, when it came to signing him, Luton hesitated and Kenny

Ronnie Whelan in his tenth league season for Liverpool.

Wimbledon, where Liverpool won 2–1, but then played the full 90 minutes against Charlton, when he hit a hat-trick in Liverpool's 4–0 win to become the new Reds' hero.

Sandwiched in between those last two league fixtures, Liverpool met Crystal Palace at Villa Park for a place in the FA Cup final. The talk was all about Liverpool's 9–0 win earlier in the season but, as everyone should know, the Cup is a very different animal. It was Liverpool's third consecutive FA Cup semi-final and the 18th in their history. The day began well enough, with Ian Rush shooting them into an early lead, but when the Welsh international striker went off injured a little later the warning bells began to clang. The second half also began with another Liverpool substitution as the injured Gary Gillespie remained in the dressing room. And with the Reds still reorganising their defence, Palace took full advantage, stealing in to equalise almost before they had drawn breath. Palace were now in full flight, constantly harrying Liverpool with their set pieces and high crosses. It was almost inevitable that they would score again and, as expected, it resulted from a free kick in the 69th minute. But then came as dramatic a finale as anyone could have wished to see. With just nine minutes remaining, Liverpool equalised as Steve McMahon slammed a shot beyond Nigel Martyn. Then, 60 seconds later, Liverpool were ahead as Steve Staunton was tripped in the penalty area. John Barnes stepped up to take the kick and Liverpool were leading 3–2. Surely there was no way back for Palace now. But no, with virtually the last effort of the game, Palace stole the prize from under Liverpool's noses as Andy Gray hit Palace's equaliser from yet another free kick. Extra time was necessary. A massive TV audience watching at home sat glued to their sets. For the first period, Palace looked as if they might have given their all, as Liverpool again began to control the game. But Palace's aerial bombardment was still causing the Liverpool defence problems and, with only ten minutes remaining, Alan Pardew headed Palace into the final from a corner kick.

So Liverpool were out of the Cup in the shock result of the competition. Palace had taken their revenge, clearly learning a few lessons from their 9–0 drubbing earlier in the season. But what a difference it might have made had Rush and Gillespie not been forced to retire from the game. And with their semi-final defeat went Liverpool's hopes of another Double. Three years in succession they had come within a whisker of emulating their double triumph of 1986.

So it was back to the league and the mundane business of chalking up another championship. In their next match at Anfield against Nottingham Forest, it was

Dalglish was in like a shot to offer him his chance at Anfield. He was an instant hit, making an immediate impression in the reserves before his debut against Southampton. Rosenthal was again on the bench against

Rosenthal again who struck as the two old foes drew 2–2. At Liverpool they take one game at a time and don't worry about the championship. But, as they travelled to Highbury to face Arsenal, there was no denying that this was one of the most crucial games of the season. Liverpool simply could not afford to lose and, thanks to a late goal from John Barnes, they salvaged a draw that virtually ended Arsenal's title dreams. That left Liverpool with three successive home fixtures plus an away match at Coventry to clinch the title. First came Chelsea, beaten 4–1, leaving Liverpool needing just four points from three games.

Queens Park Rangers came next and threatened to spoil the party when they took an early lead, but Ian Rush and John Barnes from the penalty spot put Liverpool in front. Meanwhile, down at Villa Park, Aston Villa faced a stubborn Norwich side not prepared to surrender. From a 3–1 deficit Norwich began a fightback that would finally decide the venue of the league championship. Thousands on the Kop listening to their transistor radios began to relay the dramatic scoreline to the players. Suddenly, with minutes to go, it was 3–2 and then came a thunderous roar from the Kop. There seemed no reason. But there was. Norwich had

struck a last-minute equaliser. The word spread around Anfield like a bushfire. Suddenly everyone was on their feet. Nerves jangled and the final moments seemed an age as everyone recalled the game with Arsenal of the previous season. But this time, Liverpool would not be denied. They defended bravely, if not nervously, and then came the final whistle and the short wait for confirmation that Villa and Norwich had drawn. Finally, the tannoy announcement declared that Liverpool had clinched their 18th championship.

There was the usual lap of honour, the rush of photographers, the singing and the chanting for 'Kenny'. Liverpool rounded off the season by formally receiving the trophy before beating Derby County 1–0 and, in the season's last fixture, went to Coventry where they put on a dazzling display to win 6–1. John Barnes struck a hat-trick, with Ronnie Rosenthal hitting a couple to add to the five he had already scored. It had been a magnificent performance all round. Seventy-eight goals had been scored in the league, another 20 in the FA Cup and eight in the Littlewoods Cup, making a total of 106 goals. Barnes ended the season top scorer with 28 goals, while Ian Rush chalked up 26 and Peter Beardsley 15. But although the season had stretched from August, it was perhaps the introduction of the bustling Ronnie Rosenthal towards the climax that provided that final inspirational burst to the title.

Ronnie Rosenthal with his end-of-season goals helped Liverpool clinch their 18th title.

20
GOODBYE KENNY

It was a season that began with so much promise yet ended in despair. A season that kicked off with ten straight wins and finished with a wave of defeats; a season opening with one manager and ending with another; a season that began with Liverpool as champions and ended with them as runners-up.

Liverpool opened their account at Sheffield United where a spirited performance by the first division's new boys held the Reds to a goalless first half. But an injury to the Blades' goalkeeper, who was carried off after just 15 minutes, eventually told and Liverpool finally ran out 3–1 winners. In their first home game, a 2–0 win over Nottingham Forest, the Reds edged into top spot. A few days later they entertained the previous season's runners-up Aston Villa at Anfield. But much had changed in the four months since Villa's success and under new manager Jozef Venglos the Midlanders crashed to a 2–1 defeat as Barnes inspired some devastating Liverpool play. Next in line were Wimbledon, always tricky opponents for Liverpool, but, for once, the Reds overcame the long ball tactics of the south Londoners and by half time were two goals up and on their way to victory thanks to John Barnes and Ronnie Whelan.

Next in line were Manchester United, lying third in the table, and desperate for revenge after Liverpool had scraped a 1–1 draw in the Charity Shield at Wembley. By half time, though they hardly deserved it, Liverpool were three goals ahead. Beardsley added a fourth in the second half to add to his two before the interval, giving Liverpool a 4–0 victory, their best win over United for 65 years. Liverpool travelled across Stanley Park for their next fixture and, although they were three goals in front with only 15 minutes remaining, they contrived to almost give the game away and ended up scrambling the ball off the goalline in the dying seconds as they clung desperately to a 3–2 lead. That was six league wins in a row, but their run almost came to a sensational end at Anfield as humble Crewe of the third division took an early lead in the first leg of the second round of the Rumbelows Cup. A lethargic-looking Liverpool struggled to find their shooting boots, but eventually Ian Rush struck to open the floodgates and the Reds wound up 5–1 winners. League victories then followed over Sunderland and Derby County to give Liverpool a six-point lead over Arsenal. In the second leg of the Rumbelows Cup, Ian Rush helped himself to a hat-trick

as the Reds cantered to an easy 4–1 victory. Ten wins out of ten, but that was where it stopped as Liverpool faltered against Norwich at Carrow Road and struggled to hold on to a 1–1 draw. A week later, however, they were back to their winning ways with an impressive 2–0 win over Chelsea, thanks to some excellent work by John Barnes.

In the next round of the Rumbelows Cup, the Reds travelled to Old Trafford where, against a rampant United, they gave one of their most inept performances in years. Two goals adrift at half time they had barely an attack to talk of in the first 45 minutes. Although they improved after the interval, there was no stopping United who went on to win 3–1. For the televised clash against Tottenham, Dalglish responded by choosing what was almost a seven-man defence. His team selection surprised everyone, yet it worked, with David Burrows blotting out the effervescent Paul Gascoigne. The Reds stormed to a 3–1 win, Rush grabbing a couple. The following week Rush struck two more as they cuffed Luton 4–0, bringing his tally to 12 goals in 15 games. And as Arsenal and United faltered, Liverpool raced six points clear.

Their unbeaten league run continued the following week as Coventry were beaten 1–0 at Highfield Road and then, in an exciting tussle at Anfield, Manchester City and Liverpool fought out a dramatic draw. A goal down with just eight minutes remaining, Rush finally struck an equaliser and then, with less than a minute to go, Ronnie Rosenthal lobbed what seemed a winner only to be denied with the last touch of the game as Niall Quinn headed City's equaliser. In early December Liverpool visited Highbury but, although the Gunners had been thrashed 6–2 in mid-week by Manchester United, they recovered sufficiently to overcome Liverpool 3–0, reducing the gap at the top to three points. Liverpool, again packing their defence, had held out well until a couple of disputed goals saw them trailing 2–0. After that they were simply overrun. It was their first league defeat of the season, but they followed it up with wins over Sheffield United and Southampton before drawing at Queens Park Rangers.

However, in honesty, Liverpool weren't functioning as normal and, in an end-of-the-year televised clash with high-fliers Crystal Palace, they crashed to a 1–0 defeat that underlined their vulnerability. January brought little luck other than an impressive 3–0 win over third placed Leeds United. In the third round of the FA Cup

Exciting Irish full back Steve Staunton.

they travelled to Blackburn and seemed on the point of a sensational exit until a last second own goal saved their embarrassment. The replay proved a little easier and a 3–0 win saw Liverpool into the fourth round where they faced Brighton at Anfield. But again Liverpool made heavy weather of their second division opponents, giving two goals away in the final 20 minutes after leading 2–0. The replay proved even more hazardous, with Liverpool equalising only in the final minute of normal time before going on to win 3–2 in extra time. In the league they could do no more than draw 0–0 at Aston Villa and then allowed Wimbledon to sneak in for a last minute equaliser at Anfield.

With Liverpool looking increasingly uncomfortable, Dalglish plunged into the transfer market, snapping up Jimmy Carter, the Millwall winger, then young Jamie Redknapp, the promising Bournemouth player and finally lashing out £750,000 for David Speedie of Coventry. Earlier in the season he had signed Tony Cousins, the Irish Under-21 international from Dundalk and Don Hutchison of Hartlepool. But what Liverpool probably needed was a central defender to hold together a creaking defence. David Speedie, for all the criticism levelled at his surprise transfer, made an immediate impact, scoring on his debut at Old Trafford to give Liverpool a deserved draw. A week later he was on the scoresheet again, netting a couple as Liverpool powered to a 3–1 win over Everton to ease three points clear at the top of the table.

But it was victory at a cost as Ronnie Whelan paid with an injury that was to keep him out for the remainder of the season. The following week the two old rivals met again, this time in the fifth round of the FA Cup, where they fought out a goalless draw. But, sadly, there were further injury problems as Steve McMahon limped off to be sidelined for the rest of the campaign. Three days later the two teams faced each other at Goodison Park in what was to be one of the most momentous games in Liverpool's history. Many reckoned it was the finest Cup tie seen since the war. Liverpool were never behind and most of the time had their noses in front, but last-minute equalisers by Everton in both normal and extra time took the tie to a third game. It ended 4–4, with Peter Beardsley, making his first appearance in months, twice on the scoresheet. But the question being asked by fans was how Liverpool could so easily concede four goals. What nobody knew, however, as they watched enthralled was that this was to be Kenny Dalglish's final game in charge of Liverpool.

The following morning Dalglish broke the news to Liverpool chairman Noel White and, at a hurriedly arranged press conference the next day, Friday 22

February, Dalglish told the football world that he could no longer continue as manager of Liverpool – the strain was too much, he was exhausted, for once he was putting himself before Liverpool. The news came as a bombshell. Nobody could believe it. It was like history repeating itself as minds flashed back to the day Bill Shankly had calmly announced his retirement. Liverpool supporters everywhere were stunned. After almost six years in charge that had brought Liverpool the double and two more league triumphs, Dalglish was quitting Anfield. He was not even waiting until the end of the season. He was going that morning, leaving the team at the penultimate stage of the season without a manager.

Dalglish's contribution to the Anfield story is almost without parallel, ranking alongside the great Scots of Liverpool's history – Raisbeck, Liddell and Shankly. As

Surprise signing David Speedie made an instant impact for the Reds after his £750,000 transfer.

a player, arriving in 1977, he had gone on to help Liverpool clinch a galaxy of silverware that included five league championships, three European Cups and four League Cups. Then, taking over from Joe Fagan in May 1985 in the aftermath of the Heysel disaster, he steered the club to a league and cup double in his first season in charge. Two seasons later they almost clinched a second double, winning the league title but going down to Wimbledon at Wembley. And then, the following season, in the wake of the Hillsborough tragedy, Dalglish managed Liverpool to another Cup triumph, again over Everton, before losing the league title to a last-minute goal against Arsenal. Finally, in 1990, came a third league championship as Liverpool took their revenge. With a record number of caps and goals for Scotland, Dalglish was rated one of the finest footballers since the war. Liverpool were indeed lucky to have had his services. But now, after 14 years, he was gone and Liverpool would simply have to cope without him.

Kenny Dalglish faces a barrage of questions from the press following his shock resignation.

Not surprisingly, they did not cope well. Twenty-four hours after his resignation they lost 3–1 at Luton. A few days later they were out of the Cup as Everton won their fifth round replay by the game's only goal. That was followed by a 1–0 defeat at Anfield by Arsenal. Three defeats in a week and the loss of a manager; it marked the turning point in Liverpool's season. Arsenal were now three points ahead in the title race, but, as if that were not enough, a week after Dalglish's resignation, Alan Hansen announced his retirement. There had been some press stories about Hansen taking over from Dalglish, but, having long decided his future was outside football, Hansen announced his retirement before the speculation increased. Like Dalglish, Hansen had enjoyed a long and distinguished career at Anfield. Arriving from Partick Thistle in April 1977 for £100,000 he had gone on to play more than 600 games in Liverpool's defence. A tall, calm, elegant figure, Hansen had been one of the most formidable defenders in English football. Capped 26 times by Scotland he was also one of the most honoured players in soccer, collecting 17 medals that included eight league championships, four League Cup, three

European Cup and two FA Cup. The loss of Dalglish and Hansen brought to an end an era of incomparable honours that will forever be difficult to emulate.

For the time being, the Liverpool managerial seat remained vacant. Ronnie Moran gallantly stepped into the fray as caretaker manager and there were rumours about the possibility of John Toshack returning to Anfield. But, as events later showed, the Anfield board had long decided on Dalglish's successor. Before any announcement was made, Liverpool surprisingly jumped back to the top of the table with a thoroughly undeserved win over Manchester City at Maine Road, thanks to a couple of dubious penalty decisions. A week later they beat Sunderland 2–1 at Anfield, though again it was hardly deserved. But you certainly could not say that about their next result, as they thrashed Derby County 7–1 at the Baseball Ground in one of the club's best-ever away wins. Liverpool, thanks to a considerable degree of fortune, were still in with a chance for the title but all that evaporated in one of Liverpool's worst Easter periods for many a year. A defeat at home by QPR and then defeat at Southampton followed by a 1–1 draw at Anfield with Coventry virtually wiped out any remaining hopes of Liverpool retaining the title. Arsenal stormed ahead in the race, with the gaps in Liverpool's defence now the talking point of the terraces. The following week the problem was again emphasised as Liverpool let slip a 4–0 lead at Elland Road to see Leeds United almost snatch a draw. But in the end the Yorkshiremen lost 5–4.

Within days of that result, news leaked out that Liverpool were about to appoint their new manager and the surprise was that it was to be old boy Graeme Souness. Although Souness's name had been mentioned early on as a possible successor, he had immediately dampened any speculation with a strong denial and a firm commitment to Glasgow Rangers. Souness appeared to be firmly entrenched at Ibrox, with a seat on the board, a large shareholding and a high salary. But Liverpool knew the man they wanted and kept plugging away until he eventually reconsidered. The intention was for Souness to take over at the end of the season, but, with news leaking out and Rangers, to say the least, not too happy, it was decided to make a public announcement. Within the day Souness had packed his bags and was back at Anfield in time to take charge of their fixture with Norwich. There were immediate changes. Glenn Hysen was dropped and Jan Molby was given the role of sweeper. It worked, Liverpool ran out 3–0 winners, though it was clear they were still desperately missing McMahon and Whelan. The good news of Souness's appointment was followed by more welcome news, this time from UEFA, who announced that, after a six-year ban from European football, Liverpool could be re-admitted to European competition the following season. All they had to do now was to finish either first or second.

They took a major step to finishing as runners-up by defeating third-placed Crystal Palace 3–0 at Anfield. The title was still a mathematical possibility, although by now it meant relying on Arsenal losing. But, in their next game, Liverpool crashed 4–2 at Stamford Bridge having pulled back a two-goal deficit to level the scores. It was typical of Liverpool's season that they should then concede two more goals. The title race ended conclusively two days later when Liverpool visited Nottingham Forest and lost 2–1. Arsenal were crowned league champions later that evening and Liverpool had to be content with second spot.

The tongues had been wagging about Liverpool's performances since January. Dalglish's reluctance to play either Peter Beardsley or Ronnie Rosenthal mystified many pundits, while the defence was leaking goals like a side fighting off relegation. Fortunately their forwards compensated, scoring 77 goals, the highest in the first division. Ian Rush was again leading scorer with 26 goals while John Barnes struck 19. There was also much talk of Liverpool's ageing stars and the club's inability to discover new young talent. But much of this criticism was misplaced. The loss of Whelan and McMahon had been crucial, far more significant in many ways than the resignation of Dalglish. On top of this they had, in recent years, lost the service of some of football's finest defenders in Phil Neal, Mark Lawrenson and now Alan Hansen, while injury had limited Gary Gillespie's appearances. Replacing them was an impossible task. Souness was probably correct when he argued that it was Liverpool who had lost the title rather than Arsenal who had won it. Prior to Dalglish's resignation they had been beaten just twice, but after his departure and the injuries to Whelan and McMahon the Reds lost seven of their remaining 15 fixtures. So, the title went to north London, but with Graeme Souness promising to embark on a major rebuilding programme, most expected that it would not be long before the title returned to Anfield.

Old boy Graeme Souness and Ronnie Moran celebrate a goal during Souness's first match in charge.

21

DECLINE AND FALL

1991–92

Graeme Souness' style was about change. At Ibrox he had swept aside the old order and replaced it with a new attitude. He had had his problems, especially with the authorities, but he had widened the horizons of Rangers, bringing fresh ideas and vision to the club. Liverpool also had to adapt to the times, he said shortly after arriving, adding that the world had moved on since Shankly and there was no point in thinking back to those days or trying to recapture them.

Souness had been influenced by Sampdoria and Italian football but he was to forget that Liverpool had more than proved themselves. As winners of so many European trophies, they were already on equal playing terms with their great continental counterparts.

As the 1991–92 season kicked off there was little doubt as to who were the favourites to lift the title. During the close season Souness had swooped into the transfer market with a double deal, as potentially exciting as any Anfield had seen in years.

Liverpool had been eyeing Derby County's Mark Wright for some time. Desperately short of a central defender following the sudden retirement of Alan Hansen, Liverpool realised the signing a top-class defender was a priority. England international Mark Wright was the obvious choice. It was common knowledge that he was to leave Derby at the end of the season and Liverpool were always favourites for his signature. Wright duly signed in July 1991 for a fee of £2.2 million. It looked an astute signing.

At the time that Derby County were unloading Wright there were hints that they might also sell their Welsh international striker Dean Saunders, especially as they had just been relegated. All the press talk linked him to other clubs, with Everton the firm favourites to sign him. Liverpool already boasted Ian Rush, Peter Beardsley, John Barnes and Ronny Rosenthal for the two spots

£2.2 million signing Mark Wright battles with Sunderland's Peter Davenport in the 1992 FA Cup Final.

upfront. They hardly needed an additional striker. But Souness was keen, spurred on by the interest of other clubs. As the Wright deal was nearing completion it suddenly developed into a double-deal as Souness dramatically put in an offer of £2.9 million to bring a second Derby County player to Anfield, the most expensive player in Liverpool's history.

There is no doubt that the signing of Saunders sent a shiver of anticipation through the city. After all Saunders had a proven track record as a prolific goalscorer. His father, Roy Saunders, had once played for Liverpool and with his Welsh international striking partner Rush set to play alongside him, it seemed that Saunders would find Anfield to be his natural home.

To pay for the outlay on Wright and Saunders, Souness surprised almost everyone by selling Kop favourite Peter Beardsley to neighbours Everton a few weeks later. Beardsley had not enjoyed the best of seasons in 1990–91 and had looked a shadow of the player he was when he first arrived at Anfield, but nevertheless it seemed a rash move to off-load him, especially when the asking price was a mere £1 million. Souness argued that at 30 years of age Beardsley was at the back end of his career and that the club needed to invest in youth. At his best, Beardsley was one of the most exciting players in British football. In 131 League appearances for Liverpool he had scored 46 goals, and memories of the way he linked up with John Barnes and John Aldridge will live forever with Liverpool fans. Beardsley never really settled at Everton and soon found himself returning to Newcastle where he took on a new lease of life, even winning further international honours.

Also shown the door was Steve Staunton, the young Irish full back. In another surprise move he was sold to Aston Villa for £1.1 million, having made 65 League appearances for the Reds. The transfer of Staunton seemed especially puzzling given that he was only 22 and the emphasis was supposed to be on youth. Staunton had shown considerable promise as an attacking full back and over the next few years would prove time and again that Liverpool should never have sold him. The transfer of Gary Gillespie and David Speedie, however, did seem to make sense. Gillespie was sold to Glasgow Celtic for almost £1 million. Given his injury problems, and especially the price Liverpool negotiated, Gillespie's departure was not surprising. At his best Gillespie could hold his own in any Liverpool defence but sadly his career was dogged by injury and he never quite fulfilled his promise. The sale of Speedie was also understandable. He was sold to Blackburn for £500,000.

With their new signings Dean Saunders up front to give them added variety and Mark Wright at the back to

Dean Saunders became the most expensive player in Liverpool's history when he signed for £2.9 million from Derby.

strengthen their one weak area, Liverpool began the season as favourites to capture Arsenal's crown. They made a promising start, even though they lost their second fixture; after half a dozen games they were in second place. But by then the injuries were beginning to mount. The first to limp off was John Barnes in the second game, followed almost immediately by Mark Wright. A few games later Ronnie Whelan joined them.

Mike Marsh scores against Auxerre in the second leg of the UEFA Cup. Liverpool went through 3–2.

To solve their long term injury problems Souness dipped into the transfer market again. Days before the season kicked off Souness had returned to his old club Glasgow Rangers to sign Mark Walters for £1.25 million. The former Aston Villa winger, with one international cap to his credit, began the season as substitute but once Barnes was injured he quickly found himself drafted into the side. Next to arrive, in September, was Rob Jones from Crewe Alexandra for £300,000. Jones made his debut in the cauldron of Old Trafford but gave a magnificent performance in a goalless draw against United. Although questions were being asked about Souness' early signings – Saunders, Wright and Walters – it was clear that in Rob Jones he had uncovered a gem. It would not be long before Jones was pulling on an England shirt.

By the end of September, Liverpool had lost a second game and had slipped into mid-table as Manchester United and Leeds began to open a gap at the top. Two months later Liverpool's position had barely improved. They had won a mere five of their fifteen League games, drawn seven and lost three. The pattern had been set. Autumn was barely over and Liverpool were already fourteen points off the top and well out of contention. In

previous seasons Liverpool sides might have been able to pull back that sort of gap but with so many injuries and new players it was not now a realistic prospect.

Michael Thomas also joined the club, signed from Arsenal for £1.5 million in December 1991. It was a signing that raised a few eyebrows. It was not that the fans had no respect for his undoubted talents but they retained the memory of his last-minute goal at Anfield in the final match of the 1988–89 season, a goal that robbed Liverpool of a second successive double. It was a painful memory although by the end of the season Thomas would have helped ease the pain a little. In January Souness returned to Scotland to make another signing, this time to buy the Hungarian international Istvan Kozma from Dunfermline at a cost of £300,000. There was one more notable signing: Lee Jones from Wrexham for £300,000. By the end of the season Graeme Souness had invested £8.7 million in eight talented new players.

This season Liverpool were back in Europe. The ban on English clubs competing in Europe following the

Heysel Disaster had been lifted the previous season, although Liverpool had been forced to serve a further year's ban. As runners-up in the League Championship Liverpool had been rewarded with a place in the UEFA Cup, a tournament they had twice won in the past. But this was a far different Liverpool. They began with a 6-1 pasting of Kuusysi Lahti at Anfield. The scoreline looked impressive on paper but it was not until the last 15 minutes that the Finns fell apart. Saunders, who had looked out of place and had managed only two goals so far that season, hit four against the Finns and eased a few anxious minds on the Kop. In the second leg Liverpool lost 1-0, an embarrassment even if it hardly mattered. In the next round they faced Auxerre of France and again went down in the away tie, this time 2-0. It looked to be all over for Liverpool but in the second leg, in front of a flag-waving, noisy Kop, they pulled off a remakable 3-0 win. It was one of the finest European victories at Anfield since the dramatic win over St Etienne.

Liverpool's season looked to be on course again, but only until they went to Third Division Peterborough United for a Rumbelows Cup game and were humiliated, losing 1-0. By then Mark Wright had returned from injury though John Barnes would come back only briefly before injury again struck while Ronnie Whelan would be sidelined for the rest of the campaign. Rush was also injured and missed more than 20 games after a cartilage operation, and Jan Molby was out for ten weeks following a similar operation. By the end of the season Liverpool had used 26 players in total in League matches.

Liverpool's European campaign continued with a comfortable win over Swarovski Tirol of Austria with Saunders hitting five goals in all. Liverpool's exploits in the UEFA Cup finally came to an abrupt end in March when they faced Genoa in the fourth round. In Italy, where they had enjoyed so many triumphs, Liverpool were totally outclassed, losing 2-0. Back home there were hopes of another fightback but instead quality triumphed again as the Italians had the audacity to come to Anfield and win 2-1; it was only the fourth time Liverpool had lost a European tie at Anfield in 25 years.

Liverpool eventually wound up in sixth spot in the League, 18 points behind champions Leeds United, having lost 10 games and drawn 16. Saunders was top scorer with ten League goals. It was many years since a Liverpool top scorer had managed only ten goals, although Saunders had scored another nine goals in his five European outings. The one success of the season was undoubtedly Steve McManaman, a teenage winger. A Dalglish signing, he began the season in fine style with

Graeme Souness walks out at Wembley after his heart bypass operation, accompanied by his doctor.

his exciting runs and although he tired in mid-season he was to end it with a glorious performance at Wembley and a Cup winner's medal that promised much for his future at the club.

For while the League was slipping from Liverpool's grasp, hope was rising elsewhere. In the FA Cup the luck of the draw found them facing lower division opponents. Crewe Alexandra, Bristol Rovers and Ipswich were all dealt with – the last two forcing replays – before Liverpool faced a First Division outfit, and then, as luck would have it, they were drawn at Anfield. Aston Villa were their opponents and a 1–0 victory was enough to set up a semi-final against Second Division Portsmouth. The first game was drawn 1–1 at Highbury with Liverpool riding their luck through a late equaliser.

Before the replay took place came the astonishing news that manager Graeme Souness had suffered a mild heart attack and was about to enter hospital for an emergency bypass operation. Souness' condition immediately raised a question mark over his future and whether he would be able to continue as manager of a top club like Liverpool.

Liverpool had barely deserved a second chance against Pompey and in the replay they pushed their luck again. Portsmouth were desperately unlucky not to win but after a goalless 90 minutes followed by a further goalless period of extra time, the match went to a penalty shoot out. The drama was sky high with a place at Wembley at stake, but for once in the season the Liverpool sharpshooters did their work. Liverpool were into their tenth FA Cup final, 3–1 on penalties. Souness had listened to the game from his hospital bed and now the question being asked was whether he would be able to lead his side out at Wembley.

FA Cup Final 1992 Liverpool v Sunderland

In the final Liverpool found themselves facing yet another Second Division side. Sunderland had reached the final with fine wins over Port Vale, Oxford United, West Ham, Chelsea and Norwich. Liverpool had met four lower division sides en route to Wembley, most of them offering stubborn opposition, and Sunderland with their famous cup-fighting pedigree were enough to

Ian Rush scores Liverpool's second goal in the 1992 FA Cup Final, which Liverpool won 2–0.

frighten even the best of competition. Yet surprisingly, Sunderland offered the least resistance of any of the opponents Liverpool were to meet in the FA Cup competition that season.

Liverpool arrived at Wembley not only worried about their manager's health but minus John Barnes. While Ronnie Moran lead the side out, Souness sat on the bench with his doctor ready to restrain him.

Liverpool kicked off brightly enough but as the first half wore on Sunderland began to look more confident. The Wearsiders possibly edged the first period against a docile Liverpool midfield but there was not too much to choose between them. The match changed when Souness, taking over the managerial reins in the dressing room, switched Steve McManaman to the right wing. McManaman was a revelation, carving holes in the Sunderland back four. Goals were inevitable. The first came from new signing Michael Thomas with a glorious volley that helped erase memories of his goal for Arsenal that robbed Liverpool of the Championship. The second Liverpool goal arrived via old boy Ian Rush. It was enough to give Graeme Souness' men a comfortable 2 – 0 win. It had taken Liverpool nine games to win their fifth FA Cup. Liverpool might not have won the League but they were still winning trophies. Sadly, it would be the only trophy Souness would win in his three controversial years at Anfield.

Liverpool Grobbelaar, Jones, Burrows, Nicol, Molby, Wright, Saunders, Houghton, Rush, McManaman, Thomas.
Sunderland Norman, Owers, Ball, Bennett, Rogan, Rush, (Hardyman), Bracewell, Davenport, Armstrong, Byrne, Atkinson (Hawke).

Although Liverpool had won the FA Cup, it was clear that all was not well and the performance of Souness in his first season as manager came under close scrutiny.

Within days of his arrival at Anfield, Souness had introduced his first major change. No other Liverpool manager had ever brought his own assistant with him. When Shankly had arrived at the club he had met the bootroom staff and told them that their jobs were safe. Over the years new faces were introduced as old hands retired but the changes were always from within and never disruptive. Shankly brought Roy Evans into the bootroom; Dalglish introduced Phil Thompson and Steve Heighway but only gently and never giving them any authority over first team affairs, despite all their experience of Anfield. But Souness' first decision was to introduce Phil Boersma into his set up.

Boersma had been a Liverpool player from 1965 to

Steve McManaman emerged as one of the most promising home-grown talents during 1991–92.

1975, when Bob Paisley had sold him to Middlesbrough for £72,000. At Middlesbrough Boersma met Graeme Souness. He later teamed up with some former Liverpool colleagues at Swansea but retired from football in April 1981. He trained as a physiotherapist and then found himself invited to join his old pal Graeme Souness at Ibrox. When Souness came to Anfield Boersma came as part of the package with a position that put into question the roles of Moran, Evans and Thompson. The pecking order became confused.

181

Souness was also trying out new techniques on the training field. Schedules that had been practised in Genoa and refined at Ibrox might have worked in those places, but nobody could see the sense of changing things at Anfield when their own system had been so successful over the years. Melwood became a more important place in the Souness era. He had seen the set-ups in Italian soccer where everything revolved around the training camp. As a result the club transferred all its training and medical facilities to Melwood. But it was a move that meant an important break with tradition.

It was also during the first full season of Souness' rule that injuries began to dog the club, mounting each week until they reached a peak in 1993. Nobody could ever recall so many. Liverpool had always been a club that had prided itself on turning out the same eleven players week after week. It was one of the club's greatest strengths with continuity vital to its success. Over the years Liverpool had rarely used more than 20 players a season. Indeed in the 30 years between 1960 and 1990 they had used more than 20 players on only a handful of occasions and in 1965–66 had used only 14 men in the entire season. The new trend was to get so bad however, that in the 1993–94 season Liverpool used 21 players in the first dozen League games. It was impossible to pick the same 11 men for two matches running. The chopping and changing inevitably had an effect. The Liverpool style of accurate passing and intelligent running off the ball became impossible.

It had never been Liverpool's policy to blame poor results on injuries yet even Souness was forced to concede that the spate of injuries were dictating his season almost from day one. Young players, like McManaman had to be blooded far sooner than was ideal and were forced to continue turning out week after week when really they should have been given the occasional rest.

Injuries also forced Souness into the transfer market all too readily in search of replacements and quick solutions, only adding to the confusion. It was clear that once the injured were fit, Liverpool would have a squad of 20 or so first team players. The wages bill of simply maintaining the squad alone was now exceeding £5 million a year.

Inevitably, before the season was out other players had left Anfield. The most surprising was Steve McMahon, who was sold to Manchester City for £900,000 in

OPPOSITE: David James gathers a high ball in a 1–0 victory over Arsenal at Highbury.

ABOVE: Paul Stewart joined Liverpool from Spurs for £2.5 million as a replacement for Steve McMahon.

December. McMahon had been the iron in Liverpool's midfield, playing more than 200 League games for the club. A Liverpool lad, he had arrived at Anfield from Aston Villa, having kicked off his career with Everton. McMahon had been the natural replacement for Graeme Souness and over the years was to give more than his share of fully committed performances, becoming a vital member of the side. Souness argued, as with Beardsley, that McMahon was on the wrong side of 30, yet McMahon was still playing three years later and with as much gusto as he had shown at Anfield.

Three other players left. They were Jimmy Carter,

Norwegian international defender Stig Bjørnebye was signed by Souness in autumn 1992.

players had been signed for £8.7 million and eight players had been offloaded, bringing in £5.65 million. Anfield had seen nothing like it since the first few months of Bill Shankly's reign. But at least at the end of the season Liverpool had the FA Cup back in their trophy room and there was still plenty of optimism that once all the injuries had been resolved Liverpool would again be challenging for the League title.

For Graeme Souness the season ended on a sour note. Following his heart bypass operation he had sold his story to *The Sun*, a paper scorned on Merseyside for its appalling coverage of the Hillsborough disaster. The article about Souness appeared on the third anniversary of the tragedy. It was hardly sensitive and there was outrage. Letters poured into the club and local newspaper offices. To his credit Souness immediately apologised and donated his fee to the Alder Hey Children's hospital. But that was not the end of the affair. Remarks about Souness' behaviour were now being made privately by some club directors and three days after the Cup final Souness appeared before the board to explain himself. One director was calling for his resignation. In the end the board decided to give Souness the benefit of the doubt, accepting that although it had been a difficult year, they had just won the FA Cup. But it was apparent that all was not well inside Anfield. Souness had had his knuckles rapped and there was open and persistent speculation about how long he could remain in charge.

1992–93

Just as the 1991–92 season had opened with so much optimism, so too did the following season. There had been a few encouraging signings, including David James, the young Watford goalkeeper, who had arrived during the close season for £1.3 million as the eventual successor to Bruce Grobbelaar. A few weeks after signing James, Liverpool had snapped up Paul Stewart, the Spurs midfielder for £2.5million. Stewart had begun his footballing career with Blackpool before joining Manchester City. Tottenham had paid £1.7 million for him and successfully converted him into a midfielder. In search of some desperately needed midfield bite after the sale of Steve McMahon, Souness decided that Stewart might be the man for the role. He was looking to Stewart to perform the same role as Ray Kennedy had done so well, picking up the loose chances in and around the edge of the area. But it quickly became clear that Stewart was no Kennedy. Stewart was dropped, injured, returned to the first team and dropped again.

The summer also saw the departure of a couple more players. The most surprising was Ray Houghton, who

generally regarded as a panic signing by Dalglish. Carter was sold to Arsenal for £500,000, having made only five League appearances for Liverpool. Full back Gary Ablett was also sold, joining Everton for £750,000, while the stylish Glenn Hysen returned to Sweden on a free transfer muttering about dressing room rows at Anfield.

All this activity brought great change to Anfield. Eight

had enjoyed a particularly productive season. Indeed he was the one Liverpool player who had looked consistent throughout the campaign. But now Houghton was gone, sold to Aston Villa for the knock down price of £850,000. Over the years Houghton had proved an inspired buy, working feverishly in the midfield. He had provided width to the attack and commitment in defence in more than 150 League games for the club.

Another veteran saying goodbye to Anfield was full back Barry Venison who, after missing the early part of the previous season through injury, had returned to play a useful role. Venison was a strong attacking full back who had taken over from Phil Neal and his sale to Newcastle seemed puzzling. Liverpool received only £250,000, and four years later Venison would be the dynamo of the Newcastle midfield, winning international honours.

There was another departure that was to cause increasing tremors as the months wore on. It was the sacking of Phil Thompson as reserve team coach. Former captain and Kop favourite Thompson had been drafted in by Dalglish to replace Chris Lawler in 1986. He had proved to be a popular choice and many of the youngsters he had been coaching had made the breakthrough into the first team. But in the summer of 1992 Souness decided to dispense with his services. It was to be an acrimonious parting and was public recognition that all was not well behind the scenes.

After six games of the new season, Liverpool had only one win to their credit. After ten games they had lost five and drawn three and had managed only one more win. David James, who had arrived at Anfield expecting little to do, found himself picking the ball out of the net four times against Villa. It was an appalling start; their League campaign was over virtually before it had begun. In the past Liverpool had recovered from unimpressive starts. But anyone watching Liverpool in the autumn of 1992 knew that this was not the Liverpool of the 1970s and 1980s. In fact the side was in serious trouble, hovering just above the relegation zone.

During the autumn Souness, searching frantically for further defensive cover, ventured abroad, first to sign the Dane Torben Piechnik and then the Norwegian Stig Inge Bjornebye. Both were international players, yet neither looked particularly impressive in the red of Liverpool. The players sold seemed every bit as good as those being bought.

To finance these deals Souness decided to cut his losses with Dean Saunders. The transfer had not worked out. Saunders seemed to lack that vital first touch. The statistics told the tale. In 42 League appearances Saunders had scored only 11 goals. Ron Atkinson, the

Jamie Redknapp shouldered considerable midfield responsibility as an injury crisis hit Liverpool.

manager of Aston Villa, came in with a £2.3 million offer and Saunders was off to join ex-Liverpool stars Staunton and Houghton at Villa Park.

Almost without saying, there were further injuries. John Barnes had damaged his Achilles tendon, this time while on international duty during the summer, and did not put in an appearance until the end of November.

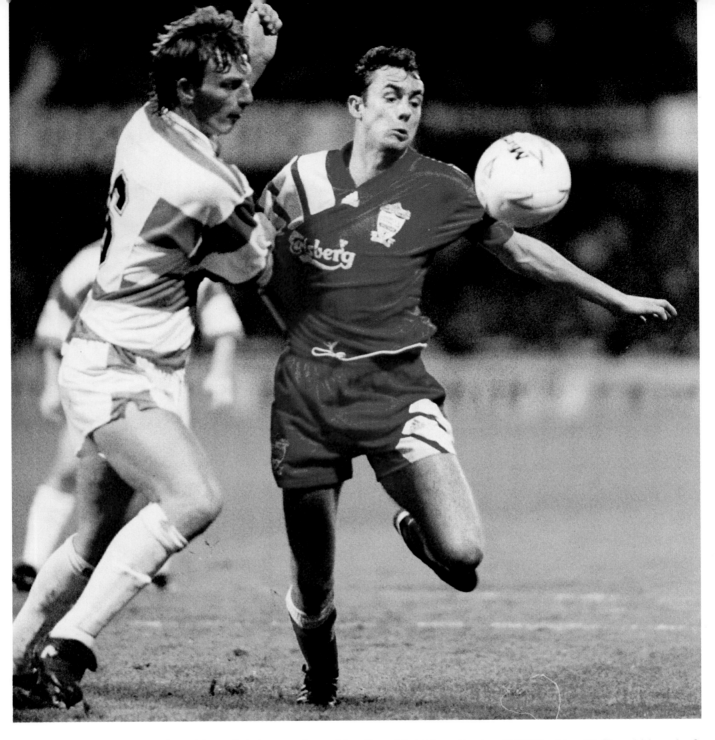

Don Hutchison fends off QPR's Alan McDonald in a 1–0 victory at Loftus Road.

Rob Jones was absent with a shin split injury and would also be out of action until shortly before Christmas. Ronnie Whelan had reappeared briefly at the beginning of the season, only to be injured yet again. Michael Thomas would also miss large chunks of the season as would Mark Wright, Jan Molby, David Burrows and new boy Paul Stewart. It was left to a crop of emerging youngsters to hold the team together. Steve McManaman continued to make positive progress, as did Jamie Redknapp, while Mike Marsh, Steve Harkness and Don Hutchison were all developed steadily. In all 25 players would be used in the League that season.

If the League looked a lost cause from the beginning, there was still Europe. After their Cup triumph of the previous season Liverpool went into the draw for the European Cup Winners Cup, the one European trophy they had never won. They began with an effortless 6–1 win at Anfield over Limassol, followed by a 2–1 win in Cyprus. But in the next leg they faced Spartak Moscow and suffered one of the most depressing defeats in the club's many European campaigns. Spartak won 4–2 in Moscow after Bruce Grobbelaar had been shown a red card. Graeme Souness made matters worse when he voiced his disapproval to the referee. Back at Anfield, Souness cranked the Kop into action, hoping for a repeat of the Auxerre result of the previous season. Liverpool began promisingly but faded when the early goal failed to materialise. In the end Spartak won 2–0.

By Christmas Liverpool were out of the Coca-Cola Cup, beaten by Crystal Palace, and by mid-January they were also out of the FA Cup, humbled 2–0 at Anfield by Bolton Wanderers in one of the biggest Cup upsets in years. Liverpool had a habit of drawing against lowly opposition away from Anfield in the Cup but always snatching victory at home. This time it would be different. Bolton outclassed them both at Burnden Park and at Anfield.

Liverpool's season was effectively over. The New Year had just begun and they had nothing to play for, except avoiding relegation. In the end they dragged themselves clear of the relegation zone to finish in a respectable sixth place, thanks to a spirited end of season run of only three defeats in their final dozen games, though in fact they finished only ten points away from relegation. The highlight of the season came in the final game when they trounced Tottenham 6–2 in front of a packed Anfield. Souness was absent, his resignation seemingly imminent.

Liverpool had lost 15 games and won only 16, with Ian Rush as top scorer with 15 League goals. What made it all worse was that Manchester United topped the League, a massive 25 points ahead of Liverpool.

There is an old saying at Anfield: 'first is first, second is nowhere'. In May 1993 the knives were out for Souness. It wasn't just that Liverpool had ended the season without a trophy or that they had failed to qualify for Europe for the first time in 30 years. It was simply the way they were playing. Souness was as baffled as anyone. There was no doubt that the glut of injuries had not helped matters but the biggest concern was why so many of the manager's signings had failed to deliver. Huge amounts of money had been spent to revive the team with almost £5 million spent that season alone. In all the manager had so far paid out £13.5 million on new players. Yet, instead of improving, Liverpool seemed to be getting worse.

It was just as bad off the field. The bootroom, the very soul of the club, had been knocked down to make way for a new press room and although they built a new bootroom, further down the corridor, it would never be the same. And if the bootroom was the soul of Liverpool Football Club, then its heart was the Kop. The Taylor Report, following the Hillsborough disaster, had ruled that Premiership clubs had to provide all-seater stadiums for the start of the 1994–95 season. Nobody really liked the idea of tearing down the Kop but it was incumbent

Souness, Boersma and Moran on the bench. Roy Evans replaced Boersma as Souness' number two.

on Liverpool to set an example. Plans were drawn up to build a new all-seater Kop. Fans campaigned against the decision, but they knew that they were fighting a losing battle. It seemed that their part in the years of glory was being snatched from under their feet.

David Moores, now installed as chairman of the board, had accumulated a majority shareholding in the club through a series of share issues which he had underwritten. Eventually he would end up with more than 50 per cent of the club's shares, making him not only by far the largest shareholder but in effect the owner of Liverpool Football Club. It was the first time in its history that Liverpool had virtually been in the hands of one individual, and was another cause of public dissatisfaction and anxiety.

Souness' departure looked inevitable. Shortly before the end of the season the board met and took a decision to end the manager's contract. But it was not quite so easy. It would be an expensive business and there was no obvious successor in line. Kevin Keegan insisted that he was not interested and Kenny Dalglish also rejected a return. Confronted by these problems, and Souness' insistence on seeing out his contract, the board met on more than one occasion in an attempt to resolve matters. Finally the board changed its mind and decided to give the manager one last shot, but on the condition that Roy

Nigel Clough joined Liverpool from Forest after the Nottingham club were relegated.

Evans stepped up and became his number two, the first assistant manager in the club's history. Evans, who had for so long been serving his apprenticeship as a bootroom boy, was now clearly in line for the top job. It simply seemed a case of how long it would be before he took over as manager.

1993–94

After almost 30 years of unprecedented success, Liverpool were now beginning to realise what it was like to be just one of the pack. Before it could get any better it was destined to get worse. And yet, Liverpool got off to a good start, winning their three opening fixtures of the 1993–4 season to go top of the Premiership.

The season opened with Sheffield Wednesday beaten at Anfield, followed by Queens Park Rangers, beaten 3–1 at Loftus Road. And then newly promoted Swindon were trounced 5–0 on their own ground. Liverpool were back where they belonged at the top of the table and it looked as if manager Graeme Souness had finally turned the corner. His success was largely down to two men, Nigel Clough and Neil Ruddock.

Clough had all the hallmarks of a Liverpool player. Thoughtful, full of commonsense and commitment, he seemed certain to introduce a dash of flair to the attack. A move to Anfield had been widely predicted, and with Forest just relegated, Souness spent £2.75 million on the England international. It looked as if Liverpool had struck gold with Clough off to a roaring start, scoring four goals in his first four games. But apart from an inspired second half against Manchester United later, he would suffer bitter disappointment. Before the season was over he had been substituted, dropped and injured with open talk of either swapping him or selling him. Clough, like so many of Souness' signings, had arrived with a sky-high reputation only to look mediocre soon after pulling on a red shirt.

Weeks after signing Clough, Souness also snapped up Neil Ruddock, the Tottenham central defender for £2.5 million. The combative Ruddock had experienced a mixed career with Millwall, Tottenham and Southampton, often marred by an alarming lack of discipline followed by frequent suspensions.

With talk of championship trophies in the air, more than 42,000 turned out at Anfield for the fourth game of the season, the visit of Tottenham. But dreams of the title were to be shortlived. Liverpool went down 2–1 and within ten days they had suffered a second defeat. They had been toppled from their perch at the top of the table and seen Manchester United draw clear of them. Then when Kenny Dalglish's Blackburn Rovers arrived at Anfield, Liverpool came a cropper again, going down to their third defeat and their second at home. Seven games played and three defeats already. It may have been too early to write off their title dreams but it meant that they could not afford to lose more than a couple more games all season.

But there was another disturbing development. Over the years Liverpool had had hard players like Tommy Smith, Jimmy Case and even Graeme Souness, but they had never set out to destroy their opponents with physical intimidation. But suddenly all that had changed. Rob Jones had been sent off in the defeat at Coventry and now he was being shown another yellow card after flashing his studs at a Blackburn player. And to make matters worse, in the same game new signing Neil Ruddock was seen dashing 20 yards to have his say and swing a punch. It all resulted in a major confrontation as players measured up to each other. Such scenes had not been witnessed at Anfield for decades. It was not in the Liverpool tradition.

It seemed that Graeme Souness was encouraging his players to 'get stuck in' and show some mettle. Or perhaps the cause was frustration born out of their own failings. Liverpool were no longer invincible at Anfield and they did not like it.

In the past the solution might have been to slap a few culprits into line. Instead Liverpool supporters woke up days later to read that their manager had put in a bid for Julian Dicks of West Ham, a defender whose disciplinary record was, to say the least, appalling. He had been sent off on eight occasions and had collected dozens of yellow cards. The prospect of Ruddock and Dicks in the Liverpool defence might have frightened a few strikers but it only dismayed Liverpool supporters. The deal was soon confirmed and to make matters worse, David Burrows and Mike Marsh were going in the opposite direction. It may have been necessary to unload players but few could see the sense in the departure of Burrows and Marsh.

Burrows had arrived at Anfield as a teenager, recruited by Dalglish from West Bromwich Albion. Although he had never quite blossomed into the player he promised, there was a good argument for keeping him, at least as a utility player. There was an even better argument for hanging on to Mike Marsh. He had barely begun his first team career and was a bright prospect.

Dicks duly made his debut the following day at Goodison Park in the Merseyside Derby. Liverpool lost 2−0 with what was undoubtedly their poorest performance so far that season. Time and again Everton cut through the midfield with the new defence exposed. But there was worse than this. Two Liverpool players should have been sent off for fighting. Astonishingly they were fighting each other. After Everton's opening strike goalkeeper Bruce Grobbelaar laid into midfielder Steve McManaman for failing to deal with a ball close to the edge of the area. Cottee had leapt on the ball for Ward to rifle it into the net. It was hardly McManaman's fault but Grobbelaar told him in no uncertain terms who was to blame. A punch was swung, McManaman retaliated and a disgraceful scene was captured for millions to watch later that evening on television.

Souness answered his critics with drastic action. Ronnie Whelan found himself transfer-listed while Steve Nicol, Steve McManaman and Mark Walters were relegated to the substitutes' bench. For Whelan it was humiliating after a long and distinguished Anfield career, it seemed unfair that he should have been forced to shoulder the blame. Over the years he had picked up a bagful of medals at Anfield and although he was not always popular on the terraces, the side had missed his thoughtful distribution and tackling back in defence during his enforced absence through injury. The decision effectively marked the end of his Liverpool career. The following year he joined Southend United.

Souness snapped up Neil Ruddock, the Spurs central defender, for £2.5 million.

Initially the wholesale changes seemed to improve matters as Liverpool travelled to London to take on Fulham in the Coca-Cola Cup. They won 3−1 although their victory had its share of anxious moments. The one success of Souness' purge was the introduction of the 18-year-old Robbie Fowler, who not only scored on his debut but gave a performance that showed much promise for the future. The following Saturday, however Liverpool came back down to earth with a bump as they returned to the capital to tackle a spirited Chelsea side. The Londoners won 1−0, although Liverpool deserved at least a draw. Luck was continuing to desert them as they plunged into the lower half of the table.

Liverpool suffered their worst September in 90 years, with not one League point to show for all their endeavours. With only nine games played they had already used 20 players. The goals had all but dried up and expensive new signing Nigel Clough was looking distinctly anonymous. The following week Liverpool entertained Arsenal and although Liverpool might well have pinched the points, in the end they had to settle for a goalless draw. By now they had gone five League games

ABOVE: Marsh (left) and Burrows (right) became part of the Liverpool–West Ham connection of the Souness years.
OPPOSITE: John Barnes returned to first team action after a long lay off through injury.

without a goal, their worst such run for 40 years. The record books were being rewritten every game.

The deadlock was finally broken two weeks later as they entertained relegation candidates Oldham at Anfield. Although Liverpool were to win, it was thanks only to a couple of goals in the last three minutes, including an own goal. Earlier they had fallen behind to an Oldham goal and had given a performance that many rated the poorest Anfield had seen since the unsuccessful pre-Shankly days.

Things could not get worse and Liverpool made steady progress up the table during the autumn without ever looking convincing. There always lurked the feeling that sooner or later their luck was going to run out. It finally did, at St James' Park. Within five minutes they were a goal down and after 30 minutes had conceded three as Newcastle tore them apart. It was embarrassing to watch, especially as Newcastle boasted three ex-Liverpool players – Venison, Hooper and Beardsley – all Souness cast-offs. Besides which, the side was managed by two other former Liverpool stars, Kevin Keegan and Terry McDermott.

Souness was quick to lay the blame on injuries. Admittedly he was only able to field one of his usual back

four. Jones, Dicks and Wright were all injuried. Dicks had been at the club only a few weeks and already he was limping. It had a depressing familiarity about it.

Two weeks later there was a repeat of the Newcastle humiliation as Sheffield Wednesday ran in three goals at Hillsborough, thanks to the remarkable generosity of the Liverpool defence. Sandwiched in between the Newcastle and Sheffield defeats were a painful victory over Aston Villa which owed more to luck than anything else and a fortuitous draw against Wimbledon in the Coca-Cola Cup at Anfield, when Liverpool plumbed new depths. If their win over Oldham had been talked of as one of their most bankrupt performances in a quarter of a century, then the game against Wimbledon plunged Kopites into deep gloom. In the second half Liverpool failed to even create a single opportunity. Their inconsistency was incomprehensible. After the defeat at Sheffield they returned to Anfield and in a mid-week fixture, played in driving rain and wind, produced some

Julian Dicks shuts out Arsenal's Kevin Campbell in a 0 – 0 draw at Anfield.

of their best football of the season to notch up a 3 – 2 win over Queens Park Rangers. Then four days later they lined up against bottom of the table Swindon, the team they had crushed at the County ground early in the season. Swindon, still searching for their first away win in the Premier League, showed few inhibitions at fortress Anfield. They even had the audacity to take the lead and only a looping Mark Wright header four minutes from time saved Liverpool from further humiliation as they hung on for a draw.

Souness was reported to be in despair. Throughout the month he had chopped and changed the line-up as he battled to find a solution. Rush, Clough, Stewart, Nicol, Redknapp and Dominic Matteo had all been dropped as he shuffled his pack around to find a winning hand. On the plus side John Barnes returned from his long lay off

but still the midfield seemed unable to create chances for the front runners. Steve McManaman also returned from injury but looked only half the player of two seasons before.

Predictably Liverpool fell to Wimbledon in the replayed Coca-Cola Cup tie at Selhurst Park with penalty misses once more playing their part. This time it was John Barnes missing from the spot in extra time when the scores were level, followed by Jamie Redknapp and Mark Walters who failed to make their spotkicks count in the penalty shoot out.

With Christmas still a fortnight away, Liverpool were out of the League and one cup competition, with only the FA Cup to play for. A third round away tie at Bristol City could not be regarded as a foregone conclusion, with the previous year's encounter with Bolton in mind.

Meanwhile Liverpool's dismissal from the Coca-Cola Cup inspired a further symphony of calls for Souness' resignation. But there were no indications from chairman David Moores that the manager's future might be in any doubt. In January, Ronny Rosenthal was sold to Tottenham for £250,000. Signed by Dalglish in the spring of 1990, he had provided the surge that clinched the Championship for Liverpool in his first season. After that he had trouble holding down a regular spot, especially under Souness, but he remained a great favourite of the Kop, who always appreciated his have-a-go attitude. He left having played just over 60 League games for the club and having scored some vital goals.

You could hardly blame Souness for all the inconsistencies. On occasion, as at the beginning of the season and against QPR at Anfield, they had shown commendable passing and determination. But it would all too often be followed by the most depressing of performances. There was no denying that there were quality players at Anfield, some brought in by Souness himself. Mark Wright, Dean Saunders, Paul Stewart and Nigel Clough had all looked intelligent signings. But somewhere along the line they had lost their appetite and desire to win.

Liverpool–Manchester United fixtures have long carried the stigma of being the bloodiest battles in the entire Football League. The Anfield clash of January 1994 was to go down as one of the most exciting games seen in Britain for years. Both sides could take satisfaction from the proceedings if not the result, though Liverpool emerged the happier. Points may have been at stake but more important were pride and honour. Liverpool, by now 21 points adrift of United, began brightly, Robbie Fowler spurning a golden opportunity in the first minute. And yet despite their positive opening Liverpool found themselves a goal behind after eight minutes as their defence failed to deal with a corner. It was a devastating blow; shoulders dropped and fifteen minutes later Liverpool were three goals down as a rampant United began to fire in shots from every angle. Liverpool looked set to be engulfed but in a remarkable come-back, urged on by the Kop, they suddenly found an extra yard of pace. The result was two splendid strikes by Nigel Clough and a half-time scoreline that looked far more respectable than many had imagined possible 20 minutes earlier. If the first half had belonged marginally to United, then the second half belonged to Liverpool as they stormed the United goal. An equaliser was inevitable and Anfield erupted when it came.

Liverpool had shown commendable courage and character to retrieve a three goal deficit. Souness was euphoric while Nigel Clough had emerged from his shell to give a performance that finally made him look value for money. The Kop went home happy, hopeful that events were about to turn their way.

It did not last long. After United came a flattering win at Ipswich and a last-gasp victory over Manchester City at Anfield. In between, Liverpool's third round Cup-tie at Bristol City had been halted as the floodlights failed. But there were enough signs to suggest that the First Division outfit would be no pushovers. And in the rearranged fixture Liverpool were lucky to survive a City onslaught. It should have been a warning. Even so few would have put money on their chances in front of a packed Anfield.

But history was set to repeat itself. At Anfield, Bristol City continued where they had left off. Chances came, only to be wasted. Had Liverpool been beaten against the run of play or put up a determined fight, then perhaps all might have been forgiven. As it was they simply gave in. A goal was inevitable and when Brian Tinnion struck in the 67th minute Souness' days were numbered. It was the only goal of the game. It had been an abysmal performance from Liverpool, yet it was only 21 days since their stirring fightback against arch-rivals Manchester United.

Liverpool's luck had finally run out. Free of injury, free of boardroom squabbles and money worries, for years they had simply got on with the job as professionally as they knew. But suddenly in the 1990s it all went wrong. First Dalglish resigned, sending tremors through Anfield. Then Souness arrived and the trusted system began to fall apart. Too many changes were made in too short a period. Famed for years for their players fitness, the club suddenly experienced a rash of long-term injuries. In addition every player they signed seemed to lose form as soon as they pulled on a red shirt while those sold found an extra lease of life elsewhere. With a new chairman came worrying financial restraints. Liverpool found it increasingly difficult to compete in the transfer market. The dressing room rows that simmer in most clubs had suddenly became public. The board had hesitated about sacking Souness, only to see results continue to deteriorate. It was all so unlike Liverpool. There was a lack of direction both in the offices and on the field. After 25 years of success, Liverpool fans had to learn to be second best.

The Kop's patience finally ran out. This time they could be neither understanding nor forgiving; their venom was directed at one person – Graeme Souness. As the Liverpool team trooped off the field to a chorus of booing after the Cup defeat, it was clear that the Souness reign was all but over.

It all happened very quickly. After a three-day break Souness returned to Anfield and the inevitable. At 6pm on the Friday evening the verdict emerged from a hastily arranged board meeting. Souness was going, the first Liverpool manager to be sacked since 1956 when Don Welsh was forced out of office. In his 33 months at the club Souness had spent just over £21 million on 15 players and had sold 18 players raising £12 million. The club was £9 million out of pocket from his deals in the transfer market.

Within 24 hours Souness' successor had been named. It came as no great surprise to anyone when Roy Evans was paraded before the cameras. He was the Kop's choice, heralding a return to basics, the old Liverpool style, and hopefully the old Liverpool success. The only question was whether it was now too late to recreate the old system.

Roy Evans on the bench in his first game in charge, a 2–2 draw at Norwich.

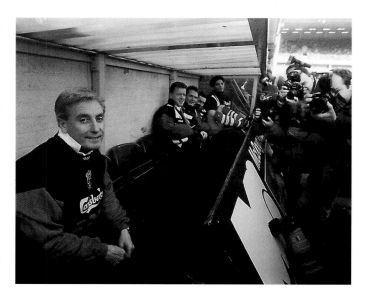

THE BOOTROOM BOY TAKES OVER

1994-95

Roy Evans took charge of his first game as the new Liverpool manager as the team travelled to Norwich. It was an encouraging start, a 2–2 draw, but over the next three months there was little else to cheer. It was to be a case of watching and waiting. On the plus side Everton were beaten 2–1 at Anfield but there were also some embarrassing defeats, with even relegation threatened Sheffield United snatching a surprise win at Anfield. Evans' 16 League games to the end of the season brought only five victories with nine defeats. Liverpool eventually finished in eighth spot, having conceded an astonishing 55 goals. They could not even manage a win at Anfield for the Kop's final game. The flags were out in force, the songs and chants as glorious as they had ever been from over 44,000 spectators, but Norwich stole all three points in one of the most lacklustre performances that Liverpool produced all season.

As the new campaign approached, the newspapers went in for their usual pre-season speculation on the championship. They all agreed that Manchester United were odds-on favourites for the title again with Blackburn Rovers likely to give them a close call. Newcastle were mentioned as possibles along with Aston Villa and Arsenal. But again one name was missing. Nobody mentioned Liverpool. Liverpool were among the also rans; the bookmakers had chalked them up at 20–1. On the eve of the championship it seemed that Liverpool were most definitely not title contenders. It was something you could hardly have dreamed in the previous 30 years.

What probably influenced the football writers more than anything was that Liverpool had not been in the transfer market for months. It was clear from the

John Scales shuts out Ryan Giggs in Liverpool's 2–0 win over Manchester United.

previous season that changes and additions to the squad were vital. Yet the summer had come and gone and nothing had happened. Players had changed hands for vast fees elsewhere but at Anfield all had been quiet. What's more Liverpool had hardly been linked with any of the big summer signings. The only addition to the squad had been the young Danish goalkeeper Michael Stensgaard who had come highly recommended by United's Danish international keeper Peter Schmeichel.

Perhaps even more worrying was that hardly anyone had left Anfield. The legacy of Souness was still proving expensive. Paul Stewart had been out on loan to Crystal Palace for a period but had proved too expensive for anything more permanent than a couple of months. The London club had made an inquiry following their promotion to the Premiership but the £1 million plus transfer tag and his salary were way beyond their means. As it was Liverpool stood to lose more than £1.5 million on the deal that had brought him to Anfield in the first place. There were no other inquiries for Stewart either, until Wolves stepped in to take him on loan to Molineux later in 1994. By November Stewart's valuation had slipped even further with Liverpool finally agreeing to an £800,000 offer from Wolves only for the deal to fall through at the last minute as Stewart reported yet another injury. Mark Walters was another priced out of the market. Bought by Souness for £1.25 million from his old club Glasgow Rangers, he made only a handful of appearances under new manager Roy Evans before being loaned out to Stoke City. But again the proposed fee proved too prohibitive. Wolves also took Walters on loan but returned him some months later without even making an offer.

The only two players to leave were goalkeeper Bruce Grobbelaar, who had joined Southampton on a free transfer, and Torben Piechnik who had moved back to Denmark, also on a free transfer. The transfer of Grobbelaar was not altogether unexpected. He was clearly nearing the end of his career and with David James returning to the side shortly after Souness' departure when Grobbelaar was injured, the odds were that he would retain the place. Grobbelaar had given magnificent service. There had been times when his eccentricity had been costly – twice Liverpool had been eliminated from the European Cup partly through his errors – but there were also times when Grobbelaar had kept Liverpool's hopes alive. The fingertip save against Everton at Wembley in 1986 and his knee-shaking antics in the penalty shoot-out at the 1984 European Cup final stay in the memory, two of

Phil Babb was an important signing from Coventry, boosting the Liverpool defence.

his many triumphs. In all he had played almost 600 games for Liverpool and when he left Anfield he went with a bagful of medals.

Grobbelaar was later at the centre of investigations into match-fixing, after a former business associate had made accusations in *The Sun*. One of the matches concerned a game at Newcastle the previous season when Liverpool had lost 3–0 though it was difficult to

Ian Rush congratulates Robbie Fowler on another goal. Fowler was nominated PFA Young Player of the Year.

see how Grobbelaar could be blamed for any of the goals. Graeme Souness and Liverpool were quick to deny any knowledge of anything suspicious.

The other player to disappear, Torben Piechnik, had made less than 30 appearances for the club. Signed by Souness from Copenhagen for £500,000, there were later to be allegations surrounding his transfer to Liverpool, with claims that illegal commissions had been levied on his fee.

After a heavy pre-season defeat by Bolton Wanderers in a warm-up for the 1994–5 season, Evans decided to get tough. Julian Dicks was slammed for his lack of fitness and weight while Mark Wright was also told that he was not up to scratch. Both players were furious, complaining bitterly to the newspaper journalists. Within a few months Dicks was on his way back to his old club West Ham for £500,000, significantly less than Liverpool had paid for him. As for Mark Wright, the former England international continued to languish in reserve team football, with nobody showing much interest in him, although he emerged to give a splendid performance against Manchester United late in the season. But he remained the forgotten man of English football.

Don Hutchison, although not a Souness signing, was another who would soon move on. A poor disciplinary record, both on and off the field, finally came to a head early in the new season and Hutchison was offloaded to West Ham United to join Julian Dicks. It was a clear indication that Evans expected high standards at Anfield and that anyone failing to comply would be shown the door.

Given the turmoil, it was a surprise that Liverpool should begin the season in style, slamming six goals past newly promoted Crystal Palace at Selhurst Park. Everyone was impressed, but a more serious test for Liverpool was around the corner with the visit of Arsenal to Anfield. It was a strange Anfield that greeted everyone for that first game of the season. The Kop which had once regularly swayed with 27,000 fans had been totally demolished and was now a building site. But if the fans found it strange the players certainly did not as they thrashed the Gunners 3–0, with Robbie Fowler scoring a record-breaking hat-trick in the space of four and a half minutes.

This was not the Liverpool of the Souness years. The players looked more confident, and there were none of the usual glances towards the bench for instructions or inspiration. John Barnes, playing in a far deeper role, was relishing his new challenge. Jan Molby, given another chance by the new manager, was rewarding him with those visionary passes that had once been his hallmark. And Steve McManaman, for so long a promising youngster run off his feet by too much football, was now maturing into a quality marauder, hitting two goals in his first game.

But the biggest revelation of all was Neil Ruddock. Under Souness Ruddock had rarely displayed any of the talent that had once had his former manager Terry Venables predicting an England career. He had looked hopelessly slow and clumsy though he later put this down to living in a hotel and indulging in too much rich food. But a new house and a club dietician had him looking slim and fit for the start of the season. Ruddock was a changed man. The Anfield faithful were suitably impressed, and Ruddock's commitment and determination soon made him a favourite.

After a third win Liverpool again found themselves top of the table. The doom merchants were quick to point out that it had been the same story the previous season – and look what had happened then. But this time the expected stumble was slow in arriving. Instead they drew with West Ham before eventually losing their fifth game, against United at Old Trafford, though only after a spirited display against the League champions that deserved some reward. Liverpool then drew with League leaders Newcastle at St James' Park before losing at Blackburn. But there were also wins, and by mid-November Liverpool were handily placed, just a few points off the top of the table.

By then Evans had further indicated the failings of Souness' side by spending £7 million on bringing Phil Babb from Coventry and John Scales from Wimbledon to strengthen the defence. From the start Scales looked as if had always been a Liverpool player, but Irish international Babb took time to readjust to his new role playing in a five-man back line.

Admittedly, Liverpool still did not look like championship material, but there was no doubting the improvement from the dark expressionless days of Graeme Souness. The side moved with purpose, passing with a pace and vision reminiscent of the Shankly/Paisley era and although they lacked penetration in the final quarter of the field they were still scoring at a healthy rate. In December seven Liverpool players found themselves picked for the England B international against Ireland, six of them in the England side. It was recognition that Liverpool were on the road back.

At Anfield the club were still counting the cost of

Souness' managerial reign. His investment in new players who initially showed much promise was causing concern. A number of new signings, dogged by injury and loss of form, found themselves playing in the reserves soon after pulling on a Liverpool shirt. They included a variety of young, high-profile players who had been assembled from clubs up and down the country. Of Souness' 15 signings at Liverpool only David James, Stig Inge Bjornebye, Rob Jones and Neil Ruddock looked to be part of Roy Evans' immediate plans, with Michael Thomas and Nigel Clough part of the squad but having to bide their time in the hope that an injury to someone might offer them a lifeline into first team football.

Liverpool's season progressed impressively. Time and again they stood on the brink of a leap to the top of the table but in the end had to settle for second or third spot. It was consistency that was lacking. At times they were capable of exhilarating performances, such as their 2–0 defeat of Newcastle at Anfield. At one point they had gone 25 games with only one

The new Kop at Anfield, redeveloped following the recommendations of the Taylor report.

Steve McManaman scores the first of his two goals in the Coca-Cola Cup Final.

defeat but then managed to lose their next two fixtures. With Babb and Scales settling to their new roles the defence looked as secure as any at Anfield in the last four years. In that 25-game run only ten goals were conceded. Up front Robbie Fowler had forged an effective partnership with Ian Rush, although the youngster was to run out of steam midway through the season.

The highlight of Liverpool's League season came with the visit of Manchester United, aiming for a third consecutive League championship. United, on the tails of Blackburn Rovers, needed at least a point from Liverpool but in the end went home with nothing, beaten 2–0. Liverpool had given one of their finest displays in years as they harried and hassled United, a display that promised much for the future. By then an impressive all-seater stand capable of holding 11,000 spectators had risen from the rubble of the Kop, which was almost as noisy and taunting as it had ever been.

All season there was a feeling that Liverpool would claim a trophy. Nobody really imagined it would be the title but there were high hopes of the League Cup or the FA Cup. In the event it was the League Cup, now known as the Coca-Cola Cup, that came

Liverpool's way. It had begun in a quiet way as Liverpool won their first leg encounter with Burnley by two goals to nil at Anfield. A fortnight later they put four past the Lancashire side at Turf Moor to set up a third round game with Stoke City at Anfield. Liverpool did just enough to win 2–1.

If the draw had favoured Liverpool so far it certainly did not in the next round as they faced top of the table Blackburn at Ewood Park. But Liverpool gave one of the most impressive performances of the season as they outplayed Kenny Dalglish's hopefuls to win 3–1 with all three goals coming from Ian Rush. Liverpool's name now looked to be as good as carved on the trophy. They feared no one and when drawn against Arsenal at Anfield, the Gunners were swept aside with Ian Rush hitting the only goal of the game. That win put Liverpool into the semi-finals with a two-legged match against Crystal Palace. At Anfield Liverpool struggled to find goals. Chances came but nobody seemed capable of delivering the killer punch. Then seconds into injury time, with a goalless draw looking inevitable, Steve McManaman chased a ball down the right flank, crossed and Robbie Fowler struck. It was a vital goal. In the second leg, with Liverpool anticipating a Crystal Palace onslaught, the Reds opened the scoring early on. There was only one side in it after that, although for all their superiority Liverpool were unable to turn half a dozen chances into goals.

Liverpool's opponents in the final were Bolton Wanderers from the Endsleigh League First Division, who a couple of seasons before had embarrassed Liverpool at Anfield in the FA Cup. Bolton, pushing for promotion to the Premiership, had taken the scalp of Liverpool, Everton, Arsenal and Aston Villa in the previous two seasons, and had a posse of youngsters equal to any in the country. It turned out to be as entertaining a final as everyone had anticipated, with both sides committed to passing the ball and running at defences. But if there was any difference between the sides it was Steve McManaman, Liverpool's pencil-thin winger, who tore at the Bolton defence at every opportunity. Wembley seemed to suit him with its wide open spaces and time and again he jinked his way down the wing, cutting inside then outside. Inevitably it was McManaman who opened the scoring with a brilliant solo goal, as he raced almost from the half-way line. With everyone screaming for him to pass the ball, he simply continued on his way and unleashed a shot that sneaked inside the post. In the second half McManaman continued where he had left off, giving Liverpool a 2–0 lead with an almost identical goal. It looked as if it was all over but within minutes Bolton had pulled a goal back and then began a desperate assault on Liverpool for an equaliser. But luck was with the Reds and at the final whistle they had won the League Cup for a record fifth time. It was mainly thanks to Steve McManaman, who had given a performance to equal any that the day's guest, Sir Stanley Matthews, had given at Wembley in his illustrious career. New manager Roy Evans had won his first trophy and Liverpool had qualified for a European competition.

After all the excitement of Wembley Liverpool's season petered out. They had been knocked out of the FA Cup, shortly before their Wembley appearance against Bolton. But it had been an exciting run that had taken the Reds to the sixth round with victories over Birmingham, Burnley and Wimbledon. In the quarter finals they faced Tottenham at Anfield and although they might have been favourites German international Jürgen Klinsmann provided an 88th minute killer punch that knocked Liverpool out.

Liverpool had already booked themselves a spot in Europe and there was little to be gained in the League. In the end they finished in fourth spot. But Anfield hosted one of the most remarkable finishes to a championship ever seen, equal in excitement to the 1989 finale, also at Anfield. Blackburn Rovers needed to win to clinch the title – anything else would probably hand it to Manchester United. Liverpool played brilliantly to overcome a 1–0 half-time deficit to win 2–1 with a last-minute winner from Jamie Redknapp. The despair of Blackburn fans immediately changed to joy, however as thousands of transistor

Ian Rush and Robbie Fowler celebrate Liverpool's win over Bolton in the Coca-Cola Cup Final at Wembley.

Liverpool's talented youngsters, Fowler, Redknapp and McManaman promise much for the future.

radios brought them the news that at Upton Park West Ham United, managed by Jamie's father Harry Redknapp, had held on to draw with United, thus giving Blackburn the title by one point. Blackburn's manager, Kenny Dalglish, said that if the championship could not have been won at Ewood Park, then Anfield was the nest best place. Thousands of Liverpool fans (the gate was 40,000) joined Kenny and the Blackburn brigade in their celebrations.

The season had been more than a promising start for Evans. Liverpool's youngsters – Fowler, McManaman and Redknapp – were now maturing into quality players with McManaman and Redknapp aleady called into the England squad. Fowler had notched up 31 goals and was second highest scorer in the Premiership, an impressive start in what was his first full season in football, especially as he was still only 20 years old. Towards the end of the season Liverpool dipped into the transfer market, paying £2 million for 18-year-old Mark Kennedy of Millwall, a further sign that the club were building for the future. Youth was the key and as the season ended it was in anticipation that this Liverpool could surely only get better.

1995–96

After their Coca-Cola Cup triumph and a respectable fourth place in the league, Liverpool finally seemed to have shaken off the traumas of the Souness era. During the close season manager Roy Evans had splashed out a record fee of £8.5 million on Nottingham Forest's goalscoring ace Stan Collymore, beating off rival bids from Everton and Blackburn. It was a sign that Liverpool meant business, all eyes focused on the title. In Liverpool's opening game of the season, against Sheffield Wednesday, Collymore looked to be a bargain as he curled in a shot from outside the penalty area which gave Liverpool all three points. Unfortunately his influence was to be short-lived. In the second game he limped off at Elland Road with an ankle injury and never really returned to form until the second half of the season. It was another multi-million pound signing who did the damage, Tony Yeboah scoring for Leeds with

Stan Collymore became England's most expensive player after signing for £8.5 million from Nottingham Forest.

one of the most spectacular long range goals of the entire season.

But if Liverpool fans had been depressed by that defeat they were soon upbeat again as the Reds travelled to London, beating a spirited Tottenham 3–1 and Queens Park Rangers 1–0. But in early September, a visit to bogey team Wimbledon resulted in another 1–0 defeat. Despite these two setbacks it was still early days and a few more encouraging results, particularly in Europe, helped keep things in proportion.

Against Spartak Vladikavkaz, about to become champions of Russia, a Steve McManaman shot from the tightest of angles and a sizzling Jamie Redknapp long-range shot gave Liverpool a 2–1 lead in the first leg. It was an impressive result that had the pundits waxing lyrically about Liverpool's patience and how their passing game had taken the sting out of the Russian attack. In the return at Anfield, however, Liverpool looked nowhere near as convincing and in the end were lucky to escape with a goalless draw that was enough to take them through to the next round.

Back in the league, there were further wins with Collymore hitting another spectacular goal in the 3–0 win over Blackburn in a game that also saw Jason McAteer make his debut for Liverpool. The £4.5 million signing of the Bolton player had long been anticipated and he brought with him pace, energy and a never-say-die attitude that would serve Liverpool well over the season. Ironically Liverpool's next league encounter was against Bolton and although McAteer was only named as substitute, Fowler struck four times in Liverpool's 5–2 win.

Liverpool's next league clash was at Old Trafford for the much publicised return of Eric Cantona following his lengthy suspension. Within minutes Cantona had helped United to a 1–0 lead. Liverpool battled back with Robbie Fowler's two stunning goals threatening to oust Cantona from the headlines but a controversial late penalty, converted by the Frenchman, ensured him a place on the back pages. Liverpool were despondent, having done more than enough to win, and still unable to take all the points.

After that came another draw, this time with Coventry City. But if that was a lacklustre performance, Liverpool returned to their best with a 3–1 win at the Dell and then a 6–0 hammering of Manchester City at Anfield – this after they had beaten them 4–0 in a midweek Coca-Cola Cup tie. Yet although the scoreline looked convincing, Liverpool flattered to deceive, taking all their chances against a weak City defence. Reality was about to strike home. Liverpool's season was to be torn apart as they faced Danish side Brondby at Anfield in the second round of the UEFA Cup. In the first leg in

Jason McAteer quickly settled into the side after signing from Bolton, delighting the fans with his pace and energy.

Denmark, Liverpool had put up stout resistance to draw 0–0 and might well have pinched the tie had they taken their chances. The second leg seemed a mere formality but the days when Liverpool were invincible at Anfield were long gone and to the astonishment of everyone, Brondby sneaked away with a 1–0 win. Liverpool were out of Europe; and it was about to get worse.

November would turn out to be one of the most miserable months in recent history as Liverpool failed to win one game. It became known around the corridors of Anfield as 'Black November'. It began with a visit to St James' Park to face a Newcastle side riding high at the top of the table. Within minutes Newcastle were a goal ahead but Liverpool fought back to level the score, totally outplaying the home side. They looked impressive but in the final minute Newcastle struck again and Liverpool, despite dominating the game, lost. Even Newcastle manager Kevin Keegan had to admit his team had been fortunate. It was much the same story as the Old Trafford game, though at least a point had been gained from that match.

The Newcastle result, coming on top of Liverpool's European dismissal, was a shattering blow. They had now lost three league games and the season was only a

dozen fixtures old. Could it get worse ? The answer was 'yes'. In their next match, at Anfield, against neighbours Everton, they lost 2–1. The disappointment was there for all to see.

Then came a goalless draw at West Ham followed by yet another defeat, this time at Middlesbrough where Liverpool were unlucky enough to come up against a rampant Boro side inspired by new Brazilian signing, Juninho. Had the game been played a few weeks later, Liverpool would have met a far less confident Middlesbrough. As it was they lost 2–1. Collymore had returned to the side but seemed a far different prospect from the player who had kick-started the season in such thrilling form. He looked lethargic, out of place and disinterested in playing.

Liverpool's decline was further underlined in their next match, a Coca-Cola Cup fourth round tie against Newcastle at Anfield. Liverpool had been making steady progress in the competition they had won the previous year, beating Sunderland home and away before eliminating Manchester City 4–0 at Anfield. After running Newcastle ragged at St James' Park, Liverpool were favourites to take revenge for the league defeat but instead it was Newcastle who took their chance in an evenly contested match. The Liverpool defence failed to challenge Steve Watson who, with no-one to turn to, simply looked up and floated a glorious shot beyond David James.

Out of Europe, the Coca-Cola Cup, and now seemingly out of the league, Liverpool's season looked to have fallen apart. In their five games in November they could only manage one draw. They had slumped to sixth spot, more than a dozen points behind leaders Newcastle. December did not begin much better either as they could manage only a draw with Southampton at Anfield. But if luck had deserted them then, it returned in abundance as they faced relegation threatened Bolton Wanderers at Burnden Park. Liverpool barely deserved a point from the game but Collymore cashed in on a defensive error to steal all three points. Liverpool's season was on course again. A week later they faced Manchester United at Anfield and, in one of the games of the season, gave as an impressive a display as they had done all season, beating United 2–0 thanks to a couple of goals from Robbie Fowler. Indeed, without a world-class performance from United keeper Peter Schmeichel, Liverpool might have scored six. They were now set to make an assault on the championship.

Arsenal were the next Anfield victims as Fowler repeated his goalscoring feats against the Gunners with a hat-trick in the 3–1 defeat of the London side. Then after a 2–2 draw at Chelsea, Nottingham Forest were beaten 4–2 with Fowler, continuing his great form, picking up a couple more goals. On 13 January Liverpool travelled to Sheffield Wednesday but could only come away with a draw. A week later they trounced Leeds United 5–0 at Anfield, a result that again flattered to deceive. Leeds had held Liverpool to a single goal deficit until the dismissal of Gary Kelly, but the resulting penalty turned the game firmly in Liverpool's favour. Fowler added a third, with Collymore and Ruddock finding two more in injury time.

By late January, Liverpool had moved into second spot but still trailed leaders Newcastle by 12 points, a seemingly impossible gap to bridge. United lay in third place with only goal difference separating them from Liverpool. The title looked destined for St James' Park after an absence of almost 70 years. Liverpool could only keep the pressure on and hope that Newcastle might slip up. But judging from the way Kevin Keegan's team was playing, there seemed little possibility of that. If Liverpool were to have any hope of the title they could not afford any more defeats, but the confidence that had visibly drained away from them in November had now clearly returned. In their next fixture, away to high-flying Aston Villa, they produced one of the displays of the season to win 2–0.

Spurs were next on the agenda, at Anfield, but despite all the striking talent on display, neither side could muster a goal and Spurs went away the more satisfied. The gap with Newcastle had now stretched to 14 points, with Manchester United easing into second place, five points ahead of Liverpool. Points may have been squandered, but now Liverpool were putting together an impressive unbeaten run. It continued with wins at Queens Park Rangers and Blackburn, where a fluke goal that left Tim Flowers red-faced had given Liverpool a flying start. 3–1 ahead, Liverpool then contrived to almost throw the game away, as Blackburn pulled one goal back and were then denied one point for a draw when the referee controversially turned down a late penalty claim.

Next in line at Anfield were Aston Villa, resurgent under new manager Brian Little. But within seven minutes of kick-off, Villa were trailing by three goals. McManaman, playing as well as he had ever done in a Liverpool shirt, opened the account in the first minute, with Fowler adding two more minutes later. A shell-shocked Villa never recovered as Liverpool gave one of their finest performances since the days of Dalglish. Liverpool had now gone 16 games without defeat, and with Manchester United beating Newcastle, the gap between Liverpool in third place and leaders Newcastle was down to just six points. After a 2–2 draw with Wim-

Rob Jones proved highly effective for another season, making strong runs from his wing-back position.

bledon ten days later, winning the title was still a distinct possibility.

Next in line were Chelsea at Anfield and a 2–0 win. The gap was now just two points, with Manchester United and Newcastle topping the table jointly with 61 points, although Newcastle still had two games in hand. But having made giant strides up the table in an unbeaten run that stretched over four months, Liverpool dramatically tossed away their gains in a 1–0 defeat at Nottingham Forest. Suddenly the gap opened up to five points and only the most passionate Kopites still dreamt of a title triumph.

But Liverpool have rarely been a club to concede defeat. With the visit of Newcastle United to Anfield just a few days after the Reds had reached the FA Cup final, everyone knew that a defeat would certainly destroy any lingering championship dreams. Little did they know that that evening would also end Newcastle's title ambitions. Their clash was one of the most thrilling matches seen at Anfield in years and one rated by some commentators as the finest game in the past decade. It was 90 minutes packed with breathtaking football. Liverpool opened the scoring with a Robbie Fowler goal in the second minute. Eight minutes later, Les Ferdinand

levelled the scores and, before a quarter hour had gone, French winger David Ginola put Newcastle into the lead. After the interval, Fowler struck his second of the evening, only for Newcastle's Colombian import, Faustino Asprilla, to put them ahead again at the other end a minute or so later. The game was now spinning from one goalmouth to the other, and in the heat of the contest, it was Stan Collymore who proved the hero, converting McAteer's curling cross to level the scores once more. With 40,000 people roaring both sides on, the two teams battled to find a winner in the last fifteen minutes. But just as a draw seemed inevitable, up stepped Collymore to give Liverpool a 4–3 victory and all three points. Former Liverpool idol Kevin Keegan buried his head in his hands, knowing full well that Newcastle's title chances had taken a severe set-back.

Liverpool were on a high but in their next match, away to struggling Coventry City, they repeated their failings, going down to the only goal of the game. A severe injury to defender Steve Harkness, one of the successes of the Liverpool season, undoubtedly unsettled the side as he was stretchered off with a badly broken leg, following a challenge from John Salako.

Now there was only third position to play for and a UEFA Cup place. Liverpool ended the season with a win over West Ham, a frustrating draw against Everton, an unconvincing win over Middlesbrough and then finally a draw at Maine Road that put paid to Manchester City's Premiership place. Liverpool had to be content with third spot, seven points behind runners up Newcastle and eleven points adrift of champions Manchester United.

But at least the side had given the fans something to cheer about. The frustrations of recent seasons were now well behind them. There had been a couple of new faces in Collymore and McAteer but many of the Souness signings had disappeared during the course of the campaign. Nigel Clough had gone to Manchester City for £1.2 million, Mark Walters to Southampton on a free transfer and Paul Stewart had joined Sunderland. The ever-popular Jan Molby also left to become player–manager of Swansea, while Ronnie Whelan, winner of so many honours, had joined Southend United with Steve Nicol going to Notts County.

LEFT: Steve McManaman was inspirational during 1995–96, terrifying defences with his fast attacking runs.

BELOW: Robbie Fowler picked up the PFA Young Player of the Year award for the second year in succession.

Mark Wright enjoyed a fantastic return to form during 1995–96, earning him a recall into the England squad.

However, most tears would be shed for Ian Rush, who announced his intention to quit Anfield at the end of the season. In his final league game in front of the Kop he was given a send-off to match any in the club's long history. It was fitting that the Kop should salute their hero who in his Anfield career had scored a record 345 goals. In all, he had collected five championship medals, three FA Cup-winning medals, five League Cup medals and one European Cup medal. He had also broken the record for the most FA Cup goals, while his five goals in the finals also stands as a record.

Despite all the goals, the truth was that Liverpool had rarely looked like realistic championship contenders. There had been moments when they had outclassed their opponents with their stylish passing but equally there had been many occasions when they had passed the ball once too often. Newcastle and United seemed to take a more direct approach. November, when they managed just one point out of 12, had been their downfall; the injury to Redknapp and the loss of form by Stan Collymore perhaps unsettled the side more than can be quantified. Their end-of-season slow-down was no doubt due in part to the realisation that the championship was beyond them. Had they still been in contention they may well have steeled themselves for a more purposeful finale as well as showing more passion

in the FA Cup final. Against sides of the highest quality they seemed to raise their game but against struggling teams, who usually packed their defences, they often ran out of ideas.

There had been some memorable successes though, especially the youngsters. Robbie Fowler, in only his second full season, struck 28 goals to make him the second highest scorer in the Premiership, and was rewarded with a place in the England side. Steve McManaman had rarely put a foot wrong all season, tantalising and tormenting defences wherever he went, while new signing Jason McAteer had slotted into the side, promising much for the future with his darting runs and energetic pace. Jamie Redknapp, injured for most of the second half of the season, might well have provided the necessary inspiration had he been fit. The defence had proved as mean as any team in the Premiership, with Mark Wright winning a recall to the England side. Indeed, it had been a fine year for Liverpool's England men with Wright, Scales, Collymore, Ruddock, Fowler, Barnes, Redknapp and McManaman all getting call-ups for England. The feeling was that, with so many youngsters, things could only get better in the years ahead.

But there was to be one sad moment in the season when news came of the death of former manager Bob Paisley who died, aged 77, in a Liverpool nursing home in February. He was the most successful manager, not just in Liverpool's history, but in English football, winning a total of 19 trophies over nine seasons as manager. He had served the club in various roles for 50 years from player, to coach, to manager and finally as a director. 'Nobody,' said manager Roy Evans, 'has served this club better.'

FA Cup Final 1996 Liverpool v Manchester United
Liverpool's road to Wembley began on a bitterly cold Saturday afternoon in January. Third division Rochdale were the visitors to Anfield with everyone anticipating a cricket-like score. They would not be disappointed, although they would have to wait 20 minutes before Liverpool finally found the net. But when the goals did arrive they came in abundance. Collymore hit a hat-trick, his first for the club, while Jason McAteer scored his first goal for the Reds. But the day belonged to Ian Rush who wrote himself yet another chapter in the history books as he struck his 42nd FA Cup goal to break

Ian Rush made his last appearance for Liverpool in the FA Cup final. His goalscoring record has made him a legend.

Denis Law's 20th Century record. Next in line were Shrewsbury Town, a game finally played after postponements due to the arctic weather conditions, against the emotional backdrop of Bob Paisley's recent death. But on a difficult pitch and in freezing conditions Liverpool came through comfortably, winning 4–0. The fifth round brought Charlton Athletic to Anfield and again it was Collymore and Fowler who were on target, although this time they were made to work for their goals. Liverpool eventually won 2–1 against a spirited side, packed with impressive youngsters. In the quarter-finals Liverpool visited Leeds United for what looked a difficult tie, but held them to a goalless draw in what was one of the poorest televised Cup games in years. But back at Anfield for the replay, Liverpool showed more commitment, and once Steve McManaman had opened the scoring, Leeds were finally forced to attack. The result was two more goals for Liverpool and a place in the last four.

Liverpool's opponents in the semi-final were Aston Villa who had already lost twice to Liverpool in the league. Liverpool's chances of a third victory over the high-flying Midlands club looked doubtful but a brilliantly headed first-half goal from Robbie Fowler eased any fears. In the second half he added another with McAteer finally putting the game beyond Villa's reach.

David James saves brilliantly from Cantona in the FA Cup final, but could not keep the Frenchman's next shot out.

On paper it looked a comfortable win but as with so many results that season, Liverpool were made to work for their victory. Thanks to Fowler, Liverpool went through to the next round.

And so it was off to Wembley with Liverpool's opponents none other than the mighty Manchester United, who had clinched the Premiership title just six days before. With United now poised to lift an historic second double, it was always going to be a difficult task for Liverpool but nobody quite expected them to be so uncommitted in their approach. Both sides seemed afraid of losing, allowing each other far too much time on the ball. It was the tamest Liverpool–United game seen in years. There were few chances for either side. Eventually it was decided by a stroke of genius from Eric Cantona in the 86th minute. David James punched

the ball out from a cross, but the Frenchman was on hand to rifle the ball into the net. While United fans raised the roof, Liverpool supporters were left wondering why their side had performed with so little passion and commitment.

Liverpool James, Wright, Scales, Babb, Jones, McAteer, Redknapp, McManaman, Barnes, Collymore (Rush), Fowler.

Manchester United Schmeichel, P Neville, Pallister, May, Irwin, Giggs, Butt, Keane, Beckham, Cantona, Cole (Scholes).

1996-97

With just weeks of the 1996–97 season remaining Liverpool looked to be heading for their first league title in seven seasons as well as a European final. But then in a disastrous collapse to their season they tossed away everything they had worked for. In Paris they were humiliated by Paris St Germain in one of their poorest ever European performances while at Anfield they crashed 3-1 to Manchester United and waved goodbye to all hope of the championship. Time and again the Reds were handed an opportunity to steal a march on United but each time they failed to put any distance between themselves and the champions. In the end, it was all they could do to finish in fourth spot, even missing out on the runners-up place and a chance of competing in the following season's Champions' League. So much promise, so little to show for it.

Like so many recent seasons Liverpool began well enough although various pre-season tournaments highlighted problems that would crop up time and again, particularly their defeats by FC Porto and by PSV Eindhoven. But when it came to the domestic game it never seemed so bad. They kicked off at newly promoted

Liverpool's 3-0 triumph away to recently promoted Leicester was one of a string of early season victories.

Middlesbrough who boasted expensive imports Ravanelli and the Brazilians Juninho and Emerson. But it was the Italian Ravanelli who was to be the bane of Liverpool's efforts as three times he pulled the new boys level at Boro's Riverside stadium. Eventually it ended 3-3. Liverpool might have been frustrated and probably should never have thrown points away but they could hardly grumble. Two days later at home to championship hopefuls Arsenal, Liverpool eventually slotted into gear although it took them the best part of the game before they finally struck. McManaman scored twice and Liverpool's season was underway. But then came a frustrating goalless draw at Anfield against Premiership new boys Sunderland, managed by ex-Evertonian Peter Reid. It was to be typical of Liverpool's season where at home they squandered more points than they had in years.

After that the Reds conjured up a string of wins that would take them to the top of the table and make them championship favourites. Coventry, Southampton, Leicester, Chelsea and West Ham were all beaten. In between they twice defeated MyPa 47 of Finland to ease into the next round of the Cup Winners' Cup. They had played seven games in September and won all seven matches. The highlight had been the 5-1 thrashing of Chelsea at Anfield. Boasting an international squad that included Italians Gianluca Vialli and Roberto Di Matteo, Chelsea were simply overwhelmed by a rampant Liverpool. And the man inspiring Liverpool to new heights was their new £3 million signing, Patrik Berger. The Czech Republic international, signed from German champions Borussia Dortmund, had been one of the stars of Euro 96 and his arrival had injected some well-needed pace and directness into the Liverpool midfield. On his debut against Leicester he was the architect of a 3-0 victory as he replaced Stan Collymore to score two goals. Berger, the only new addition to the side that summer, looked to be the answer to Liverpool's prayers.

Liverpool had yet to be beaten, but against Manchester United at Old Trafford they would suffer their first defeat, losing 1-0 although they could count themselves unlucky. They dominated for much of the game but in the end it's goals that count and it was David Beckham who clinched the points for United.

Liverpool's season really came unstuck in November, as it had the previous year. They lost 3-0 at managerless Blackburn in a pitiful performance and then dropped two vital points at home to Everton when a win would have put them back on top. A week later they drew again at Anfield, this time to Wimbledon. They had managed only one Premiership win in the whole month.

December would be another month of mixed fortunes. After winning at White Hart Lane they then lost at home to Sheffield Wednesday with a performance that left much to be desired. But a week later they followed that up with a superb 5-1 victory over Middlesbrough. Fowler hit four, and might have had more. Then came a win over Nottingham Forest before they dropped two points at Newcastle, Liverpool were saved by Robbie Fowler on the stroke of half-time as he

Czech Republic international Patrik Berger, a £3 Million signing from Borussia Dortmund, was an instant hit with the fans.

Berger and co celebrate a 4-1 win on aggregate over the Finnish side MyPa 47 to progress in the Cup Winners' Cup.

home to struggling West Ham which produced a goalless draw and more frustration for the 40,000 crowd.

In the League Cup Liverpool started with a 1-1 draw at Charlton before winning the replay 4-1 at Anfield. In the next round they gave a mighty performance to beat Arsenal 4-2 at Anfield that suggested they might go all the way to the final. But in the fifth round at Middlesbrough they lost 2-1 to the team who would go all the way.

After a useful 3-0 win over Aston Villa they then faced Chelsea again, this time in the FA Cup. They had reached the fourth round after a lacklustre 1-0 win over Burnley. It didn't augur well, but after a splendid first half the Reds went into the dressing room 2-0 up. They should in fact have been three ahead with at least one golden chance fluffed. But then in the second half Chelsea introduced the indomitable Mark Hughes. You could see the terror in Liverpool's eyes and within minutes Hughes had turned the tables. Zola added a second and before anyone knew what had happened Chelsea were 4-2 ahead and looking likely to score even more. It had been an appalling second half display by Liverpool

netted his 19th goal of the season. But on Boxing day against Leicester City they could only draw at Anfield and another opportunity to gain ground had been lost.

Liverpool's progress in the European Cup Winners' Cup was steady. After defeating the Fins of MyPa 47, they faced Sion of Switzerland, winning the away leg 2-1. At Anfield the Reds went on the rampage to win 6-3 on aggregate although giving three goals away seemed a far cry from the Liverpool of old. The writing was on the wall, but at least they were through to the quarter-finals and could forget about Europe until March.

The New Year began at Stamford Bridge with a 1-0 defeat as a Michael Thomas back pass presented Roberto Di Matteo with a simple opportunity. You would hardly have guessed that this was the same Liverpool who in September ran Chelsea ragged at Anfield. Liverpool's form barely improved in their next fixture at

The guile and graft of players like Jason McAteer sent the Reds to the top of the table early on in the 96–97 season.

A dejected David James was to come in for much criticism for his end-of-season performances and the 3-0 defeat at Paris St Germain.

as they dropped back and allowed Chelsea to swarm all over them. It was more than 30 years since they had led 2-0 and finished up losing.

After that there were marginal improvements including a 4-0 win over Leeds United but equally points were dropped when Blackburn visited Anfield and when Liverpool went to Villa.

The goalless draw with Blackburn looked to seal Liverpool's fate. While United had gone down to London and beaten high-flyers Arsenal and then taken a point away to Chelsea, Liverpool had struggled against lowly Blackburn. In truth they should have won by a canter but Fowler was guilty of missing a succession of chances. Twice they hit the post and the bar but it was to be one of those days. Had they been there until midnight they would never have scored. 'Rarely have I seen so many chances created without scoring,' claimed an exasperated Roy Evans after the game. So instead of ending the week with a comfortable lead over their rivals, Liverpool found themselves a point behind United and with a mighty hill to climb.

Liverpool's challenge at the top looked to have come to an effective end at the beginning of March. As United comfortably beat Coventry at home to take a four point lead at the top of the table, Liverpool had to wait until the following day before they travelled to Aston Villa. The pressure was now on them to come up with a result – but they couldn't manage it. Fowler missed a golden opportunity to put them ahead but late into the second half Villa scored and Liverpool went down 1-0.

It didn't get much better later that week as they travelled to Norway to face Brann Bergen in the quarter finals of the Cup Winners' Cup. After almost conceding a goal in the opening minutes, they composed themselves and began to pass the ball with some accuracy and invention. So much so that in the ninth minute Robbie Fowler struck with what must have been his best goal of the season, flicking the ball over the stranded Norwegian defender before running on to it to volley it past the helpless keeper. At half time Liverpool still led despite a barrage of Bergen opportunities. An equaliser was inevitable and shortly after the break it appeared. Liverpool continued to withstand some torrid Norwegian pressure but held out, more through luck than anything else.

In the second leg Liverpool were more convincing though there was always the danger that Bergen would sneak a vital away goal. It was the introduction of substitute Stan Collymore that turned the game as the tall striker powered his way into the area brushing everyone aside before slotting the ball past the keeper. Fowler added a couple more and in the end Liverpool finished up easy 3-0 winners and earned a place in the semi-finals, and a possible ninth European final.

But in France against Paris St Germain Liverpool came hopelessly unstuck with one of their poorest performances in years. Goalkeeper David James bore the brunt of most criticism as Liverpool crashed to a 3-0 defeat, but he wasn't the only one. The defence again looked hesitant and uncertain while the midfield looked ponderous and devoid of ideas.

If the first leg had been a disaster the second leg at Anfield was to go down as one of the great European nights. Nobody gave Liverpool a chance of pulling back a three goal deficit but under the Anfield lights and with a changed format Liverpool almost pulled off the impossible. Roy Evans throwing caution to the wind, ditched the wing back system and opted instead for a traditional 4-4-2 line-up. Barnes was also dropped. The transformation was startling although within a minute or two Liverpool might well have been out of the contest as Patrice Loko latched on to a through ball and was all alone on goal. Fortunately he missed. Then in the 11th minute Liverpool scored the early goal they so desperately needed when Robbie Fowler volleyed a low cross into the net. Anfield erupted and for the remaining hour and a quarter there was bedlam. Liverpool hurled everything into attack but a second goal did not come until the final ten minutes when Mark Wright headed them into a 2-0 lead. The noise was deafening. Anfield had not heard anything like it for years. Liverpool now needed just one more goal to force extra time. With the entire stadium on its feet the Reds pounded the PSG goal but sadly could not find a third and at the final whistle Paris were into the final. At the end of the match they cursed their bad luck and their wretched performance in Paris.

In between their two European ties had been sandwiched what was surely the Premiership game of the season when Newcastle came to Anfield. In the previous season Liverpool had beaten Newcastle in a see-saw game that had ended 4-3 as Stan Collymore struck a late winner. Of course it couldn't happen again. But astonishingly it did. In the first half Liverpool were superb as they quickly built up a three goal advantage. It was possibly their best performance so far as they outplayed and outbattled Kenny Dalglish's new charges. In the second half Liverpool picked up where they had left off but failed to add any more goals to their score sheet. Then, with minutes remaining, Newcastle scored what looked like a consolation goal. But then, minutes later, as the Liverpool defence fumbled, Newcastle struck again. Panic set in and suddenly it was 3-3 as Newcastle sensationally drew level. Liverpool had astonishingly

Robbie Fowler hurls his boot into the crowd after a memorable night at Anfield. Despite a 2–0 win the match ends in dismay as PSG go through 3–2 on aggregate.

Michael Thomas battles at the heart of the Liverpool midfield – too little, too late as the title slips away again.

thrown away a three goal lead and the way they were playing might even finish up being beaten. But it was not all over. In the final seconds Fowler leapt to head home a Bjornebye cross to make it 4-3 to Liverpool. It had been a repeat of the previous season's scoreline in a game that had been every bit as breathtaking. But although everyone poured out of Anfield delighted with the scoreline, there was no denying that the Liverpool defence had gifted Newcastle three goals and, but for Fowlers' last gasp effort, they would have thrown away three vital points. It was not really championship form. A few weeks earlier they had tossed away a two goal lead at Chelsea when they were in total control. Now they'd done it again.

Fortunately for Liverpool neither Manchester United nor Arsenal seemed capable of capitalising on their errors. Even up until the last few matches the Reds were still in with a shot at the title. Hopes were raised yet again when they went to Highbury and beat Arsenal but in their next Premiership game they lost at home to

Coventry and then after beating Sunderland dropped two points at Everton in a game they needed to win to stay in touch.

Their challenge effectively ended on an April Saturday morning at Anfield against Manchester United. It was a game Liverpool simply had to win. A draw or a defeat was of no use to them. United had to be stopped, though judging by the unusual silence inside Anfield you sensed that most Kopites already believed that their challenge was over. United began the better side and soon swept into the lead as Gary Pallister leapt above everyone to head United in front. But then came a period of sustained pressure from Liverpool. Barnes equalised and Liverpool began to press for a second goal. Then United won a corner and up stepped Pallister with a repeat of his first goal. After that it was a foregone conclusion. Liverpool were overwhelmed by a rampant United. Their heads dropped and in the second half Andy Cole added a third after David James fumbled the ball. The Liverpool goalkeeper's nightmare continued.

United had now put distance between themselves and the chasing pack and had a game in hand. They would stumble once or twice more before the season ended but the gap was too much for Liverpool. They simply had to win every game after that and hope that United would lose a few. It was mission impossible, especially with away games coming up at Wimbledon and Sheffield Wednesday. As their season wound to an end they would drop 11 points in their final five matches. They finished their programme losing at Wimbledon and then scraping a draw at Sheffield Wednesday when a win would have given them the runners-up spot and a place in the Champions' League. As it was they finished a disappointing fourth behind United, Newcastle and Arsenal, to qualify for the UEFA Cup.

The fact was that Liverpool barely deserved to win the title. They had spluttered and stalled for much of the season, never showing much consistency. On only a handful of occasions had they ever resembled the Liverpool of old. They were slow, with far too many balls played sideways instead of forward. With the exception of McManaman the midfield rarely broke into the penalty area. All the goals came from Fowler and Collymore with the rest contributing a mere handful. Fowler ended the season with a total of 31 goals, Collymore with 16. Berger had been dropped, his confidence suffering in the process and towards the end of the season McManaman looked a shadow of the man who could dance around defenders. Fowler also missed the final three games, sidelined through suspension after being sent off at Everton. After the Paris St Germain victory Barnes had failed to regain his place with Liverpool reverting to a more familiar 4-4-2 system. It seemed to herald an end to Roy Evans' long flirtation with wing backs. It also seemed to suggest that John Barnes' days as an automatic choice were numbered.

The one bright spot on the horizon was the emergence of some promising youngsters. Seventeen-year-old Michael Owen became the talk of the Premiership at the end of the season, emerging from previous season's cup-winning youth team to the first team in less than 12 months to become Liverpool's youngest ever player. Even before he'd pulled on a first team jersey the talk was that he might one day be better than Rush and Fowler. On his debut, coming on as a substitute against Wimbledon he scored a perfectly executed goal. It was a promising start.

Bjorn Tore Kvarme was another success. Signed from Rosenborg on a free transfer early in the new year, he immediately slotted into the right of defence and looked as calm and skilful a player as Liverpool had had in that position for years. Jamie Carragher was another young success coming from the youth side while

Newcomer Jamie Carragher hits his first goal for Liverpool in the 3–0 home win over Aston Villa.

Dominic Matteo was also a promising beginner, looking every bit an Alan Hansen as he calmly strode out of defence and upfield with the ball.

Two days after the season ended Stan Collymore, for so long an enigma at Anfield, was sold to Aston Villa for £7 million. His days at Anfield had never been satisfactory. He had arrived in a blaze of glory and his early goals seemed to herald a bright new era for Liverpool. But it had all evaporated. Collymore had become homesick, refusing to move from the Midlands to Liverpool, preferring instead to do a round 160–miles journey each day. It took its toll. Then his mother was ill. He didn't seem to settle. There were reports of bad feelings towards him in the Liverpool camp. It was also reported that he failed to turn up for training and on one occasion failed to show for a reserve match. He was fined, rebuked and so forth. He didn't help either by voicing his own concerns in a magazine article. Yet he still scored 35 goals in 81 appearances for the club. At times Collymore looked lethargic and disinterested. He seemed to lack the commitment, the do or die resolve. Yet the Kop loved him and willed him to succeed – but it didn't work. Perhaps in the end his style was simply not suited to Liverpool. Collymore liked the ball played long and fast to him. He liked to be chasing balls

Bjorn Kvarme fitted in well in defence and proved to be one of the successes of Liverpool's season.

The first of many to come. Seventeen-year-old Michael Owen scored on his debut.

whereas Liverpool's style, exacerbated by the use of wing backs, relied on a steady build up that at times was about going sideways rather than forwards. Time and again Collymore found himself having to drop back into the midfield to find the ball. It wasn't his style. A parting of ways was inevitable. After their disappointing season major changes were always going to result. It wasn't however simply Collymore's fault; Liverpool's problem was far more deep-rooted.

The wing back system which Liverpool had adopted in the past couple of years had never been wholly successful. It had allowed them to control games, as no other club in the Premiership could, but it did not necessarily bring results. Far too often opposing defenders had time to get behind the ball or swamp the midfield. The build up was slow and wearisome and Liverpool would run out of imagination as they approached the area. They would be left passing the ball around the perimeter of the box not sure how to break into the area. Nobody seemed to have that penetrative pass into no-man's land or the ability to take the ball to the bye line.

Liverpool had looked exciting only once in the season as they destroyed Paris St Germain but even then, on reflection, there had been far too many long balls played over the top of the defence for Collymore to chase, and not enough thoughtful inventive passing.

The season ended with Roy Evans desperately disappointed and much talk about wholesale changes. The side that had shown so much potential had failed to deliver. For a couple of seasons they had been threatening. But even though the likes of Fowler, McManaman, Redknapp and McAteer had matured the team had still fallen short. Time and again they had been given an opportunity to climb over United and make a break for the title. But on each occasion they had failed. It was going to be a busy and expensive summer for Liverpool.

1997–98

The departure of Stan Collymore to pastures new came as a surprise to no one. The tall striker had never fulfilled his price tag. At times he seemed disinterested, reluctant to commit himself either on the field or off it. He'd started well enough but the promise had soon evaporated. There was no doubting that he had talent with pace, strength and a powerful enough shot but the Liverpool passing game did not seem to suit him. At best he was a player more inclined to run at a ball played in front of him. The fans remained loyal but in the end everyone had to agree it simply had not worked out and Liverpool were fortunate enough to recoup most of his buying price when they sold him to Aston Villa. Nevertheless, Collymore had managed 35 goals in 71 appearances for the club.

The loss of Collymore, however, left Liverpool seemingly short of firepower up front. Although young Michael Owen looked a bright prospect there was no telling how he might progress. A few indelicate tackles from strong, experienced Premiership defenders might well stifle his enthusiasm and anyhow, at seventeen, too much Premiership football might not be advisable. Owen was still an apprentice in the business of football.

For much of the summer a variety of strikers names were associated with Liverpool but it would not be until almost the start of the new season before a suitable recruit was enlisted. And just like the good old days, when the man arrived, it was without the usual speculation and pre-publicity.

The new addition turned out to be Karlheinz Riedle, the man who had scored two goals in the European Cup final against Juventus to win the trophy for Borussia Dortmund. Riedle was also a World Cup winner with Germany. He might have been the wrong side of 30, but his experience of European football and his £1.25 million price tag made him look the bargain of the season.

It was enough to set Liverpool hearts fluttering, especially given that Riedle was not the only big-name signing during the summer. After much hype and a transfer saga that stretched over months, Paul Ince, formerly of Manchester United but then with Inter Milan, finally signed on the dotted line for a fee of £4.2 million. Ince seemed to be the final piece in the jigsaw, the iron man in the middle of the park, a player the equal of Smith, Souness or McMahon. He was just what Liverpool had been lacking since McMahon had been prematurely sold.

Also coming on board were Norwegian international Oyvind Leonhardsen from Wimbledon, a right-sided midfielder who enjoyed running at defences, and Danny Murphy the highly promising young midfielder

The new season saw the arrival of the stylish England under-21 star Danny Murphy from Crewe for £3 million.

from Crewe. Norwegian international Leonhardsen cost Liverpool a massive £4 million while Murphy was signed from under the nose of former Liverpool star Kenny Dalglish for £3 million. But Dalglish did surprise everyone by snatching former Anfield favourite John Barnes on a free transfer.

In the summer of 1997 it seemed that at last Liverpool had the blend of experience, youth, enthusiasm and talent to wrest the title from United, although the talk of signing a much-needed central defender never materialised. It was little wonder the bookies made them the favourites for the Premiership.

But although Liverpool boasted a galaxy of new stars they were forced to kick off the new season not only without Robbie Fowler, badly injured during a pre-season friendly in Norway, but also without Jamie Redknapp still recuperating from a broken ankle received while on England duty in June against South Africa.

Initially the darling of the Kop, Patrik Berger, fell out of favour during 1997/98 and sought a transfer.

In Fowler's absence Michael Owen, who had made his debut at the back end of the previous season, stepped in for just his second full appearance with the seniors partnered by new signing Karlheinz Riedle. And it was the youngster, Owen, who saved Liverpool's blushes converting a penalty to give them a 1–1 away draw at Wimbledon.

Any championship ambitions Liverpool might have harboured, however, were soon put into sharp perspective by a 2–1 defeat at home to Coca-Cola Cup holders Leicester City. Liverpool's performance, to say the least, was well below what was expected of championship contenders. Next in line was a tricky away tie at Blackburn and again Liverpool failed to take three

points, managing a second draw. Three games played and only two points to show; it was beginning to look like a repeat of the previous season. However, a few days later Liverpool began to look more like the finished article when they went to Elland Road and returned with a 2–0 win, albeit somewhat fortunate even though at times they had showed some quality football. Liverpool's poor form on the field was matched by growing intrigue off the field as Steve McManaman jetted off to Spain with rumours of a transfer to Barcelona. In the end nothing came of it but it was nonetheless unsettling and speculation about his future would linger for most of the season. Liverpool's appalling inconsistency continued into September. Against Sheffield Wednesday at Anfield, however, they spluttered and started and having taken a two-goal lead eventually hung on and were a little fortunate to win 2–1.

Next in line were Celtic in the plum tie of the UEFA Cup first round. Liverpool began superbly with Michael Owen, in his first European game, taking only six minutes to put the Reds ahead before a pulsating audience at Parkhead. For 45 minutes Liverpool looked a class above Celtic but as the game wore on Liverpool's dominance began to evaporate. In the second half Celtic equalised, then went ahead through a penalty as the Liverpool defence began to creak under the strain. But then in the final minute Steve McManaman raced the entire length of the pitch and slammed in a dazzling equaliser that swung the odds in Liverpool's favour.

In the return a fortnight later at Anfield a vast, noisy crowd of red and green, reminded everyone of what European football was all about and rekindled memories of a famous night at Anfield in 1966 when Liverpool had beaten Celtic to reach the Cup Winners' Cup final. This time it was even closer with neither side able to break the deadlock and although Liverpool went through, courtesy of their away goals, there really had been little to choose between the two sides.

Sandwiched between the two epic games with Celtic had been another run of poor results, with a draw at Southampton, a creditable 3–0 win over Aston Villa and a 2–1 defeat at West Ham.

Although October began with a flourish and a 4–2 win at Anfield over Ruud Gullit's Chelsea, it was against 10 men and a side without a striker for much of the game. Patrik Berger who had scored two against the Londoners in the previous season went one better, hitting a hattrick. A fortnight later they lost to Everton and then travelled to France to meet RC Strasbourg in the next round of the UEFA Cup. It turned out to be a disaster as a wobbly Liverpool defence caved in to concede three goals. The finger of blame pointed at Neil

Steve McManaman scores his wonder-goal during a thrilling UEFA Cup tie at Parkhead that finished 2–2.

Ruddock; it effectively ended his Anfield career. Liverpool's European exploits for the season were all but over. It was Paris St Germain once more. They even won the return leg by the same 2—0 scoreline but never really threatened to overhaul Strasbourg.

The pattern for the season had been set. Everywhere you looked there seemed to be questions. In goal David James continued to look uncertain and would not improve as the season wore on, while in front of him the need for an experienced quality central defender looked even more pressing than it had the previous season. The midfield looked much the same, lacking in pace and invention while up front the goals were in short supply. The new signings had hardly raised the pulse. Paul Ince had begun well but had petered out while Leonhardsen, apart from a goal or two, had contributed little. Danny Murphy had come into the side early on with some impressive performances but had then mysteriously been left out. Karlheinz Riedle looked formidable enough but was barely scoring. In recent seasons it had

been the midfield who had failed to hit target but this season it was the strikers. Apart from Michael Owen who had been a revelation, Liverpool looked no better than the side that had finished in fourth spot the previous season.

Then in November came the result that really summed up Liverpool's season, a 1–0 defeat at home by bottom of the table Barnsley. The newly promoted Yorkshire side had been on the wrong end of some embarrassing scorelines and although they barely deserved their win, it plunged the knife into Liverpool's championship hopes. For much of the game Liverpool had laid siege to the Barnsley goal but the ball simply would not go in with Karlheinz Riedle guilty of a succession of missed opportunities. Prior to that catastrophe, Robbie Fowler had been sent off at Bolton after putting the Reds a goal up inside 50 seconds. But there were good moments. Tottenham were beaten 4—0 at Anfield in Liverpool's best win so far, while they ended the month by going to Highbury and defeating championship contenders Arsenal 1–0.

But if anybody imagined Liverpool were genuine title hopefuls that was answered a week later when

Oyvind Leonhardsen, a £4 million scoop from Wimbledon, returned to Selhurst Park in December against Crystal Palace to begin a run of four successive victories.

Manchester United came to Anfield and repeated their 3–1 victory of the previous season. Again it was Liverpool's failure to deal with corners that led to their downfall. There was a gulf between the two clubs and nobody but the most optimistic imagined it could be bridged in the forthcoming months. One minute Liverpool were flying high, the next they were crashing to earth.

Following the defeat by the champions, successive wins over Crystal Palace, Coventry, Leeds and Newcastle had briefly resurrected hopes that Liverpool were at last finding their consistency. But as the New Year rolled in Liverpool, in fourth spot, still trailed United by nine points. Then, in the third round of the FA Cup against Coventry, the Reds were given a lesson in team spirit, losing 3–1 and that after Jamie Redknapp had shot them into the lead. It was a deeply disappointing result.

Out of the cup, out of Europe and looking increasingly out of the league, Liverpool's only hope was in the Coca-Cola Cup. Liverpool had not come into the competition until the third round when they disposed of West Bromwich Albion 2–0 at the Hawthorns, although Liverpool's first goal did not arrive until after half time and the second came in the final minute. Up until that moment West Brom were always in with a chance. The next round was far more comfortable with a 3-0 win over Grimsby at Anfield to put them into the quarter-finals. That pitted Liverpool against Newcastle at St James' Park, as tough a tie as you could have wished for but Liverpool were always the likely winners. After 90 minutes it was goalless, but in extra time Michael Owen edged them ahead and Fowler finished the job as Newcastle ran out of steam. It seemed that Liverpool's name might be written on the trophy, especially as they drew First Division Middlesbrough out of the bag for the semi-final. But in the first leg at Anfield Liverpool never looked convincing. Middlesbrough went ahead through Paul Merson. Redknapp quickly equalised and in the 82nd minute Fowler gave them some breathing space, but there was always a suspicion that such a narrow lead would not be sufficient in front of a boisterous Teesside crowd. Sure enough it wasn't, although even Liverpool could not have expected the sudden onslaught from the kick off that brought a couple of goals in as many minutes. Liverpool never recovered from the shock and with Fowler out of sorts, failed to capitalise on what opportunities they did create. It was a bitter disappointment; Liverpool's one realistic chance of a trophy had disappeared.

Where there was any mathematical possibility of the title, there was still hope, albeit desperate. But even that came effectively to an end in February. A 3–2 defeat at home by Southampton, followed by a 3–3 draw at Hillsborough and then another draw, this time against Everton and defeat at Villa Park, saw Liverpool's chances finally disappear. Whenever United stumbled, and stumble they did more frequently than they liked, Liverpool failed to capitalise. As if that was not bad enough Robbie Fowler's season came to a tragic end in front of the Anfield Road when he collided with Everton goalkeeper Thomas Myrhe and limped off with what proved to be a serious cruciate ligament injury to his knee. It just about summed Fowler's season up. It had been appalling. He had been injured before the season kicked off but had then returned towards the end of September to bag a few vital goals. Then he had been sent off against Bolton and after returning from suspension seemed to lose his form. He looked lethargic and heavy legged, missing chances that he would normally

RIGHT Paul Ince, bought for £4.2 million from Inter Milan, was seen by many as the man to give Liverpool's midfield the bite it had been lacking for many years.

slot away without a second thought. Roy Evan's stood loyally by his man when other managers might have dropped him but just as Fowler was beginning to show signs of emerging from his nightmare came that collision and an injury that left his personal World Cup dreams in tatters.

Also injured a few weeks earlier had been Jason McAteer who had broken a leg against Blackburn Rovers, an injury that put paid to his season. And then, as the season drew to its climax, Jamie Redknapp suffered yet another injury, this time to an ankle, that looked to cast a serious doubt over his World Cup availability.

As with the previous season Liverpool's campaign ended with a whimper. On Good Friday at Old Trafford they salvaged some pride with a spirited 1–1 draw against United that effectively ended the champions' hopes of retaining their title. Yet in the process Michael Owen was sent off. With United dropping points left, right and centre, Arsenal, who earlier had looked to be well out of the title race, had seized their opportunity and in a storming run finally overtook the Manchester side to become Premiership champions.

After the draw with United came an unconvincing win over bottom placed Crystal Palace at Anfield. In the end it took a goal from young substitute David Thompson five minutes from the whistle to give Liverpool the three points. It was typical of Liverpool's season with an inability to see off lower placed sides with any conviction. A week later a draw at Coventry even ended any hopes Liverpool might have had of second spot. That was followed by an appalling 4–1 defeat at Chelsea which had Roy Evans accusing them of being 'gutless'. They responded with a 5–0 win over West Ham and a 4–0 win over the newly crowned champions Arsenal but typically ended the campaign losing 1–0 at Derby to wind up in third place, 13 points behind Arsenal.

In an otherwise gloomy season there were few highlights. The brightest note was undoubtedly the emergence of Michael Owen as a player of exceptional quality. He had made his debut for Liverpool as a seventeen-year-old at the end of the previous season; six months later he became the youngest England international this century at just eighteen years of age, and at the end of the season was joint top scorer in the Premiership. He had enjoyed a meteoric rise and as the season closed held hopes of a World Cup call. Breathtakingly fast, tricky and mature well beyond his years,

Michael Owen in a dazzling first full season netted 18 league goals and became the youngest player to earn a full England cap since 1881. He also won the PFA Young Player of the Year and ended with a trip to the World Cup Finals.

Owen was a revelation, a player who promised to be around for at least another 10 years. Jamie Redknapp was also someone to be singled out. For so many years he seemed not to fulfil his promise but with Barnes departed he began to relish his new freedom and responsibility, though yet again injury deprived him of being an even greater influence.

It was also cheering to see the new Anfield Road stand emerge from behind the billboards. Now a double-decker stand, it increased the ground capacity to 45,000, giving many more fans the opportunity to visit and watch their favourites. It also brought an end to a six-year phase of development that had seen Anfield turned into one of the most modern stadiums in the country.

Days before Christmas, Liverpool had finally won their long-running battle with the Department of Employment to secure a work permit for American goalkeeper Brad Friedel. The American international arrived from Columbus Crew for a fee of £1 million but surprisingly did not go straight into the Liverpool line-up. Indeed it would be another two months before Roy Evans finally grew weary of David James and handed the responsibility to Friedel. But by then it was really too late to turn things around. Czech international Patrik Berger had also grown tired of being left on the sidelines and by March was demanding a transfer. Mark Kennedy was another who wanted away from Liverpool but with no firm offers coming in he spent most of the season in the wilderness until Queens Park Rangers took him on loan. The change did him good. At Loftus Road he began to regain his confidence and with injuries galore at Anfield he returned to be handed his opportunity against Bolton. He seized it, his appearance from the bench helping to revive the side and turn a one goal deficit into a 2–1 win. A week later he joined Wimbledon for £2 million. Speculation over the future of Jason McAteer and Steve McManaman hung around for most of the season.

So much had been expected from Evans' £12 million close season spending spree but sadly few of the new signings came up to promise. Despite his undoubted pedigree Karlheinz Riedle failed to deliver the goals with only a season's total of seven. Much of his time seemed to be spent either on the substitute's bench or the injury table. Oyvind Leonhardsen was another who looked little better than the array of players already at Anfield, managing only six goals all season. Youngster Danny Murphy was given an early opportunity, but although he showed promise and enthusiasm he was dropped and did not reappear until the end of the campaign. Even Paul Ince, touted by many as the final piece

A three-month wrangle over a work permit finally ended in late December when USA International 'keeper Brad Freidel signed for Liverpool.

in the jigsaw, never really looked quite as commanding as he had with United or England.

True, the club had their share of bad luck with long-term injuries to Redknapp, Fowler and McAteer, but what finally cost Liverpool was their alarming propensity to leak goals, particularly from set pieces. In all they conceded 42 goals, compared to Arsenal's 33 and United's 26. Since the beginning of the season Roy Evans had been searching for a top class central defender but nothing had materialised. Throughout the season questions had also been raised about manager Roy Evans' future. The board had guaranteed him a job for life at Anfield but quite where that job might be, remained in doubt. As the season closed there was much speculation about a clear-out and quite how many of those who had finished the season would still be there in September was anyone's guess.

THE HISTORY OF ANFIELD

Anfield is one of the most famous soccer grounds in Britain, as well known as Wembley, Hampden or Old Trafford. Over the years so many outstanding football occasions from the ground have been televised across Britain and Europe, and visiting supporters always relish the prospect of a trip to Liverpool. Ask any goalkeeper his favourite away ground and he will say Anfield, with its sporting supporters on the Kop.

The patch of land now known as Anfield was originally owned by John Orrell, a brewer and friend of John Houlding, who agreed to let Everton rent the land for a small fee. That was in 1884 and the first game played on the ground was between Everton and Earlstown on 28 September with Everton winning 5–0. Everton continued to use the ground until 1892 when a dispute with Houlding over a rent increase led to their leaving and purchasing another nearby plot of land, known as Goodison Park. During those eight years, Houlding, who had been the motivating force behind Everton, had been pouring money into the ground and had erected a small stand for some of the 8,000 spectators regularly attending games. When Everton moved on, Houlding was left with his empty ground and made the wise decision to form a new team to use it. Liverpool's first game at Anfield was a friendly played on the Thursday evening, of 1 September, 1892 against Rotherham Town. Liverpool won that game by seven goals to one.

After a highly successful season in the Lancashire League, Liverpool were admitted to the Football League, and their first league game at Anfield was played on 9 September, 1893. They defeated Lincoln City by four Goals to nil in front of 5,000 spectators.

As the crowds began to flock to Anfield the club built a new stand in 1895 capable of seating 3,000. It was constructed on the site of the present Main Stand and remained until 1973, although many changes were made to it over the years. Another stand was built at the Anfield Road end in 1903, constructed from timber and corrugated iron. After Liverpool had won their second League Championship in 1906 the directors rewarded the fans by building a new banking at the Walton Breck Road. A local journalist, Ernest Edwards, of the Liverpool Daily Post and Echo christened it the Spion Kop, after a famous hill in South Africa where a local regiment had suffered heavy losses during the Boer War.

The ground remained much the same for the next twenty years until 1928 when a major redevelopment occurred. The Kop was redesigned and extended to accommodate 30,000 with a huge roof erected. It was without question the largest Kop in the country, able to hold more supporters than some entire football grounds. The top mast of the Great Eastern, one of the first iron ships, was rescued from the breakers' yard at Rock Ferry and was painstakingly hauled up the Everton Valley by a team of horses to be erected alongside the new Kop where it stood for many years.

In 1957 floodlights were installed and on 30 October switched on for a game against neighbours Everton for a special trophy to commemorate the 75th anniversary of the Liverpool County FA. But there were few other changes around Anfield until the team forced its way

The original Kop – Anfield's spiritual home witnesses its last match in May '94 (top). The terracing was replaced by a grand all-seater stand (bottom) which houses the same vociferous support.

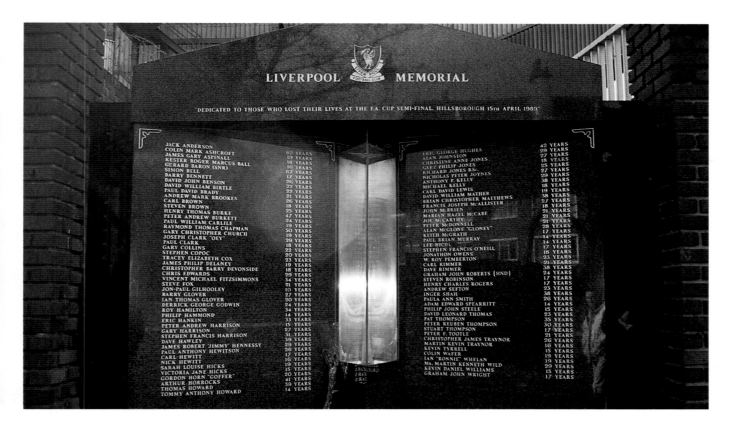

The Hillsborough Memorial dedicated to those who lost their lives during the tragic FA Cup semi-final of 1989.

back into the First Division. In 1963 the old Kemlyn Road stand was replaced by a cantilevered stand, seating 6,700 and built at a cost of £350,000. A couple of years later alterations were made at the Anfield Road end, turning it into a large covered standing area. But the biggest redevelopment came in 1973 when the old Main Stand was ripped down and a magnificent new one constructed. It was officially opened on 10 March, 1973 by the Duke of Kent.

The next major change came in the early 1990s when a second tier, costing £10 million, was added to the old Kemlyn Road stand, turning it into a magnificent 11,000 all-seater stand. The new stand was equipped with executive boxes, dining lounges and bars, making it one of the finest stands in the country.

In May 1994 came the most dramatic change of all, with the old Spion Kop torn down to be replaced by an all-seater stand, built to comply with the recommendations of the Taylor Report following the Hillsborough disaster. It was a sad day for Liverpool when they played their final match in front of a noisy flag-waving Kop, knowing that it would never be quite the same again. The times when 27,000 sang and swayed on those great European nights were gone forever. But in its place the

club did the fans justice with a new 10,000 all-seater stand. Then during the 1997/98 season the Anfield Road end was redeveloped with a new stand constructed on the old stand and a top tier added, bringing the grounds capacity to 45,000.

All these changes in recent years have led to a fall in the crowd capacity of Anfield. The record attendance of 61,905 to see Wolverhampton Wanderers, then one of the outstanding teams of the day, play Liverpool in a fourth round FA Cup game in February 1952 will now stand forever.

Liverpool's biggest victory at Anfield was in the European Cup Winners' Cup when they beat Stromgodset 11–0 on 17 September 1974 while their biggest home defeat came in April 1930 when Sunderland beat them 6–0. Over the years Anfield has entertained many famous visitors. King George V and Queen Mary came to watch an FA Cup semi-final in 1921, while many politicians have also visited the ground. Surprisingly, only five FA Cup semi-finals have been played at Anfield. The first was 1888 when the ground still belonged to Everton.

Anfield has hosted many internationals, the first in 1889 when England beat Ireland by six goals to one. England have also played Wales there on three occasions, in 1905, 1922 and 1931, winning all three games. In 1926 Ireland forced a memorable draw against England but perhaps the finest international to have grace

Anfield was the World Cup game between Wales and Scotland in October 1977 when 50,000 saw Scotland win 2–0 to capture a place in the finals. During the Second World War England and Wales fought out a 2–2 draw in front of 38,000. There have also been six inter-League games with the Football League playing the Irish League on all those occasions and winning all bar one. Anfield was also chosen as a venue for the 1996 European championships, and featured games between Italy and Russia, the Czech Republic, and Italy, Russia and the Czech Republic, as well as the quarter final match between France and Holland.

Anfield has also been the venue for many other events and during the inter-war years boxing matches were regularly held there. A number of British championships were contested and on 12 June, 1934 Nel Tarleton fought for the World Featherweight title against the American holder, Freddie Miller. The fight went to a points decision; Miller kept his title. Professional tennis was also played on boards on the pitch with the American champion, Bill Tilden and Wimbledon champion, Fred Perry, entertaining the crowds.

An unusual football occasion at Anfield was the fifth round FA Cup clash between Everton and Liverpool in 1967. The game was played at Goodison in front of 64,000 but with four giant television screens erected at Anfield in order to show it live, a further 40,000 saw Everton win by a single goal.

Television arrived at Anfield on 22 August, 1964 when the BBC chose Anfield for the first *Match of the Day*. The cameras saw Liverpool beat Arsenal by three goals to two.

Perhaps most bizarre of all Anfield stories concern the regular requests for the ashes of dead supporters to be sprinkled behind the Kop goal.

For the more lively, singing was first reported at the ground as long ago as the championship-winning season of 1905–06. But the tradition did not really establish itself until Liverpool won the Second Division championship in 1962.

A number of features have been added to the ground in recent years reflect the strong bond between the club, its supporters and players. Following the death of Bill Shankly, the club erected a memorial to him in the form of the Shankly Gates which were formally opened by his widow, Nessie. 'You'll Never Walk Alone' is the message which tops the fine wrought-iron gates. In 1998 a statue to the late Bill Shankly was also unveiled. It stands fittingly outside the Kop. After the Hillsborough tragedy in 1989 when 96 died, a memorial was erected close to the Shankly Gates with an eternal flame. Alongside it are the names of all those who died.

The Shankly Gates (top) and the statue of the man himself standing victorious outside the Kop (above) provide fitting tributes to Liverpool's greatest ever manager.

The many thousands who visited Anfield following the disaster will never forget the sight of thousands of scarves and flowers covering the pitch and the Kop, or hanging from the Shankly Gates in tribute. It was the supporters' own way of remembering.

LIVERPOOL RECORDS

LIVERPOOL IN THE FOOTBALL LEAGUE

	P	W	D	L	F	A	Pts.	Pos.
DIVISION TWO								
1893–94	28	22	6	0	77	18	50	1
DIVISION ONE								
1894–95	30	7	8	15	51	70	22	10
DIVISION TWO								
1895–96	30	22	2	6	106	32	46	1
DIVISION ONE								
1896–97	30	12	9	9	46	38	33	5
1897–98	30	11	6	13	48	45	28	9
1898–99	34	19	5	10	49	33	43	2
1899–1900	34	14	5	15	49	45	33	10
1900–01	34	19	7	8	59	35	45	1
1901–02	34	10	12	12	42	38	32	11
1902–03	34	17	4	13	68	49	38	5
1903–04	34	9	8	17	49	62	26	17
DIVISION TWO								
1904–05	34	27	4	3	93	25	58	1
DIVISION ONE								
1905–06	38	23	5	10	79	46	51	1
1906–07	38	13	7	18	64	65	33	15
1907–08	38	16	6	16	68	61	38	8
1908–09	38	15	6	17	57	65	36	16
1909–10	38	21	6	11	78	57	48	2
1910–11	38	15	7	16	53	53	37	13
1911–12	38	12	10	16	49	55	34	17
1912–13	38	16	5	17	61	71	37	12
1913–14	38	14	7	17	46	62	35	16
1914–15	38	14	9	15	65	75	37	14
1919–20	42	19	10	13	59	44	48	4
1920–21	42	18	15	9	63	35	51	4
1921–22	42	22	13	7	63	36	57	1
1922–23	42	26	8	8	70	31	60	1
1923–24	42	15	11	16	49	48	41	12
1924–25	42	20	10	12	63	55	50	4
1925–26	42	14	16	12	70	63	44	7
1926–27	42	18	7	17	69	61	43	9
1927–28	42	13	13	16	84	87	39	16
1928–29	42	17	12	13	90	64	46	5
1929–30	42	16	9	17	63	79	41	12
1930–31	42	15	12	15	86	85	42	9
1931–32	42	19	6	17	81	93	44	10
1932–33	42	14	11	17	79	84	39	14
1933–34	42	14	10	18	79	87	38	18
1934–35	42	19	7	16	85	88	45	7
1935–36	42	13	12	17	60	64	38	19
1936–37	42	12	11	19	62	84	35	18
1937–38	42	15	11	16	65	71	41	11
1938–39	42	14	14	14	62	63	42	11
1939–40	3	2	0	1	6	3	4	4
1946–47	42	25	7	10	84	52	57	1
1947–48	42	16	10	16	65	61	42	11
1948–49	42	13	14	15	53	43	40	12
1949–50	42	17	14	11	64	54	48	8
1950–51	42	16	11	15	53	59	43	9
1951–52	42	12	19	11	57	61	43	11
1952–53	42	14	8	20	61	82	36	17
1953–54	42	9	10	23	68	97	28	22
DIVISION TWO								
1954–55	42	16	10	16	92	96	42	11
1955–56	42	21	6	15	85	63	48	3
1956–57	42	21	11	10	82	54	53	3
1957–58	42	22	10	10	79	54	54	4
1958–59	42	24	5	13	87	62	53	4
1959–60	42	20	10	12	90	66	50	3
1960–61	42	21	10	11	87	58	52	3
1961–62	42	27	8	7	99	43	62	1
DIVISION ONE/PREMIER LEAGUE								
1962–63	42	17	10	15	71	59	44	8
1963–64	42	26	5	11	92	45	57	1
1964–65	42	17	10	15	67	73	44	7
1965–66	42	26	9	7	79	34	61	1
1966–67	42	19	13	10	64	47	51	5
1967–68	42	22	11	9	71	40	55	3
1968–69	42	25	11	6	63	24	61	2
1969–70	42	20	11	11	65	42	51	5
1970–71	42	17	17	8	42	24	51	5
1971–72	42	24	9	9	64	30	57	3
1972–73	42	25	10	7	72	42	60	1
1973–74	42	22	13	7	52	31	57	2
1974–75	42	20	11	11	60	39	51	2
1975–76	42	23	14	5	66	31	60	1
1976–77	42	23	11	8	62	33	57	1
1977–78	42	24	9	9	65	34	57	2
1978–79	42	30	8	4	85	16	68	1
1979–80	42	25	10	7	81	30	60	1
1980–81	42	17	17	8	62	42	51	5
1981–82	42	26	9	7	80	32	87	1
1982–83	42	24	10	8	87	37	82	1
1983–84	42	22	14	6	73	32	80	1
1984–85	42	22	11	9	68	35	77	2
1985–86	42	26	10	6	89	37	88	1
1986–87	42	23	8	11	72	42	77	2
1987–88	40	26	12	2	87	24	90	1
1988–89	38	22	10	6	65	28	76	2
1989–90	38	23	10	5	78	37	79	1
1990–91	38	23	7	8	77	40	76	2
1991–92	42	16	16	10	47	40	64	6
1992–93	42	16	11	15	62	55	59	6
1993–94	42	17	9	16	59	55	60	8
1994–95	42	21	11	10	65	37	74	4
1995–96	38	20	11	7	70	34	71	3
1996–97	38	19	11	8	62	32	68	4
1997–98	38	18	11	9	68	42	65	3

LIVERPOOL IN THE FA CUP

1892 – 93
1st Qualifying Round
v Nantwich (a) 4 – 0
2nd Qualifying Round
v Newton (h) 9 – 0
3rd Qualifying Round
v Northwich V (a) 1 – 2

1893 – 94
Round 1
v Grimsby Town (h) 3 – 0
Round 2
v Preston North End (h) 3 – 2
Round 3
v Bolton Wanderers (a) 0 – 3

1894 – 95
Round 1
v Barnsley St Peter's (a) 2 – 2 aet
Replay
v Barnsley St Peter's (h) 4 – 0
Round 2
v Nottingham Forset (h) 0 – 2

1895 – 96
Round 1
v Millwall (h) 4 – 1
Round 2
v Wolverhampton Wanderers (a) 0 – 2

1896 – 97
Round 1
v Burton Swifts (h) 4 – 3
Round 2
v West Bromwich Albion (a) 2 – 1
Round 3
v Nottingham Forest (h) 1 – 1
Replay
v Nottingham Forest (a) 1 – 0
Semi-final
v Aston Villa (Bramall Lane) 0 – 3

1897 – 98
Round 1
v Hucknall St John's (h) 2 – 0
Round 2
v Newton Heath (a) 0 – 0
Replay
v Newton Heath (h) 2 – 1
Round 3
v Derby County (a) 1 – 1
Replay
v Derby County (h) 1 – 5

1898 – 99
Round 1
v Blackburn Rovers (h) 2 – 0
Round 2
v Newcastle United (h) 3 – 1
Round 3
v West Bromwich Albion (a) 2 – 0
Semi-final
v Sheffield United (Nottingham) 2 – 2

Replay
v Sheffield United (Bolton) 4 – 4
v Sheffield United (Fallowfield) 1 – 0
Match abandoned
Replay
v Sheffield United (Derby) 0 – 1

1899 – 1900
Round 1
v Stoke City (a) 0 – 0
Replay
v Stoke City (h) 1 – 0
Round 2
v West Bromwich Albion (h) 1 – 1
Replay
v West Bromwich Albion (a) 1 – 2

1900 – 01
Round 1
v Notts County (a) 0 – 2

1901 – 02
Round 1
v Everton (h) 2 – 2
Replay
v Everton (a) 2 – 0
Round 2
v Southampton (a) 1 – 4

1902 – 03
Round 1
v Manchester United (a) 1 – 2

1903 – 04
Round 1
v Blackburn Rovers (a) 1 – 3

1904 – 05
Round 1
v Everton (h) 1 – 1
Replay
v Everton (a) 1 – 2

1905 – 06
Round 1
v Leicester Fosse (h) 2 – 1
Round 2
v Barnsley (h) 1 – 0
Round 3
v Brentford (h) 2 – 0
Round 4
v Southampton (h) 3 – 0
Semi-final
v Everton (Villa Park) 0 – 2

1906 – 07
Round 1
v Birmingham (h) 2 – 1
Round 2
v Oldham Athletic (a) 1 – 0
Round 3
v Bradford City (h) 1 – 0
Round 4
v Sheffield Wednesday (a) 0 – 1

1907 – 08
Round 1
v Derby County (h) 4 – 2
Round 2
v Brighton (h) 1 – 1
Replay
v Brighton (a) 3 – 0
Round 3
v Newcastle United (a) 1 – 3

1908 – 09
Round 1
v Lincoln City (h) 5 – 1
Round 2
Norwich City (h) 2 – 3

1909 – 10
Round 1
v Bristol City (a) 0 – 2

1910 – 11
Round 1
v Gainsborough Town (h) 3 – 2
Round 2
v Everton (a) 1 – 2

1911 – 12
Round 1
v Leyton (h) 1 – 0
Round 2
v Fulham (a) 0 – 3

1912 – 13
Round 1
v Bristol City (h) 3 – 0
Round 2
v Arsenal (a) 4 – 1
Round 3
v Newcastle United (h) 1 – 1
Replay
v Newcastle United (a) 0 – 1

1913 – 14
Round 1
v Barnsley (h) 1 – 1
Replay
v Barnsley (a) 1 – 0
Round 2
v Gillingham (h) 2 – 0
Round 3
v West Ham United (a) 1 – 1
Replay
v West Ham United (h) 5 – 1
Round 4
v Queens Park Rangers (h) 2 – 1
Semi-finals
v Aston Villa (White Hart Lane) 2 – 0
Final
v Burnley (Crystal Palace) 0 – 1

1914 – 15
Round 1
v Stockport County (h) 3 – 0
Round 2
v Sheffield United (a) 0 – 1

1920 – 20
Round 1
v South Shields (a) 1 – 1
Replay
v South Shields (h) 2 – 0
Round 2
v Luton Town (a) 2 – 0
Round 3
v Birmingham (h) 2 – 0
Round 4
v Huddersfield Town (a) 1 – 2

1920 – 21
Round 1
v Manchester United (h) 1 – 1
Replay
v Manchester United (a) 2 – 1
Round 2
v Newcastle United (a) 0 – 1

1921 – 22
Round 1
v Sunderland (a) 1 – 1
Replay
v Sunderland (h) 5 – 0
Round 2
v West Bromwich Albion (h) 0 – 1

1922 – 23
Round 1
v Arsenal (h) 0 – 0
Replay
v Arsenal (a) 4 – 1
Round 2
v Wolverhampton Wanderers (a) 2 – 0
Round 3
v Sheffield United (h) 1 – 2

1923 – 24
Round 1
v Bradford City (h) 2 – 1
Round 2
v Bolton Wanderers (a) 4 – 1
Round 3
v Southampton (a) 0 – 0
Replay
v Southampton (h) 2 – 0
Round 4
v Newcastle United (a) 0 – 1

1924 – 25
Round 1
v Leeds United (h) 3 – 0
Round 2
v Bristol City (h) 1 – 0
Round 3
v Birmingham (h) 2 – 1
Round 4
v Southampton (a) 0 – 1

1925 – 26
Round 3
v Southampton (a) 0 – 0
Replay
v Southampton (h) 1 – 0

Round 4
v Fulham (a) 1 – 3

1926 – 27
Round 3
v Bournemouth (a) 1 – 1
Replay
v Bournemouth (h) 4 – 1
Round 4
v Southport (h) 3 – 1
Round 5
v Arsenal (a) 0 – 2

1927 – 28
Round 3
v Darlington (h) 1 – 0
Round 4
v Cardiff City (a) 1 – 2

1928 – 29
Round 3
v Bristol City (a) 2 – 0
Round 4
v Bolton Wanderers (h) 0 – 0
Replay
v Bolton Wanderers (a) 2 – 5 aet

1929 – 30
Round 3
v Cardiff City (h) 1 – 2

1930 – 31
Round 3
v Birmingham City (h) 0 – 2

1931 – 32
Round 3
v Everton (a) 2 – 1
Round 4
v Chesterfield (a) 4 – 2
Round 5
v Grimsby Town (h) 1 – 0
Round 6
v Chelsea (h) 0 – 2

1932 – 33
Round 3
v West Bromwich Albion (a) 0 – 2

1933 – 34
Round 3
v Fulham (h) 1 – 1
Replay
v Fulham (a) 3 – 2 aet
Round 4
v Tranmere Rovers (h) 3 – 1
Round 5
v Bolton Wanderers (h) 0 – 3

1934 – 35
Round 3
v Yeovil & Petters (a) 6 – 2
Round 4
v Blackburn Rovers (a) 0 – 1

1935 – 36
Round 3
v Swansea Town (h) 1 – 0
Round 4
v Arsenal (h) 0 – 2

1936 – 37
Round 3
v Norwich City (a) 0 – 3

1937 – 38
Round 3
v Crystal Palace (a) 0 – 0
Replay
v Crystal Palace (h) 3 – 1 aet
Round 4
v Sheffield United (a) 1 – 1
Replay
v Sheffield United (h) 1 – 0
Round 5
v Huddersfield Town (h) 0 – 1

1938 – 39
Round 3
v Luton Town (h) 3 – 1
Round 4
v Stockport County (h) 5 – 1
Round 5
v Wolverhampton Wanderers (a) 1 – 4

1945 – 46
Round 3 1st leg
v Chester (a) 2 – 0
Round 3 2nd leg
v Chester (h) 2 – 1 agg 4 – 1
Round 4 1st leg
v Bolton Wanderers (a) 0 – 5
Round 4 2nd leg
v Bolton Wanderers (h) 2 – 0 agg 2 – 5

1946 – 47
Round 3
v Walsall (a) 5 – 2
Round 4
v Grimsby Town (h) 2 – 0
Round 5
v Derby County (h) 1 – 0
Round 6
v Birmingham City (h) 4 – 1
Semi-final
v Burnley (Ewood Park) 0 – 0 aet
Replay
v Burnley (Maine Road) 0 – 1

1947 – 48
Round 3
v Nottingham Forest (h) 4 – 1
Round 4
v Manchester United (a) 0 – 3

1948 – 49
Round 3
v Nottingham Forest (a) 2 – 2 aet
Replay
v Nottingham Forest (h) 4 – 0

Round 4
v Notts County (h) 1 – 0
Round 5
v Wolverhampton Wanderers (a) 1 – 3

1949 – 50
Round 3
v Blackburn Rovers (a) 0 – 0
Replay
v Blackburn Rovers (h) 2 – 1
Round 4
v Exeter City (h) 3 – 1
Round 5
v Stockport County (a) 2 – 1
Round 6
v Blackpool (h) 2 – 1
Semi-final
v Everton (Maine Road) 2 – 0
Final
v Arsenal (Wembley) 0 – 2

1950 – 51
Round 3
v Norwich City (a) 1 – 3

1951 – 52
Round 3
v Workington (h) 1 – 0
Round 4
v Wolverhampton Wanderers (h) 2 – 1
Round 5
v Burnley (a) 0 – 2

1952 – 53
Round 3
v Bolton Wanderers (a) 0 – 1

1954 – 55
Round 3
v Lincoln City (a) 1 – 1
Replay
v Lincoln City (h) 1 – 0 aet
Round 4
v Everton (a) 4 – 0
Round 5
v Huddersfield Town (h) 0 – 2

1955 – 56
Round 3
v Accrington Stanley (h) 2 – 0
Round 4
v Scunthorpe United (h) 3 – 3
Replay
v Scunthorpe United (a) 2 – 1 aet
Round 5
v Manchester City (a) 0 – 0
Replay
v Manchester City (h) 1 – 2

1956 – 57
Round 3
v Southend United (a) 1 – 2

1957 – 58
Round 3
v Southend United (h) 1 – 1

Replay
v Southend United (a) 3 – 2
Round 4
v Northampton Town (h) 3 – 1
Round 5
v Scunthorpe United (a) 1 – 0
Round 6
v Blackburn Rovers (a) 1 – 2

1958 – 59
Round 3
v Worcester City (a) 1 – 2

1959 – 60
Round 3
v Leyton Orient (h) 2 – 1
Round 4
v Manchester United (h) 1 – 3

1960 – 61
Round 3
v Coventry City (h) 3 – 2
Round 4
v Sunderland (h) 0 – 2

1961 – 62
Round 3
v Chelsea (h) 4 – 3
Round 4
v Oldham Athletic (a) 2 – 1
Round 5
v Preston North End (h) 0 – 0
Replay
v Preston North End (a) 0 – 0 aet
Second Replay
v Preston North End (Old Trafford) 0 – 1

1962 – 63
Round 3
v Wrexham (a) 3 – 1
Round 4
v Burnley (a) 1 – 1
Replay
v Burnley (h) 2 – 1 aet
Round 5
v Arsenal (a) 2 – 1
Round 6
v West Ham United (h) 1 – 0
Semi-final
v Leicester City (Hillsborough) 0 – 1

1963 – 64
Round 3
v Derby County (h) 5 – 0
Round 4
v Port Vale (h) 0 – 0
Replay
v Port Vale (a) 2 – 1 aet
Round 5
v Arsenal (a) 1 – 0
Round 6
v Swansea Town (h) 1 – 2

1964 – 65
Round 3
v West Bromwich Albion (a) 2-1

Round 4
v Stockport County (h) 1 – 1
Replay
v Stockport County (a) 2 – 1
Round 5
v Bolton Wanderers (a) 1 – 0
Round 6
v Leicester City (a) 0 – 0
Replay
v Leicester City (h) 1 – 0
Semi-final
v Chelsea (Villa Park) 2 – 0
Final
v Leeds United (Wembley) 2 – 1 aet

1965 – 66
Round 3
v Chelsea (h) 1 – 2

1966 – 67
Round 3
v Watford (a) 0 – 0
Replay
v Watford (h) 3 – 1
Round 4
v Aston Villa (h) 1 – 0
Round 5
v Everton (a) 0 – 1

1967 – 68
Round 3
v Bournemouth (a) 0 – 0
Replay
v Bournemouth (h) 4 – 1
Round 4
v Walsall (a) 0 – 0
Replay
v Walsall (h) 5 – 2
Round 5
v Tottenham Hotspur (a) 1 – 1
Replay
v Tottenham Hotspur (h) 2 – 1
Round 6
v West Bromwich Albion (a) 0 – 0
Replay
v West Bromwich Albion (h) 1 – 1 aet
Second Replay
v West Bromwich Albion (Maine Road)
1 – 2

1968 – 69
Round 3
v Doncaster Rovers (h) 2 – 0
Round 4
v Burnley (h) 2 – 1
Round 5
v Leicester City (a) 0 – 0
Replay
v Leicester City (h) 0 – 1

1969 – 70
Round 3
v Coventry City (a) 1 – 1
Replay
v Coventry City (h) 3 – 0

Round 4
v Wrexham (h) 3 – 1
Round 5
v Leicester City (h) 0 – 0
Replay
v Leicester City (a) 2 – 0
Round 6
v Watford (a) 0 – 1

1970 – 71
Round 3
v Aldershot (h) 1 – 0
Round 4
v Swansea Town (h) 3 – 0
Round 5
v Southampton (h) 1 – 0
Round 6
v Tottenham Hotspur (h) 0 – 0
Replay
v Tottenham Hotspur (a) 1 – 0
Semi-final
v Everton (Old Trafford) 2 – 1
Final
v Arsenal (Wembley) 1 – 2 aet

1971 – 72
Round 3
v Oxford United (a) 3 – 0
Round 4
v Leeds United (h) 0 – 0
Replal
v Leeds United (a) 0 – 2

1972 – 73
Round 3
v Burnley (a) 0 – 0
Replay
v Burnley (h) 3 – 0
Round 4
v Manchester City (h) 0 – 0
Replay
v Manchester City (a) 0 – 2

1973 – 74
Round 3
v Doncaster Rovers (h) 2 – 2
Replay
v Doncaster Rovers (a) 2 – 0
Round 4
v Carlisle United (h) 0 – 0
Replay
v Carlisle United (a) 2 – 0
Round 5
v Ipswich Town (h) 2 – 0
Round 6
v Bristol City (a) 1 – 0
Semi – final
v Leicester City (Old Trafford) 0 – 0
Replay
v Leicester City (Villa Park) 3 – 1
Final
v Newcastle United (Wembley) 3 – 0

1974 – 75
Round 3
v Stoke City (h) 2 – 0

Round 4
v Ipswich Town (a) 0 – 1

1975 – 76
Round 3
v West Ham United (a) 2 – 0
Round 4
v Derby County (a) 0 – 1

1976 – 77
Round 3
v Crystal Palace (h) 0 – 0
Replay
v Crystal Palace (a) 3 – 2
Round 4
v Carlisle United (h) 3 – 0
Round 5
v Oldham Athletic (h) 3 – 1
Round 6
v Middlesbrough (h) 2 – 0
Semi-final
v Everton (Maine Road) 3 – 0
Final
v Manchester United (Wembley 1 – 2

1977 – 78
Round 3
v Chelsea (a) 2 – 4

1978 – 79
Round 3
v Southend United (a) 0 – 0
Replay
v Southend United (h) 3 – 0
Round 4
v Blackburn Rovers (h) 1 – 0
Round 5
v Burnley (h) 3 – 0
Round 6
v Ipswich Town (a) 1 – 0
Semi-final
v Manchester United (Maine Road) 2 – 2
Replay
v Manchester United (Goodison Park) 0 – 1

1979 – 80
Round 3
v Grimsby Town (h) 5 – 0
Round 4
v Nottingham Forest (a) 2 – 0
Round 5
v Bury (h) 2 – 0
Round 6
v Tottenham Hotspur (a) 1 – 0
Semi-final
v Arsenal (Hillsborough) 0 – 0
Replay
v Arsenal (Villa Park) 1 – 1 aet
Second Replay
v Arsenal (Villa Park) 1 1 aet
Third Replay
v Arsenal (Highfield Road) 0 – 1

1980 – 81
Round 3
v Altrincham (h) 4 – 1

Round 4
v Everton (a) 1 – 2

1981 – 82
Round 3
v Swansea City (a) 4 – 0
Round 4
v Sunderland (a) 3 – 0
Round 5
v Chelsea (a) 0 – 2

1982 – 83
Round 3
v Blackburn Rovers (a) 2 – 1
Round 4
v Stoke City (h) 2 – 0
Round 5
v Brighton & Hove Albion (a) 0 – 2

1983 – 84
Round 3
v Newcastle United (h) 4 – 0
Round 4
v Brighton & Hove Albion (a) 0 – 2

1984 – 85
Round 3
v Aston Villa (h) 3 – 0
Round 4
v Tottenham Hotspur (h) 1 – 0
Round 5
v York City (a) 1 – 1
Replay
v York City (h) 7 – 0
Round 6
v Barnsley (a) 4 – 0
Semi – final
v Manchester United (Goodison Park) 2 – 2 aet
Replay
v Manchester United (Maine Road) 1 – 2

1985 – 86
v Norwich City (h) 5 – 0
Round 4
v Chelsea (a) 2 – 1
Round 5
v York City (a) 1 – 1
Replay
v York City (h) 3 – 1 aet
Round 6
v Watford (h) 0 – 0
Replay
v Watford (a) 2 – 1 aet
Semi-final
v Southampton (White Hart Lane) 2 – 0 aet
Final
v Everton (Wembley) 3 – 1

1986 – 87
Round 3
v Luton Town (a) 0 – 0
Replay
v Luton Town (h) 0 – 0

Second Replay
v Luton Town (a) 0–3

1987–88
Round 3
v Stoke City (a) 0–0
Replay
v Stoke City (h) 1–0
Round 4
v Aston Villa (a) 2–0
Round 5
v Everton (a) 1–0
Round 6
v Manchester City (a) 4–0
Semi-final
v Nottingham Forest (Hillsborough) 2–1
Final
v Wimbledon (Wembley) 0–1

1988–89
Round 3
v Carlisle United (a) 3–0
Round 4
v Millwall (a) 2–0
Round 5
v Hull City (a) 3–2
Round 6
v Brentford (h) 4–0
Semi-final
v Nottingham Forest (Hillsborough) 0–0
Abandoned after six minutes
v Nottingham Forest (Old Trafford) 3–1
Final
v Everton (Wembley) 3–2 aet

1989–90
Round 3
v Swansea City (a) 0–0
Replay
v Swansea City (h) 8–0
Round 4
v Norwich City (a) 0–0
Replay
v Norwich City (h) 3–1
Replay
v Southampton (h) 3–0
Round 6
v Queens Park Rangers (a) 2–2
Replay
v Queens Park Rangers (h) 1–0
Semi-final
v Crystal Palace (Villa Park) 3–4

1990–91
Round 3
v Blackburn Rovers (a) 1–1
Replay
v Blackburn Rovers (h) 3–0
Round 4
v Brighton (h) 2–2
Round 5
v Brighton (a) 3–2 aet
Replay
v Everton (h) 0–0
Replay
v Everton (a) 4–4 aet
Second Replay
v Everton (a) 0–1

1991–92
Round 3
v Crewe Alexandra (a) 4–0
Round 4
v Bristol Rovers (a) 1–1
Replay
v Bristol Rovers (h) 2–1
Round 5
v Ipswich Town (a) 0–0
Replay
v Ipswich Town (h) 3–2
Round 6
v Aston Villa (h) 1–0
Semi-final
v Portsmouth (Highbury) 1–1
Replay
v Portsmouth (Villa Park) 0–0
Liverpool won 3–1 on penalties
Final
v Sunderland (Wembley) 2–0

1992–93
Round 3
v Bolton Wanderers (a) 2–2
Replay
v Bolton Wanderers (h) 0–2

1993–94
Round 3
v Bristol City (a) 1–1
Abandoned after 65 minutes
v Bristol City (a) 1–1
Replay
v Bristol City (h) 0–1

1994–95
Round 3
v Birmingham (a) 0–0
Replay
v Birmingham (h) 1–1
Liverpool won 2–0 on penalties
Round 4
v Burnley (a) 0–0
Replay
v Burnley (h) 1–0
Round 5
v Wimbledon (h) 1–1
Replay
v Wimbledon (a) 2–0
Round 6
v Tottenham Hotspur (h) 1–2

1995–96
Round 3
v Rochdale (h) 7–0
Round 4
v Shrewsbury Town (a) 4–0
Round 5
v Charlton Athletic (h) 2–1
Round 6
v Leeds United (a) 0–0
Replay
v Leeds United (h) 3–0
Semi-final
v Aston Villa (Old Trafford) 3–0
Final
v Manchester United (Wembley) 0–1

1996–97
Round 3
v Burnley (h) 1–0
Round 4
v Chelsea (a) 2–4

1997–98
Round 3
v Coventry (h) 1–3

LIVERPOOL IN THE FOOTBALL LEAGUE CUP
(Since 1982 the Milk Cup, then the Littlewoods Cup, then the Rumbelows Cup, now the Coca-Cola Cup)

1960–61
Round 2
v Luton Town (h) 1–1
Replay
v Luton Town (h) 5–2
Round 3
v Southampton (h) 1–2

1967–68
Round 2
v Bolton Wanderers (h) 1–1
Replay
v Bolton Wanderers (a) 2–3

1968–69
Round 2
v Sheffield United (h) 4–0
Round 3
v Swansea Town (h) 2–0
Round 4
v Arsenal (a) 1–2

1969–70
Round 2
v Watford (a) 2–1
Round 3
v Manchester City (a) 2–3

1970–71
Round 2
v Mansfield Town (a) 0–0
Replay
v Mansfield Town (h) 3–2 aet
Round 3
v Swindon Town (a) 0–2

1971–72
Round 2
v Hull City (h) 3–0
Round 3
v Southampton (h) 1–0
Round 4
v West Ham United (a) 1–2

1972–73
Round 2
v Carlisle United (a) 1–1
Replay
v Carlisle United (h) 5–1
Round 3
v West Bromwich Albion (a) 1–1
Replay
v West Bromwich Albion (h) 2–1

Round 4
v Leeds United (h) 2–2
Replay
v Leeds United (a) 1–0
Round 5
v Tottenham Hotspur (h) 1–1
Replay
v Tottenham Hotspur (a) 1–3

1973–74
Round 2
v West Ham United (a) 2–2
Replay
v West Ham United (h) 1–0
Round 3
v Sunderland (a) 2–0
Round 4
v Hull City (a) 0–0
Replay
v Hull City (h) 3–1
Round
v Wolverhampton Wanderers (a) 0–1

1974–75
Round 2
v Brentford (h) 2–1
Round 3
v Bristol City (a) 0–0
Replay
v Bristol City (h) 4–0
Round 4
v Middlesbrough (h) 0–1

1975–76
Round 2
v York City (a) 1–0
Round 3
v Burnley (h) 1–1
Replay
v Burnley (a) 1–0

1976–77
Round 2
v West Bromwich Albion (h) 1–1
Replay
v West Bromwich Albion (h) 0–1

1977–78
Round 2
v Chelsea (h) 2–0
Round 3
v Derby County (h) 2–0
Round 4
v Coventry City (a) 2–0
Round 5
v Wrexham (a) 3–1
Semi-final 1st leg
v Arsenal (h) 2–1
Semi-final 2nd leg
v Arsenal (a) 0–0 agg 2–1
Final
v Nottingham Forest (Wembley) 0–0 aet
Replay
v Nottingham Forest (Old Trafford) 0–1

1978–79
Round 2
v Sheffield United (a) 0–1

1979–80
Round 2 1st Leg
v Tranmere Rovers (a) 0–0
Round 2 2nd Leg
v Tranmere Rovers (h) 4–0 agg 4–0
Round 3
v Chesterfield (h) 3–1
Round 4
v Exeter City (h) 2–0
Round 5
v Norwich City (a) 3–1
Semi-final 1st leg
v Nottingham Forest (a) 0–1
Semi-final 2nd leg
v Nottingham Forest (h) 1–1 agg 1–2

1980–81
Round 2 1st leg
v Bradford City (a) 0–1
Round 2 2nd leg
v Bradford City (h) 4–0 agg 4–1
Round 3
v Swindon Town (h) 5–0
Round 4
v Portsmouth (h) 4–1
Round 5
v Birmingham City (h) 3–1
Semi-final 1st leg
v Manchester City (a) 1–0
Semi-final 2nd leg
v Manchester City (h) 1–1 agg 2–1
Final
v West Ham United (Wembley) 1–1 aet
Replay
v West Ham United (Villa Park) 2–1

1981–82
Round 2 1st leg
v Exeter City (h) 5–0
Round 2 2nd leg
v Exeter City (a) 6–0 agg 11–0
Round 3
v Middlesbrough (h) 4–1
Round 4
v Arsenal (a) 0–0
Replay
v Arsenal (h) 3–0 aet
Round 5
v Barnsley (h) 0–0
Replay
v Barnsley (a) 3–1
Semi-final 1st leg
v Ipswich Town (a) 2–0
Semi-final 2nd leg
v Ipswich Town (h) 2–2 agg 4–2
Final
v Tottenham Hotspur (Wembley) 3–1 aet

1982–83
Round 2 1st leg
v Ipswich Town (a) 2–1
Round 2 2nd leg
v Ipswich Town (h) 2–0 agg 4–1
Round 3
v Rotherham United (a) 1–0
Round 4
v Norwich City (h) 2–0

Round 5
v West Ham United (h) 2–1
Semi-final 1st leg
v Burnley (h) 3–0
Semi-final 2nd leg
v Burnley (a) 0–1
Final
v Manchester United (Wembley) 2–1 aet

1983–84
Round 2 1st leg
v Brentford (a) 4–1
Round 2 2nd leg
v Brentford (h) 4–0 agg 8–1
Round 3
v Fulham (a) 1–1
Replay
v Fulham (h) 1–1 aet
Second Replay
v Fulham (a) 1–0 aet
Round 4
v Birmingham City (a) 1–1
Replay
v Birmingham City (h) 3–0
Round 5
v Sheffield Wednesday (a) 2–2
Replay
v Sheffield Wednesday (h) 3–0
Semi-final 1st leg
v Walsall (h) 2–2
Semi-final 2nd leg
v Walsall (a) 2–0 agg 4–2
Final
v Everton (Wembley) 0–0 aet
Replay
v Everton (Maine Road) 1–0

1984–85
Round 2 1st leg
v Stockport County (a) 0–0
Round 2 2nd leg
v Stockport County (h) 2–0 aet
Round 3
v Tottenham Hotspur (a) 0–1

1985–86
Round 2 1st leg
v Oldham Athletic (h) 3–0
Round 2 2nd leg
v Oldham Athletic (a) 5–0 agg 8–2
Round 3
v Brighton (h) 4–0
Round 4
v Manchester United (h) 2–1
Round 5
v Ipswich Town (h) 3–0
Semi-final 1st leg
v Queens Park Rangers (a) 0–1
Semi-final 2nd leg
v Queens Park Rangers (h) 2–2 agg 2–3

1986–87
Round 2 1st leg
v Fulham (h) 10–0
Round 2 2nd leg
v Fulham (a) 3–2 agg 13–2
Round 3
v Leicester City (h) 4–1

Round 4
v Coventry (a) 0–0
Replay
v Coventry (h) 3–1
Round 5
v Everton (a) 1–0
Semi-final 1st leg
v Southampton (a) 0–0
Semi-final 2nd leg
v Southampton (h) 3–0
Final
v Arsenal (Wembley) 1–2

1987–88
Round 2 1st leg
v Blackburn Rovers (a) 1–1
Round 2 2nd leg
v Blackburn Rovers (h) 1–0 agg 2–1
Round 3
v Everton (h) 0–1

1988–89
Round 2 1st leg
v Walsall (h) 1–0
Round 2 2nd leg
v Walsall (a) 3–1 agg 4–1
Round 3
v Arsenal (h) 1–1
Replay
v Arsenal (a) 0–0
Second Replay
v Arsenal (Villa Park) 2–1
Round 4
v West Ham United (a) 1–4

1989–90
Round 2 1st leg
v Wigan Athletic (h) 5–2
Round 2 2nd leg
v Wigan Athletic (away, played at Anfield) 3–0 agg 8–2
Round 3
v Arsenal (a) 0–1

1990–91
Round 2 1st leg
v Crewe Alexandra (h) 5–1
Round 2 2nd leg
v Crewe Alexandra (a) 4–1 agg 9–2
Round 3
v Manchester United (a) 1–3

1991–92
Round 2 1st leg
v Stoke City (h) 2–2
Round 2 2nd leg
v Stoke City (a) 3–2
Round 3
v Port Vale (h) 2–2
Replay
v Port Vale (a) 4–1
Round 4
v Peterborough (a) 0–1

1992–93
Round 2 1st leg
v Chesterfield (h) 4–4
Round 2 2nd leg
v Chesterfield (a) 4–1
Round 3
v Sheffield United (a) 0–0

Replay
v Sheffield United (h) 3–0
Round 4
v Crystal Palace (h) 1–1
Replay
v Crystal Palace (a) 1–2

1993–94
Round 2 1st leg
v Fulham (a) 3–1
Round 2 2nd leg
v Fulham (h) 5–0
Round 3
v Ipswich Town (h) 3–2
Round 4
v Wimbledon (h) 1–1
Replay
v Wimbledon (a) 2–2
Wimbledon won 4–3 on penalties

1994–95
Round 2 1st leg
v Burnley (h) 2–0
Round 2 2nd leg
v Burnley (a) 4–1
Round 3
v Stoke City (h) 2–1
Round 4
v Blackburn Rovers (a) 3–1
Round 5
v Arsenal (h) 1–0
Semi-final 1st leg
v Crystal Palace (h) 1–0
Semi-final 2nd leg
v Crystal Palace (a) 1–0
Final
v Bolton Wanderers (Wembley) 2–1

1995–96
Round 2 1st Leg
v Sunderland (h) 2–0
Round 2 2nd Leg
v Sunderland (a) 1–0 agg 3–0
Round 3
v Manchester City (h) 4–0
Round 4
v Newcastle United (h) 0–1

1996–97
Round 3
v Charlton Athletic (a) 1–1
Replay
v Charlton Athletic (h) 4–1
Round 4
v Arsenal (h) 4–2
Round 5
v Middlesbrough (a) 1–2

1997–98
Round 3
v West Bromwich Albion (a) 2–0
Round 4
v Grimsby (h) 3–0
Round 5
v Newcastle United (a) 2–0 aet
Semi-final 1st leg
v Middlesbrough (h) 2–1
Semi-final 2nd leg
v Middlesbrough (a) 0–2 agg 2–3

LIVERPOOL IN EUROPE

European Cup
1964–65
Round 1 1st leg
v Reykjavik (a) 5–0
Round 1 2nd leg
v Reykjavik (h) 6–1 agg 11–1
Round 2 1st leg
v Anderlecht (h) 3–0
Round 2 2nd leg
v Anderlecht (a) 1–0 agg 4–0
Round 3 1st leg
v FC Cologne (a) 0–0
Round 3 2nd leg
v FC Cologne (h) 0–0 agg 0–0
Round 3 Replay
v FC Cologne (Rotterdam) 2–2
Liverpool won on toss of coin
Semi-final 1st leg
v Inter Milan (h) 3–1
Semi-final 2nd leg
v Inter Milan (a) 0–3 agg 3–4

1966–67
Prelim Round 1st leg
v Petrolul Ploesti (h) 2–0
Prelim Round 2nd leg
v Petrolul Ploestl (a) 1–3 agg 3–3
Prelim Round Replay
v Petrolul Ploesti (Brussels) 2–0
Round 1 1st leg
v Ajax (a) 1–5
Round 1 2nd leg
v Ajax (h) 2–2 agg 3–7

1973–74
Round 1 1st leg
v Jeunesse D'Esch (a) 1–1
Round 1 2nd leg
v Jeunesse D'Esch (h) 2–0 agg 3–1
Round 2 1st leg
v Red Star Belgrade (a) 1–2
Round 2 2nd leg
v Red Star Belgrade (h) 1–2 agg 2–4

1976–77
Round 1 1st leg
v Crusaders (h) 2–0
Round 1 2nd leg
v Crusaders (a) 5–0 agg 7–0
Round 2 1st leg
v Trabzonspor (a) 0–1
Round 2 2nd leg
v Trabzonspor (h) 3–0 agg 3–1
Round 3 1st leg
v St Etienne (a) 0–1
Round 3 2nd leg
v St Etienne (h) 3–1 agg 3–2
Semi-final 1st leg
v FC Zurich (a) 3–1
Semi-final 2nd leg
v FC Zurich (h) 3–0 agg 6–1
Final
v Borussia Moenchengladbach (Rome) 3–1

1977 – 78
Round 2 1st leg
v Dynamo Dresden (h) 5–1
Round 2 2nd leg
v Dynamo Dresden (a) 1–2 agg 6–3
Round 3 1st leg
v Benfica (a) 2–1
Round 3 2nd leg
v Benfica (h) 4–1 agg 6–2
Semi-final 1st leg
v Borussia Moenchengladbach (a) 1–2 agg 1–2
Semi-final 2nd leg
v Borussia Moenchengladbach (h) 3–0 agg 4–2
Final
v FC Bruges (Wembley) 1–0

1978 – 79
Round 1 1st leg
v Nottingham Forest (a) 0–2
Round 1 2nd leg
v Nottingham Forest (h) 0–0 agg 0–2

1979 – 80
Round 1 1st leg
v Dynamo Tbilisi (h) 2–1
Round 1 2nd leg
v Dynamo Tbilisi (a) 0–3 agg 2–4

1980 – 81
Round 1 1st leg
v Oulu Palloseura (a) 1–1
Round 1 2nd leg
v Oulu Palloseura (h) 10–1 agg 11–2
Round 2 1st leg
v Aberdeen (a) 1–0
Round 2 2nd leg
v Aberdeen (h) 4–0 agg 5–0
Round 3 1st leg
v CSKA Sofia (h) 5–1
Round 3 2nd leg
v CSKA Sofia (a) 1–0 agg 6–1
Semi-final 1st leg
v Bayern Munich (h) 0–0
Semi-final 2nd leg
v Bayern Munich (a) 1–1 agg 1–1
Liverpool won on away goal
Final
v Read Madrid (Paris) 1–0

1981 – 82
Round 1 1st leg
v Oulu Palloseura (a) 1–0
Round 1 2nd leg
v Oulu Palloseura (h) 7–0 agg 8–0
Round 2 1st leg
v AZ 67 Alkmaar (h) 2–2
Round 2 2nd leg
v AZ 67 Alkmaar (a) 3–2 agg 5–4
Round 3 1st leg
v CSKA Sofia (h) 1–0
Round 3 2nd leg
v CSKA Sofia (a) 0–2 agg 1–2

1982 – 83
Round 1 1st leg
v Dunkalk (a) 4–1
Round 1 2nd leg
v Dundalk (h) 1–0 agg 5–1

Round 2 1st leg
v JK Helsinki (a) 0–1
Round 2 2nd leg
v JK Helsinki (h) 5–0 agg 5–1
Round 3 1st leg
v Widzew Lodz (a) 0–2
Round 3 2nd leg
v Widzew Lodz (h) 3–2 agg 3–4

1983 – 84
Round 1 1st leg
v BK Odense (a) 1–0
Round 1 2nd leg
v BK Odense (h) 5–0 agg 6–0
Round 2 1st leg
v Atletico Bilbao (h) 0–0
Round 2 2nd leg
v Atletico Bilbao (a) 1–0 agg 1–0
Round 3 1st leg
v Benfica (h) 1–0
Round 3 2nd leg
v Benfica (a) 4–1 agg 5–1
Semi-final 1st leg
v Dinamo Bucharest (h) 1–0
Semi-final 2nd leg
v Dinamo Bucharest (a) 2–1 agg 3–1
Final
v AS Roma (Rome) 1–1 aet
Liverpool won on penalties

1984 – 85
Round 1 1st leg
v Lech Poznan (a) 1–0
Round 1 2nd leg
v Lech Poznan (h) 4–0 agg 5–0
Round 2 1st leg
v Benfica (h) 3–1
Round 2 2nd leg
v Benfica (a) 0–1 agg 3–2
Round 3 1st leg
v Austria Vienna (a) 1–1
Round 3 2nd leg
v Austria Vienna (h) 4–1 agg 5–2
Semi-final 1st leg
v Parathinaikos (h) 4–0
Semi-final 2nd leg
v Parathinaikos (a) 1–0 agg 5–0
Final
v Juventus (Brussels) 0–1

European Cup Winners Cup

1965 – 66
Prelim Round 1st leg
v Juventus (a) 0–1
Prelim Round 2nd leg
v Juventus (h) 2–0 agg 2–1
Round 1 1st leg
v Standard Liege (h) 3–1
Round 1 2nd leg
v Standard Liege (a) 2–1 agg 5–2
Round 2 1st leg
v Honved (a) 0–0
Round 2 2nd leg
v Honved (h) 2–0 agg 2–0
Semi-final 1st leg
v Celtic (a) 0–1

Semi-final 2nd leg
v Celtic (h) 2–0 agg 2–1
Final
v Borussia Dortmund (Hampton Park) 1–2 aet

1971 – 72
Round 1 1st leg
v Servette Geneva (a) 1–2
Round 1 2nd leg
v Servette Geneva (h) 2–0 agg 3–2
Round 2 1st leg
v Bayern Munich (h) 0–0
Round 2 2nd leg
v Bayern Munich (a) 1–3 agg 1–3

1974 – 75
Round 1 1st leg
v Stromsgodset Drammen (h) 11–0
Round 1 2nd leg
v Stromsgodset Drammen (a) 1–0 agg 12–0
Round 2 1st leg
v Ferencvaros (h) 1–1
Round 2 2nd leg
v Ferencvaros (a) 0–0 agg 1–1
Liverpool lost on away goal

1992 – 93
Round 1 1st leg
v Apollon Limassol (h) 6–1
Round 1 2nd leg
v Apollon Limassol (a) 2–1
Round 2 1st leg
v Spartak Moscow (a) 2–4
Round 2 2nd leg
v Spartak Moscow (h) 0–2

1996 – 97
Round 1 1st leg
v MyPa 47 (a) 1–0
Round 1 2nd leg
v MyPa 47 (h) 3–1 agg 4–1
Round 2 1st leg
v Sion (a) 2–1
Round 2 2nd leg
v Sion (h) 6–3 agg 8–4
Round 3 1st leg
v SK Brann Bergen (a) 1–1
Round 3 2nd leg
v SK Brann Bergen (h) 3–0 agg 4–1
Semi-final 1st leg
v Paris St Germain (a) 0–3
Semi-final 2nd leg
v Paris St Germain (h) 2–0 agg 2–3

European Fairs Cup

1967 – 68
Round 1 1st leg
v Malmo (a) 2–0
Round 1 2nd leg
v Malmo (h) 2–1 agg 4–1
Round 2 1st leg
v TSV Munchen 1860 (h) 8–0
Round 2 2nd leg
v TSV Munchen 1860 (a) 1–2 agg 9–2

Round 3 1st leg
v Ferencvaros (a) 0 – 1
Round 3 2nd leg
v Ferencvaros (h) 0 – 1 agg 0 – 2

1968 – 69
Round 1 1st leg
v Atletico Bilbao (a) 1 – 2
Round 1 2nd leg
v Atletico Bilbao (h) 2 – 1 aet agg 3 – 3
Liverpool lost on toss of coin

1969 – 70
Round 1 1st leg
v Dundalk (h) 10 – 0
Round 1 2nd leg
v Dundalk (a) 4 – 0 agg 14 – 0
Round 2 1st leg
v Vitoria Setubal (a) 0 – 1
Round 2 2nd leg
v Vitoria Setubal (h) 3 – 2 agg 3 – 3
Liverpool lost on away goals

1970 – 71
Round 1 1st leg
v Ferencvaros (h) 1 – 0
Round 1 2nd leg
v Ferencvaros (a) 1 – 1 agg 2 – 1
Round 2 1st leg
v Dinamo Bucharest (h) 3 – 0
Round 2 2nd leg
v Dinamo Bucharest (a) 1 – 1 agg 4 – 1
Round 3 1st leg
v Hibernian (a) 1 – 0
Round 3 2nd leg
v Hibernian (h) 2 – 0 agg 3 – 0
Round 4 1st leg
v Bayern Munich (h) 3 – 0
Round 4 2nd leg
v Bayern Munich (a) 1 – 1 agg 4 – 1
Semi-final 1st leg
v Leeds United (h) 0 – 1
Semi-final 2nd leg
v Leeds United (a) 0 – 0 agg 0 – 1

UEFA Cup

1972 – 73
Round 1 1st leg
v Eintracht Frankfurt (h) 2 – 0
Round 1 2nd leg
v Eintracht Frankfurt (a) 0 – 0 agg 2 – 0
Round 2 1st leg
v AEK Athens (h) 3 – 0
Round 2 2nd leg
v AEK Athens (a) 3 – 1 agg 6 – 1
Round 3 1st leg
v Dynamo Berlin (a) 0 – 0
Round 3 2nd leg
v Dynamo Berlin (h) 3 – 1 agg 3 – 1
Round 4 1st leg
v Dynamo Dresden (h) 2 – 0
Round 4 2nd leg
v Dynamo Dresden (a) 1 – 0 agg 3 – 0
Semi-final 1st leg
v Tottenham Hotspur (h) 1 – 0
Semi-final 2nd leg
v Tottenham Hotspur (a) 1 – 2 agg 2 – 2
Liverpool won on away goal

Final 1st leg
v Borussia Moenchengladbach (h) 3 – 0
Final 2nd leg
v Borussia Moenchengladbach (a) 0 – 2 agg 3 – 2

1975 – 76
Round 1 1st leg
v Hibernian (a) 0 – 1
Round 1 2nd leg
v Hibernian (h) 3 – 1 agg 3 – 2
Round 2 1st leg
v Real Sociedad (a) 3 – 1
Round 2 2nd leg
v Real Sociedad (h) 6 – 0 agg 9 – 1
Round 3 1st leg
v Slask Wroclaw (a) 2 – 1
Round 3 2nd leg
v Slask Wroclaw (h) 3 – 0 agg 5 – 1
Round 4 1st leg
v Dynamo Dresden (a) 0 – 0
Round 4 2nd leg
v Dynamo Dresden (h) 2 – 1 agg 2 – 1
Semi-final 1st leg
v Barcelona (a) 1 – 0
Semi-final 2nd leg
v Barcelona (h) 1 – 1 agg 2 – 1
Final 1st leg
v FC Bruges (h) 3 – 2
Final 2nd leg
v FC Bruges (a) 1 – 1 agg 4 – 3

1990 – 91
Round 1 1st leg
v Kuusysi Lahti (h) 6 – 1
Round 1 2nd leg
v Kuusysi Lahti (a) 0 – 1
Round 2 1st leg
v Auxerre (a) 0 – 2
Round 2 2nd leg
v Auxerre (h) 3 – 0
Round 3 1st leg
v Tirol (a) 2 – 0
Round 3 2nd leg
v Tiral (h) 4 – 0
Round 4 1st leg
v Genoa (a) 0 – 2
Round 4 2nd leg
v Genoa (h) 1 – 2

1995 – 96
Round 1 1st leg
v Spartak Vladikavkaz (a) 2 – 1
Round 1 2nd leg
v Spartak Vladikavkaz (h) 0 – 0
Round 2 1st leg
v Brondby (a) 0 – 0
Round 2 2nd leg
v Brondby (h) 0 – 1 agg 0 – 1

1997 – 98
Round 1 1st leg
v Celtic (a) 2 – 2
Round 1 2nd leg
v Celtic (h) 0 – 0 agg 2 – 2
Round 2 1st leg
v Strasbourg (a) 0 – 3
Round 2 2nd leg
v Strasbourg (h) 2 – 0 agg 2 – 3

World Club Championship

1981
v Flamengo (Tokyo) 0 – 3

1984
v Independiente (Toyko) 0 – 1

European Super Cup

1977
v SV Hamburg (a) 1 – 1
v SV Hamburg (h) 6 – 0 agg 7 – 1

1978
v Anderlecht (a) 1 – 3
v Anderlecht (h) 2 – 1 agg 3 – 4

1985
v Juventus (a) 0 – 2
Played as a one-off Super Cup match

FA CHARITY SHIELD

1922
v Huddersfield Town (Old Trafford) 0 – 1
1964
v West Ham United (h) 2 – 2
1965
v Manchester United (a) 2 – 2
1966
v Everton (a) 1 – 0
1971
v Leicester City (a) 0 – 1
1974
v Leeds United (Wembley) 1 – 1
Liverpool won 6 – 5 on penalties
1976
v Southampton (Wembley) 1 – 0
1977
v Manchester United (Wembley) 0 – 0
1979
v Arsenal (Wembley) 3 – 1
1980
v West Ham United (Wembley) 1 – 0
1982
v Tottenham Hotspur (Wembley) 1 – 0
1983
v Manchester United (Wembley) 0 – 2
1984
v Everton (Wembley) 0 – 1
1986
v Everton (Wembley) 1 – 1
1988
v Wimbledon (Wembley) 2 – 1
1989
v Arsenal (Wembley) 1 – 0
1990
v Manchester United (Wembley) 1 – 1
1992
v Leeds United (Wembley) 3 – 4

Index